# Praise for *Brother One Cell*

"*Brother One Cell* is Mr. Thomas's affecting account of his prison experience. It's an offbeat coming-of-age story, the tale of a wide-eyed, innocent, middle-class American thrust into a world of deprivation and daily trials that speed his passage into adulthood and a deeper understanding of himself and the fallen creatures around him. . . . The detail is fascinating. . . . Sincerity and earnestness are [Thomas's] strong points. A romantic to the end, he confronts his situation with Thoreau ready to hand, drawing simple conclusions from hard lessons, taking pleasure in small things, and appreciating the unexpected turn his life has taken."                    —William Grimes, *The New York Times*

"Compelling."                                        —*Chicago Tribune*

"In his memoir, Thomas explains how that time of incarceration represented his real education. Surprisingly, he found little brutality (no rape) in Korea's penal institutions, but there were language barriers, unfamiliar foreign customs, extreme codes of social hierarchy, and almost no individual freedoms. He had to overcome all of this, as well as his own personal demons, to get to a place of higher understanding—something that, amazingly, he seemed to accomplish. His account of that journey is gripping."
                                        —*Booklist* (starred review)

"As he bides his time, awaiting release, [Cullen] ultimately comes away with invaluable life lessons—paying his debt to that society, and more importantly to himself—en route to becoming a wise and more grounded adult. Part travelogue, history lesson, prison commentary, and cautionary tale, *Brother One Cell* reminds us that travel is often an interior pursuit at heart, one of reflection and personal discovery—and that cultural authenticity can be found in the strangest of places."                    —Vagabonding.com

"Cullen's story, and that of his fellow inmates, is an extraordinary journey into an inescapable nightmare. He begins his sentence as a bitter young man—confused, scared and struggling to come to terms with his terrible lot. What transpires throughout the course of this wonderfully written memoir is at the same time provocative and entirely heartbreaking."
                                —Jeff Neumann, coauthor of *Babylon By Bus*

"Like a bastard child of Paul Theroux's travel writing and Joan Didion's crisp introspective prose, *Brother One Cell* is a scary, funny, honest-as-hell, account of growing up and paying your dues inside—gulp—a Korean prison. Cullen Thomas probes with equal intensity his own life and mistakes, incarceration's mental and physical toll, the experiences of his fellow inmates, and the humbling road to redemption, achieving a symphonic narrative harmony that makes his story impossible to forget. This is memoir at its highest level."
                                —Ray LeMoine, coauthor of *Babylon By Bus*

PENGUIN BOOKS

# BROTHER ONE CELL

Cullen Thomas's writing has appeared in *The New York Times Magazine*, *Salon*, and *Penthouse*, among other publications. He lives in Brooklyn. This is his first book.

Visit www.cullenthomas.com

# BROTHER
# ONE CELL

An American Coming of Age in South Korea's Prisons

Cullen Thomas

PENGUIN BOOKS

PENGUIN BOOKS

Published by the Penguin Group

Penguin Group (USA) Inc., 375 Hudson Street, New York, New York 10014, U.S.A.

Penguin Group (Canada), 90 Eglinton Avenue East, Suite 700, Toronto,
Ontario, Canada M4P 2Y3 (a division of Pearson Penguin Canada Inc.)

Penguin Books Ltd, 80 Strand, London WC2R 0RL, England

Penguin Ireland, 25 St Stephen's Green, Dublin 2, Ireland (a division of Penguin Books Ltd)

Penguin Group (Australia), 250 Camberwell Road, Camberwell,
Victoria 3124, Australia (a division of Pearson Australia Group Pty Ltd)

Penguin Books India Pvt Ltd, 11 Community Centre,
Panchsheel Park, New Delhi – 110 017, India

Penguin Group (NZ), 67 Apollo Drive, Rosedale, North Shore 0632,
New Zealand (a division of Pearson New Zealand Ltd)

Penguin Books (South Africa) (Pty) Ltd, 24 Sturdee Avenue,
Rosebank, Johannesburg 2196, South Africa

Penguin Books Ltd, Registered Offices:
80 Strand, London WC2R 0RL, England

First published in the United States of America by Viking Penguin,
a member of Penguin Group (USA) Inc. 2007
Published in Penguin Books 2008

10  9  8  7  6  5  4  3  2  1

Grateful acknowledgment is made for permission to reprint an excerpt from the following copy-
righted work: *The Prophet* by Kahlil Gibran, copyright 1923 by Kahlil Gibran and renewed 1951 by Administrators C.T.A. of Kahlil Gibran Estate and Mary G. Gibran. Used by permission of Alfred A.
Knopf, a division of Random House, Inc.

THE LIBRARY OF CONGRESS HAS CATALOGED THE HARDCOVER EDITION AS FOLLOWS:
Thomas, Cullen.
Brother One Cell : an American coming of age in South Korea's prisons / Cullen Thomas.
p.  cm.
ISBN 978-0-670-03827-5 (hc.)
ISBN 978-0-14-311311-9 (pbk.)
1. Thomas, Cullen.  2. Prisoners—Korea (South)—Biography.  I. Title.
HV9468.T46  2007
365'.6092—dc22
[B]     2006046735

Printed in the United States of America
Designed by Carla Bolte

FOR MY PARENTS

*A man nearing his release should avoid even falling leaves.*

—Korean prison proverb

# AUTHOR'S NOTE

I WAS ARRESTED in Seoul, South Korea, on May 27, 1994, for smuggling hashish into the country. I was twenty-three years old. In July I was convicted and sentenced to three and a half years in prison. I served my time in the Seoul Detention Center and prisons in the cities of Uijongbu and Taejon. On November 26, 1997, the final day of my sentence, I was deported to the United States. I have not been back to Korea since.

Instead of using the official system for romanizing Hangul, Korea's alphabet, I have chosen to romanize Korean words, phrases, and proper names in my own way, as this results, I believe, in a more accurate representation of the actual sound and flavor of the language. All of the events depicted here are true. However, in order to protect both the innocent and the guilty some of the names have been changed. Any similarity between the fictitious names and the names of real individuals is entirely coincidental.

# A VERSION OF THE TANGUN MYTH
## A Creation Story of Korea

Hwan-In, the god of all the Heavens, had a son named Hwan-Ung.
Hwan-Ung grew into a compassionate god who wanted to help man-
kind. He asked his father for permission to govern the Korean peninsula, and his dad let him do it.

So Hwan-Ung came down to earth with three thousand followers,
appearing near a sandalwood tree on the slopes of Taebek Mountain, in the east of Korea, near the sea. He proclaimed himself
Heaven King and established the City of God. He put followers in
charge of the wind, rain, and clouds and taught the people useful
arts: agriculture, medicine, carpentry, fishing—things to live by. He
taught them right from wrong and set down a code of law.

Near the sandalwood tree was a large cave, where a bear and a
tiger lived. Every day the animals went to the tree and prayed to
Hwan-Ung. Heaven King was moved by their homage.

He called them over one day and presented them with a challenge. Giving them twenty bulbs of garlic and a divine bunch of
mugwort, he said, "Eat these and stay out of the light of day for one
hundred days. If you do this, I'll make you human."

The animals ambled back to their cave and set themselves to the
task. But the tiger was impatient, and maybe he couldn't stomach all
the garlic (if so, he had no business living in Korea), and he dashed
out. The she-bear, however, ate the garlic and mugwort and waited
patiently inside the cave. After just twenty-one days Hwan-Ung re-
warded her, transforming her into a beautiful woman named
Ung-Nyo.

Ung-Nyo enjoyed life for a while but couldn't find anyone to pass
the time with and soon grew lonely. She went to the sandalwood tree
on the mountainside again and prayed to Hwan-Ung that she might

be blessed with a child. Given this chance to copulate with the beautiful Ung-Nyo, Heaven King found himself sympathetic to her cause.

Tangun, the son, was born, and the people rejoiced. In time, Tangun became the first human king of the peninsula, establishing his capital at Pyongyang. He called his kingdom . . . Chosun.

☰☰

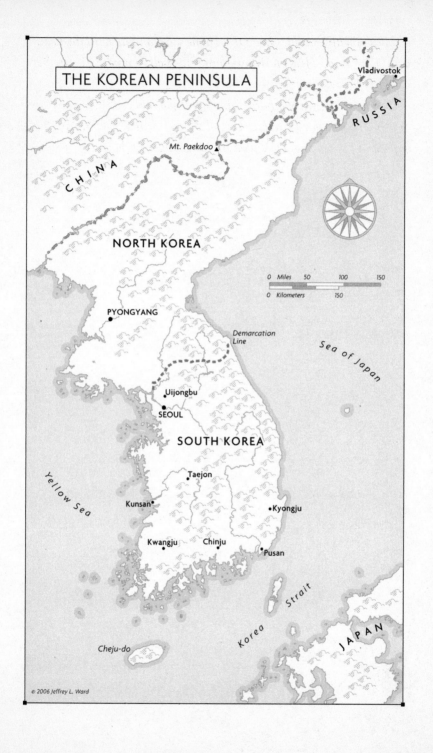

THE KOREAN PENINSULA

Vladivostok

RUSSIA

CHINA

Mt. Paekdoo

NORTH KOREA

PYONGYANG

Demarcation
Line

Sea of Japan

Uijongbu

SEOUL

SOUTH KOREA

Taejon

Yellow Sea

Kunsan

Kyongju

Kwangju    Chinju

Pusan

Korea Strait

JAPAN

Cheju-do

© 2006 Jeffrey L. Ward

# THE TIGER'S CAVE

# 호랑이 굴

THE PAIN IN my side hasn't been diagnosed, but I'm sure it's Korea. A little Korean tumor between the pancreas and liver, or maybe a Korean tear in the muscle around the ribs, a Korean hernia, a persistent Korean funk. Ultrasounds and a CT scan have shown nothing. I'm concerned because, although it seems to disappear for weeks or months at a time, it always returns, a dull throbbing that saps my energy. It reminds me that we don't escape our experiences, that they scar us quite literally and mark themselves in furrows in our soil—and that's exactly as it should be. Otherwise, how would we trace ourselves?

Aside from this strange pain in my side, though, all the physical reminders of the years I spent in prison in South Korea have faded away. I'm back in New York, years removed, and I function fairly normally; you wouldn't guess a thing by looking at me. The pus-filled boils on my chin went away, as did the large, painful ones in my crotch hair. (I thought I'd contracted the herpes that Big Green had gotten from Filipino prostitutes—had he lent me a pair of his shorts and I'd neglected to wash them first?—or that I'd gotten syphilis from somewhere in the general squalor of the jails. I was haunted by the idea that I'd never be able to love a woman again or have sex because all would be repulsed; I thought I wasn't fit for anybody.) The parasites in my stomach were killed off with medicine. No sign now of the frostbite I had. The broken fingers healed. The color returned to my skin. Most of the bizarre accent I returned with is gone.

But I am not the same. South Korea, the Hermit Kingdom of old, took a huge piece of me; she didn't *take* it really, but she vigorously broke me down and forced me to start life over. Life wouldn't be forever, Korea told me then, nor would our time as who we think we are. She showed me that I was far from invincible, that I was enormously capable of failure and weakness. I was twenty-three, not very clever or wise in the ways of the world, and the consequences of my mistake were intensely painful. I bear the scar where no one can see it, in a solitary place, an immaculate wound down below everything else. It's closed up now, but when I'm reminded of my years there—brought back by songs, faces in the crowds in New York City, overheard conversations—I split open and feel just how deep I go; out pours my heart, an almost forgotten organ of compassion and humility. It doubles me over and sits me down, keeps me straight. That scar is my greatest strength. I don't know if life will ever again give me something so pure and hard and unrelenting, so savagely true to itself, determined to test me, to burn me and make me tastier for having suffered a little, for having eaten bitter, whether I deserved it or not.

As trying as it was, I would never give the experience back. I'm convinced life showed me something rare then, opened a view into the divine, a glimpse of its breadth and our smallness, the expanse of suffering and hardship in the world, the quiet benevolence that follows us down bare hallways, through bars, into nothing. I need to remember, not to forget, my own idiocy; not to forget how, by a mixture of my own predisposition and the grace afforded by Korea herself, I took something good from the test. I would have kept my blue prison pants had they let me. I've wondered what a photograph of me then would look like. I've still got the stamps in my passport, my Korean visa. I go to them sometimes to remember—the men I came to know, the hugeness of life in the smallest of spaces, what we longed for endlessly. In my room in Brooklyn I hang maps of Korea, dangling off China, a world away now and yet in my veins. On my wall hangs Il Hwan's painting that I smuggled out of Taejon Prison—had they discovered it, the guards would have taken it from me. I'd watched Il Hwan at our table in the factory for years teaching himself how to paint in the classical Chinese style. I kept after him until he painted one for me: old thatch-roofed Korean houses beside a blue-green river, under mist and rolling mountains, a tiny fisherman sitting riverside.

ON THE STREETS of Manhattan I think I see Billy the Kid, the Colombian spitfire who'd gotten five for smuggling emeralds and cocaine; the buoyant, giant Nigerian Joseph; a Pakistani on the subway who, damned if I'm wrong, looks a little like Tracey: the proud posture, the handsome face, some faint hint of his androgynous genius. In other faces I see Koreans—guys from our shoe factory, others I never knew but would see daily for years in quick glimpses as we trudged back to our cells in long single lines through the empty stone halls: Gorilla Man's Asian eyes; the barrel chest of Panjang Nim, our warlord of a factory captain; the face of feckless little Kee Jung, our factory doorman, who'd killed his cheating wife. Faces from a dream. They walk past like secret messages out of time. I do double takes and am cast back, across the world, seven thousand miles to the east. I wonder what has happened to them and where they are now. Some, like Chang Ho and Kee Baek, are still there behind Taejon's walls. Joseph was deported and made his way to Holland. I lost touch with Reza after a couple of warm letters from Tehran. Billy disappeared back in Colombia, and like that I lost him. I stop on the street and wish it were really them somehow, that I could talk to them. We lived bare in Korea, suffered sometimes with dignity together, the flawed lot of us.

We lived like monks, often in silence and solitude; like peasants, glad for a meal with meat, subsisting, using little space, enduring the rough edge of seasons, bothering little in the world—though, of course, many of us had left outside enough wreckage for several lifetimes. We slept on stone and old wood floors, bathed with cold water even in the frigid winters; ate red-peppered cabbage and poor-man's barley rice, a hard, coarse grain, even for breakfast. We cooked dried cuttlefish on the tops of our little coal stoves. Together we sang South Korea's national song:

> *Though the East Sea should dry up and Paekdoo Mountain*
> *crumble*
> *God has blessed us, long live our country!*

When I talk to Koreans in the grocery stores and bodegas here in New York City, I remember. Korean comes out of my mouth and I feel my side throb dully and I know I was there.

"What were you doing in Korea?" they're always curious to know.

"Teaching English," I tell them.

"You are so good," they often say, beaming, while I think to myself, You have no idea what you mean to me, where I was in your country—because we did go deep, down to her underbelly, to a place few foreigners will ever see, away into Korea's more primitive past, into the proud, long-suffering grandfather hills of the peninsula.

Everything ends—seasons, pains, life sentences, championship runs on the dusty prison basketball court. We were all given an allotment of time that, like the bear and the tiger's garlic and mugwort, we had to chew through in our caves. Not only had I never been in a cave like that before, but for the most part I'd also been blinded out in happy sun: the privileges of two loving parents and nice homes out in wooded suburbs, a good education, illusions of being the golden boy. I thought I could do it all, that I'd never fail. Korea changed that. Tough little Tae Han Min Gook took me aside and showed me a different story, the hardest and best one, the one I never would have seen without her.

## 2

A long, long time ago
when tigers still smoked pipes

"I'M MR. SHIN, your prosecuting attorney in this case."

The man sitting across from me, a tall, well-groomed Korean in suspenders, with jet-black hair set perfectly on his head, starts in, using passable English. I'm handcuffed in a chair opposite him in the headquarters of the narcotics division of the Korean police, on the ground floor of the Seoul High and District Prosecutors' Office building. Six detectives on the couches alongside us look from Shin to me and back again, some grinning like idiots. Shin draws our attention to the box on the table.

"This is yours, isn't it? You sent this box yourself. Just tell us." The English is mechanical, disturbing.

"It's not mine," I say, trying to sound truthful. There are sounds of disapproval from the agents, hisses from their throats as they shift on the couches. When I was a kid, my neighbor's mom used to tease me about the way I always claimed innocence when trouble arose—a bit of a verbal song-and-dance man. No matter what I'd done, I'd convince everyone I was innocent, or at least disarm them of their blame. I didn't light and throw the M-80 that badly singed the German family's dachshund; simply wasn't me. We didn't tear the house apart. Wasn't me who busted all the stems on the living room plants; you've got the wrong guy.

"We know this is yours. Why don't you confess?" Shin says again.

In a glass case against the back wall is a display of seized drug paraphernalia: pipes, syringes, vials. Near this little museum is a poster on the wall: Earth seen from a distance, and above it, a big needle and a huge skeletal hand with its fingers splayed. Drugs are the apocalypse. These men are on a mission, and things can only get worse for me.

Shin and the men on my left speak in Korean; then one of them pulls open the top of the box and takes out a brick-shaped object wrapped in brown duct tape. The agent takes a key out of his pocket, cuts through the tape, and pulls open a small corner, just enough to reveal what's inside. He stands over me and puts that corner right under my nose.

"Look at it. What is that?" Shin asks me from the other side of the table. In my cell several days later, this incident will make me think of the treatment of young dogs, how a certain kind of owner will shove a dog's face into the mound of crap it inevitably drops in the house. I smell the black earth inside as the detective holds it up. I can see the outline of the top piece through the tape, the shape of a half-moon—what in the Philippines had seemed so seductive to me.

"What is that?" Shin presses me.

I'm trying to think of an answer. I can't say "I don't know"—that would be protesting too much. I sure as hell don't want to say the word "hashish" either; that's way too close to home. But before I pause too long and think too much, I say "Cannabis" out loud, and the word seems to explode through the silence. It detonates and sends ripples through the room.

"Cannabis?" the agents repeat, turning to one another. They don't quite understand, but then slowly they begin to. "Canna-bis?" Aahhh, "can-na-bees," yes, that's right, that's another name for it, I can see them thinking, the word registering at last.

They turn back to me collectively, only now with more resolve.

"It's yours, isn't that right?" Shin asks again.

"It's not mine, I swear." I have to lie to keep my head above water—some other people's heads, too.

The agents huff and shift on the couches. They want a quick end to this. They speak among themselves again. Then the guy nearest me on my right, a short, fat man who still has the grease of lunch on his face and the smell of liquor on his breath, pulls himself forward on the couch, slides what looks like a curling iron or baton out of his suit jacket, and leans toward me with a smile. He holds the foot-long instrument in front of my face and as a demonstration triggers it so that it buzzes to life. All I can think is *What the hell?* before he casually presses it against my upper right thigh and triggers it again with a smile. A painful blast of electric current shoots through me, shoots me right out of my chair into the middle of the room.

*"What the fuck!"* I yell, as my chair bangs against the floor beside me. I'm terrified and have to make them stop. Desperate, I blurt out, "I'm gonna report this to the *New York Times!*" It's all I can think of. I'm looking at the seven of them, checking my body internally for pain, feeling my hands cuffed behind me. Shin says something to the man holding the cattle prod, and he slides it back out of sight into his jacket. My mind breathes an enormous sigh of relief. Shin and the agents stand up and speak among themselves. Shin glares at me. "The penalty is ten years," he says bluntly, walking toward the door. "The judge can show mercy only if you confess. I will see you again."

Ten years? His words are worse than the electric shock.

Later, as part of the standard suspect interview, the investigators ask me if I've been mistreated at all during the arrest and questioning. I look at them, thinking about the cattle prod, and they look at me, waiting for my answer. I think that it will only get worse for me if I complain. If I let it go and say nothing, I tell myself, maybe they'll give me a break on something in return.

But they're going to bury me all the same. I have nothing to bargain with. Thirty thousand dollars or so to Prosecutor Shin might have done wonders, but I don't know bribery is possible in my spot. I'm still naïvely looking for the benefit of the doubt, for the detectives to realize that I'm really just a good kid and pretty damn harmless, for them to laugh this off after scaring me and let the whole thing go. I don't know about the hard-and-fast ways of the world.

But I'm getting a quick tutorial.

TWO OF THE detectives start asking for all my personal information. One takes my shoulder bag off me and finds my passport. He flips through its pages, examining the stamps.

"Mongolia, China, Russia—why you go there?" he asks accusingly.

I know my answer isn't going to work—the Trans-Siberian Railroad, the wonders of that trip. Everything I've done is now being impugned with a motivation that wasn't there before. It's all suspect; in their eyes I've always been a smuggler. To keep myself together, I hold fast to the idea that they know nothing about me or my past, that their judgments aren't the truth of the matter. But the damn weight given to those judgments—a relentless weight that will sit on me and surround me for years—my powerlessness, press hard on me, and I feel myself buckling. I don't like how my life looks through their eyes.

"I wanted to see those places," I tell the detective.

He looks at me smugly. A come-and-go traveler? Come on, what kind of life is that? he seems to say. To a Korean's mind, marriage is proper and important, a steady job to which one is unfailingly loyal is proper and important, stability and a certain social place are proper and important. I come up short in every category. I'm a piss-poor Confucian, a counterculture, a vagrant, outside the decent lines, and a foreigner to boot.

"You traveled but not working? What money?"

"I saved money from teaching."

"Teaching where?"

"At a children's school in Taechi-dong, at Dongduk Women's University . . . I taught businessmen at Hyundai, at ELS on Chongno . . ."

"If you are English teacher, why no work visa? Why did you arrive and go many times to our country?" With a pen he quickly draws a circle around my Korean visa. "Your work was illegal here."

Noncontract, no binding commitments, more money—everything I might say to explain myself would be wrong. Colored in this new light, my life looks loose and mean.

*Moo jik,* no job, the agent writes in the computer. Where am I staying? He wants to know the address. Who are my friends in Seoul? What do I do with my time? He asks the questions, then writes in his computer.

I begin to see that an irreversible process has started and that I'm caught in its machinery. I keep wishing Shin and the detectives wouldn't take the whole thing so damned seriously, but they are. I haven't harmed anyone, I argue in my head. I committed no violence. But as the private illusion of my illegal fantasy is pierced and overrun by these real-world agents, I realize, painfully, that the world at large isn't on the same page as I am, isn't as carefree and amoral and forgiving. And as this bubble is burst, the addling adolescent air drained from it, I feel myself waking in horror.

The investigator periodically stops his train of inquiry and gives me a practiced man-to-man look that says "Come on, kid; it's your package. Be a man and tell us you did it."

"It's not mine. I swear," I protest again, wishing it were the truth. "I picked it up for Jay Gallagher, an American guy I met in the Philippines. I didn't know him that well; I traveled with him for about a week. But it seemed like an easy thing to do. He said he wouldn't be back in Seoul for another couple of weeks and he wanted someone to go get his package at the general post office and hold on to it until he got here. He was young, my age maybe, with long hair and blue eyes. I had no idea of what was inside; otherwise I never would have picked it up. No, he didn't pay me anything . . ."

I'm thinking of a real character I met in the Philippines and turning him into a desperate fiction. He was a well-traveled American who never told us his real name or age. He called himself Tio and juggled everywhere we went in the Philippines—balls, bowling pins (he traveled with them), beer bottles— entertaining children in the seaside villages of Cebu and Mindanao, softening the mistrustful, curious stares. Tio had been all over Asia. Maybe he liked young boys, but he certainly didn't have anything to do with the package in question, or any other that I knew of. He never once smoked with us on those hot nights in our bungalows or on the beaches under the sheet lightning that filled the Visayan sky.

Another investigator, an athletic-looking Korean, about thirty-five and wearing a dark sweater, pulls a chair up on my left side and sits down. He looks at me sharply but also with a certain detachment: it's business as usual. He's holding a thick wooden stick in his hand, and as I give my answers each time, as I lie and equivocate, as the guy behind the computer looks at me incredulously, shaking his head, this one brings the stick up to the side of my head, threatens to strike me, then brings it down slowly onto my left shoulder and taps me with it a few times. I'm praying that he doesn't hit me. My body is useless, a danger to me. I try to draw it in, disappear. I feel my shoulders and head slumping, but all my nerve endings are tingling with fear. The agent at my side says nothing; he just sits there and menaces, first with the stick, then in the same tapping manner at the side of my head with a sneaker. I'm lucky that's all it is. A Korean would have been beaten; other foreigners were, and worse.

When I give the detective at the computer my home phone number in New York, he thinks that I'm lying. Who do you think I am? I scream silently in my head. I can't yet grasp the level of mistrust. I'm a kid who has made a large yet harmless mistake. They see me as something far more nefarious, and I can't get over the chasm of difference in our perceptions.

"That's my parents' phone number."

"Really?" the detective says provocatively. "You said it not clearly. Say again." I repeat it for him. Acting as though he has caught me, as though he's too smart for me to pull one over on him, he dials the number.

It's Friday morning in New York, and my father answers. "Hello."

"Yes, does Col-een To-ma-suh live here?"

"No, he doesn't. Who's calling?"

"This is Korea Police Inspector Lee. Do you know where he is?"

"This is Jeff Thomas, his father. This is his home, but he doesn't live here anymore. Can I help you?"

"Jep To-ma-suh?"

I turn to the agent at my left and say with some vindication, "That's my father." Pops overhears me. It's the last time he'll hear me for a long while.

"He's right there," my father says. "What's wrong? Can I talk to him?"

"He has serious trouble. You cannot talk now, but he will be permitted phone call later," the agent says before abruptly hanging up. They never give me the phone call. Korean law doesn't include a suspect's right to one. (My father still curses the man: "That bastard! He lied to me; he said you would get a phone call!")

Hours have passed since they grabbed me, and my mind is a

hot blur. I'm desperate for it to stop. Please, even just a break, I'm thinking; let me collapse for a moment, let me stop this bleeding. I feel like I've been run over. My mind has been drubbed numb; but just on the other side of that numbness I can feel self-condemnation festering, my own conscience waiting for its turn at me.

The young American the police arrested with me at the post office is in the room. They have him on a couch and are asking him questions.

"I don't even know him. He wasn't with me. He had nothing to do with it," I keep telling the detectives. After holding him for several hours, they finally let him go, and as he breathes in relief, rubs his wrists, and is escorted past me toward the door, he says to me, "Good luck." I'm sorry that because of a hello from me in the post office, he's been handcuffed, held, and threatened, but I envy him, too, because how clean is true innocence? As I watch him go by me and walk out the door, I'm thinking, How simple is that? At this moment I see how much that can mean, how our deeds spell the difference.

THE DETECTIVES CALL in a young Korean American—probably a relative of one of the men, a nephew, or the sexless, proper male friend and neighbor of one of their daughters. They bring him in to translate exactly what I'm saying and to explain their side of it clearly. I try to imagine the detectives calling him at his house in the early evening of that Friday night:

*Hi, is this little Chung Min's mother? Greetings, how are you? It's the prosecutor's office. Yes, we're looking for your son. We have this American suspect here and it's not going so well. We could use your son's English.*

*Ah, yes, okay, he's doing his schoolwork. I will get him, one moment, please.*

Mom must have been so proud of her little man.

We've been doing all right without the little hero up till now. I certainly don't need an arrogant, glasses-wearing seventeen-year-old to stop his homework so that he can come in and grill me, tell me I'm stupid, and stare disapprovingly at me in my worst hour. But that's what I get. This kid sits there with poise and translates the inspectors' questions, putting them to me in English with smug confidence—the same questions about the box, where it comes from, how I'm connected to it, who Jay Gallagher is. He doesn't stay long, but my low point comes when he is across the desk from me.

"So, you are saying that you didn't know what was inside the package? You were picking it up for the man you met in the Philippines, someone you didn't really know."

"That's right."

"Well," he sighs, reaching his summation, "you're either lying or you're really stupid." Staring right at me, this little hired prick, telling me how it is. I've suspended my ego and a good deal of pride since the process began, trying not to provoke the police any further, but there is enough still active in me to bristle at this kid. It's a bitter phrase to swallow, not least of all because he's right.

Now the detectives take my books and papers out of my bag. I have a pocket-size Bartholomew world atlas, and they smirk at me over that as if it's further proof of my criminality. I also have a list of phone numbers of friends and business contacts I've acquired in Seoul. The agents take their time going slowly down the list, quizzing me on who the people are, especially the Koreans.

I answer the detectives regarding each person in turn. "Tae Woo—he's a student of mine . . . Mr. Han—that was an institute owner I worked for . . . Hae Jin—a girl I was friends with . . . Kim Myung Sik—he's the editor of the *Korea Times*. I wrote for them." See! I'm a writer, and look! I've done good things in your country, worthy things; I'm not the unwanted element, I argue in my head.

They don't know what to make of the little book of wisdom I have in my bag: *A Practical Manual for Good and Perilous Times,* by the seventeenth-century Spanish priest Baltasar Gracián. A gift from my dad. He's always trying to wise us up. The titles of the book's sections read like warnings: "No man is wise at all hours"; "When a falsehood is exposed, accept immediate responsibility"; "To cavort with the vulgar is to infect both dignity and reputation"; "Be careful what you put in writing"; "Know that there are no secrets"; "Know how to plead your case."

I'd been unwise. I hadn't accepted. I'd cavorted, put stuff in writing, forgotten about secrets, and wasn't doing too well pleading. I'd read Gracián's book, but damned if I wasn't coming up empty on every count.

The detectives register each item in a log and post little yellow notes in Korean on them. I've always loved the precision of Koreans' handwriting, and I admired it even then. I turn my head to see Korean suspects being interrogated at another desk in the room. They look sordid. Do I look the same now? I wonder. Like me, they're handcuffed and seated on metal folding chairs, but they're wearing blue prison uniforms and have ropes around their arms. The detective at the computer in front of one suspect keeps shouting and standing up to slap him on the head.

I'm the most exhausted I've ever been. The detectives are calling it a day after some seven hours of bullying. I just want to collapse on the floor and not think or move, but it's time for dinner. The detectives order a delivery and clear off the two couches and coffee table so we can have a group meal. To pay for my share, one detective has me watch as he takes out a ten-thousand-won note (roughly twelve dollars then) from the money that's in my bag. The agents are just finishing off another day of success catching bad guys, settling down to relax over their steaming bowls. Happy them, disconsolate me. They seem pleased to know that my life is sinking before them, and I'm stunned by their callousness. I'm at the end of one couch, sitting with my head down and not much appetite, but the detectives pass me food and try to include me as though we're on a team picnic. They uncuff me so I can eat. My arms, though free now, feel lifeless. They ask if I like Korean food. I say I do and they nod approvingly. They've ordered *ja-jang myun* for me, a favorite among young Koreans: thick noodles with beef and vegetables covered in a thick black sauce. I suppose I was lucky to have been included in their meal; it was a foreigner's privilege, the first of many—each one countered by an equal and opposite foreigner's disadvantage.

They comment on the way I use the chopsticks with my left hand. All of them eat with their right. The offices are quiet except for the sound of the plastic bowls and containers, the metal of the chopsticks, and the detectives' slurping and chewing.

After dinner they give me a blanket and lock me in an empty holding cell off the main room. I lie down on the pitted wood floor and listen to the sounds of the detectives departing. The lights go off and I hear doors closing. Then the silence seems to rise in my ears like a wave and overwhelm me. It's crushing. I feel like crying, but I have nothing left (how sad is self-pity!). Within moments, I crumple into sleep.

# 3

THE NEXT MORNING, as I'm being led out into the parking lot of the Seoul prosecutors' building, several Korean attorneys in suits turn to stare at me. No matter how professional Korean justice might be, the mere sight of a handcuffed foreigner still creates an immediate, voyeuristic spectacle. I stand out. They stare and I can see their questions on their faces. This is good because I know I won't get lost in the shuffle. But I wonder what side effects this extra attention, my being a novelty, will bring.

It's late May 1994. The Korean spring is fresh, and the air feels good against my skin after my night in the holding cell. Three detectives are leading me toward a four-door silver sedan. I squint up into the sun. I'm struck by the sudden instinct to somehow memorize and store what I'm seeing out there in the open. As we drive south I watch in silence as we pass geometric Korean characters against low cement and unlit neon tubes. The detectives say nothing. Then we're out of the concrete jumble and in broader spaces, the outskirts of Anyang City, a satellite of the capital. Set back from the two-lane road about a mile, behind fields with nurseries, greenhouses, and farm equipment, the towers and solid walls of a large, faded white fort stand out against a low, rolling hill. At the four corners and halfway down the line of each wall are towers with podlike, oval battlements in the same blank, faded stone as the walls. In the center of the interior, standing high above everything else, is a main tower atop a thick column, and I can see that like a single Cyclops eye it watches everything below it in a powerful 360-degree sweep.

We drive through several gates and into a central courtyard. A blue sign above the entrance to the main building announces the

Seoul Detention House, one of several jails in and around Seoul where suspects are held during their trials and sentencing. Most of the writing in the prison, and that on my indictment and court papers, will remain inscrutable to me for months to come. My comprehension is on a serious time delay, and the lag makes life much more difficult and forces me to learn as much Korean as I can, as fast as I can.

I see guards coming and going, in dark blue uniforms, with caps bearing the symbol of Korean justice, a flower, the rose of Sharon, its rounded petals forming a pentagram. Young soldiers in fatigues pass by and take me in with glances, stares, some with an audible "Oh?" I think I hear others say things in English as they go by, dredging up words or phrases they've studied in school over the years.

The detectives lead me up the polished front steps, past the Korean flags on either side, and into a large room with dozens of desks. They turn me over to the detention house guards and walk out. In the room soldiers stomp by in thick black boots. Some of them are skinny, pimply kids, others solid and fierce looking: hard, square faces and shaved heads. It's the same with the guards: in their appearance and countenance some remind me that South Korea is a young and innocent place. They're a good-natured, tradition-bound people, and there is nothing to fear, especially for an American, I think. But in others I see the unknown and the unpredictable, the fiercer edge of justice, and the toughness and unreason of a very different Asia.

A guard tells me to sit on a couch along the wall, and as I do I feel the weight of the entire place press right down on my chest. I break down. Fear is a part of the pain. I'm crying because everything is lost, and I don't want to go to jail, not for another night, not for the long years Shin has threatened me with. I've seen movie scenes of prison. I've read some books. But I've never before been inside a prison or, to my knowledge, even seen one from the outside. I've never been in trouble with the law. Thoughts and images from my time in Seoul run through my head as I'm trying to guess what kind of prisons Koreans might run, what it will be like for me once we step outside this office. I wonder if they'll beat me. I think of tae kwon do, the deadly Korean martial art, of fights I've seen in the streets, of the legends I've heard about the ferocity of South Korean soldiers who served with U.S. forces in Vietnam. No doubt they're a passionate people with fierce tempers. I'm worried whether I'll be able to defend myself if I have to fight in here. What will the cell be like? Will I be put with Korean sociopaths? Regardless, crying isn't going to make a good first impression, I tell myself. Maybe they'll think Americans are soft.

Just then an older officer with a kind face walks over and takes a seat in a chair in front of me. He shakes his head gently and pats my leg. In halting English he asks me my name.

"Do not worry, Tomasuh," he says, still holding the hard edge that every guard tried to maintain, the attitude that says "You've done this; you've committed a crime, son. This is your rightful lot, so pick yourself up and deal with it."

I'm led into an empty room with wooden benches and told to strip. The guard looks displeased with his task. I take off my pants, shirt, shoes, then everything else. I watch as the guard rolls the items into a ball on the floor, then holds them away from his body and hurries the bundle out of the room as though it were contaminated, both biologically and morally, I suppose. I wonder when I'll see my clothes again, and instantly the thought becomes a goal. When you get your clothes back, I tell myself, you'll know this is over.

The guard asks me to bend over and he quickly half-pantomimes the action so that I understand. He's holding a small flashlight at the ready. I can see by the expression on his face that this is horrific for him. I'm not excited about it either. I bend over, and in no time to do much inspecting at all he calls the operation complete. He issues me a pair of floppy gray rubber slippers, tosses me two pairs of cheap white underwear, two undershirts, a pair of socks, and fishes out a pair of dark blue prison pants and a jacket top. The pants are too short, and the jacket sleeves don't reach my wrists. I'm a goofy-looking inmate.

The guard leads me into an adjoining gray cement room where a dozen new Korean inmates are seated on wooden benches. I take a seat behind them all in the last row. A guard at the front of the room begins to sharply inform us of the rules of the detention house. I can't understand anything he says. Old men with wrinkled faces turn and look quizzically at me. Some of the guys look like the absolutely appropriate dregs: shambling cretins with scars and tattoos of dragons, insensate and retarded faces; younger Koreans with disturbed energy, sour mouths, and misshapen heads, physiognomies that by themselves might lead to convictions. The instructor ignores me. I can't help thinking, Am I subject to these rules in the same way? If this is a purely Korean world, then where and how do I fit in?

These are questions that will never really go away, that neither side will ever fully answer.

A GUARD LEADS me into the jail's maze of empty gray hallways stretching hundreds of yards. My escort and I walk quietly, snaking our way to block 13. Numb and in a kind of trance, I watch his shoes hitting the stone and stare at the neatly trimmed hair below his cap on the back of his neck. We climb to the third floor—an empty hall with a view over the walls at the front of the jail, fifteen cells down the left side. It's the specially designated foreigners' floor, where we are segregated from the Korean inmates.

As the guard walks me down the hall, I can see faces looking out from the barred openings of each cell, guys standing up and leaning against the bars, seeing who the newcomer is, making him walk the gauntlet. I feel thin and weak in their gaze; I wonder if they can tell I'm scared and inexperienced. I try to walk tall and not turn my head to look at any of them squarely.

"What country?" someone calls out.

The guard stops at cell 12. His big metal key rattles as it enters the hole and finds the notch; there is a second of metallic strain as it works against the bolt, then the sudden power of the metal sliding, smashing against the other side of the mechanism—a deep *BANNGG* that echoes down the hall and hangs in the air. From this opening note it becomes the score to our prison lives. Bang to let us out, bang to put us back, bangs to divide the days.

I step up into the cell in which I'll spend twenty-three hours a day for the next six months. It's a two-man cell—there is a small bed frame covered by a thin green mattress on either side of the room—but I have it to myself for now, and that is a small consolation. The thought comes to me that my teaching in Korea is over; it lasted just seven months. Now it seems like it was years. And how long am I going to be here? I need to know. Nobody has broken the spell and laughed at himself, not Shin or the detectives or the guards. But the delusional part of me is still waiting for somebody to appear to snap his fingers and make it all go away.

In the year leading up to this moment, I traveled to feel the rush of discovery: searching for coffee in Moscow; staring out a huge window with blue shutters at the lights rising in a hill above Tetouan; watching a sunset from the top of a white wall in the Andalusian town of Villamartín; riding in the bicycle streams of Beijing. There was recklessness, too, and leaving things to chance. Rocket—my dynamic partner, a short spark plug of a Jewish-American girl from Brooklyn—she and I got out of Morocco on our last dollars, slept under a palm in Estepona, hitchhiked several days back to Seville. Then I actively sought an element of danger. The pitch had to be higher, the mix more intense. Just a few weeks before my arrest, I was in the southern Philippines, on the breakaway island of Mindanao, with its tales of Islamic rebels and kidnappings. I was hopping islands down the wild Sulu Archipelago, looking for pirates. Choices finally caught up with me.

In the cell I walk over and sit down on the edge of one cot. I sit there staring off, dumbfounded. In the short walk down the corridor I was struck by what I faced. It is far too much reality, and yet it seems like a perfect joke—though again, no one besides me seems to be seeing it that way (a pretty good sign that something is drastically wrong). I mean, who still puts iron bars on windows to match the picture of a prison in a dictionary? And the windows set so you can see out but not too much, just enough to tease you with the notion that the whole world is off limits? The guards' costume—their stiff military caps, the pins of rank on their collars—seems too perfect. And the metal door, the ancient lock and key; everything gray, drab, bare—all of it screams "Cliché!" at the top of its lungs. Deep below my shock—I can almost hear it—a voice inside my head is saying, "You've got to be kidding me."

Until now I've never considered the risk; worse, I managed to ignore the chance of things going wrong. Now I want to know why they have. I'm like a man shot through the chest but disbelieving it, with a stunned look on his face as he runs his hands over his body trying to find the wound. Thomas refusing to believe it was Christ risen until he could feel where his master was pierced. Why me? Why this? I keep asking myself desperately as the guard shuts the cell door. It's as if my life is caught in the frame and is cut neatly in two when the door slams shut.

# 4

"SWORDS!" I WAS yelling at my mom as she stood over her table saw in the backyard. That's where we could find her most days when we got home from school. The rough sounds of power tools going meant Mom was near and all was well.

My brother, Chris, eleven years old, and I, fifteen months younger, stood a bit away. There were rules for when she was working; we'd already broken one of them just by talking to her, but this was an emergency.

"We need more swords!" I shouted over the noise.

Mom turned off the saw and it growled to an angry stop.

"Mom, sorry, some of our swords broke yesterday. Can you make us new ones?"

"Just write down what you need. I'll do them today if I finish the shelves."

She made beds, dollhouses, bookcases, desks—finest female carpenter on the eastern seaboard. Her father was an architect, and maybe she picked it up from him—designing structures, shaping materials. She once ran her own business, Thomas Teaching Tools, creating educational crafts and toys out of wood, and once was commissioned by the town to make a wood model of an old castle on the water in Sands Point. Her replica was stunning, and after it was done and had made the local papers, we sat around the mini-castle staring, poring over its ramparts and chambers, imagining all the things that could happen in and around such a place. Mom had enormous energy, enough for her to also serve as our armorer, crafting us weapons to feed our warrior fantasies. No other mom went this far; we knew ours was the best.

Chris and I went into the kitchen and got out a piece of paper and a pencil.

"Ole, Josh, Mark, Dave . . . me and you, so we need, let's say, six short swords."

"And daggers," I said excitedly. "I definitely need a dagger. Write four!" A dagger was necessary if your sword got knocked from your hand. You could sheathe it in one of the loops on the waist of your pants.

We ran back outside and placed the paper next to the saw. Later in the day there would be a beautiful pile of wooden swords waiting for us on the deck. Mom's blades were simple yet perfect: each one with the top cut in from both sides to form a harmless but realistic point, a small piece nailed at a right angle six inches above the base to form the hilt. The short swords were about two feet long; the daggers, half that. We'd assemble the kids on our street as quickly as possible, distribute the weapons, and grab black plastic garbage-can tops to serve as shields. We'd split into groups and go berserk, staging pitched battles all around the house, over the front and back decks, down into the woods of Port Washington. Kids would be spread out in combat over the lawns and porches. We thought we were brave and battle-wise. I fancied myself a rare swordsman, a slashing piratical master. I loved it when the other kids nicknamed me Spider because I'd spin webs and dodge them all and couldn't be trapped and would cut away at unseen angles. I'd stab guys through the cracks in Mark's fence. I was going to do wonders, win kingdoms.

It was Mom who ordered Chris and me the complete set of Tintin's adventures from Little, Brown when we had to have them all. They arrived in a neat brown box, which we immediately tore open, spreading the colorful books out on the floor, throwing ourselves into them. Tintin, that little blond dandy, and his creator, Hergé, hold much of the blame for my wanderlust. Tintin was always off somewhere, on the run, investigating, deep in some intrigue. We followed him to Tibet, Scotland, Peru, the Red Sea. The names alone lit up my imagination, the stories providing some of my earliest and most memorable geography lessons. When someone spoke in a foreign language, the words were written out in the alphabet of that tongue; the native costumes (djellabas, Amazon cloth, Mongol coats, English knickers) were accurate and exotic; the streets of foreign cities were drawn to evoke the local color— all of it infused with wonder and simplicity, the kaleidoscope of the real world seen through the pure eyes of an inquisitive boy. I wanted to go where Tintin did. I could be like him, my pea brain thought; I can learn those skills, have that luck abroad, even without the little white dog of a talisman he always had with him. I'll wield my machine gun on a deserted island as he does in *Flight 714*. I'll brave the curse of the disturbed Incan mummies, make my way in disguise through the bazaar of an Arab city.

In all our minds was Tolkien's *The Lord of the Rings*, the quest, the wonder and terror of unknown places. We'd all read the books at around the same time, memorizing down to the lineage of horses the dizzying array of details. Like Aragorn or Frodo, we'd be in the thick of it. We were pirates for Halloween, with sashes and blades. Dressed as soldiers one year, we'd stabbed, crushed, and busted scores of beautiful pumpkins that people had placed in prim arrangements around their homes. A pumpkin massacre— some streets ran with seeds. Chris and I were always playing with our little cavalry figures, Union troops with guns, or with Lincoln logs, making frontier houses and forts. We made up endless games in the woods. A favorite one year was Dr. Hinton and Balldigger Jones. Hinton was an evil bastard played by Chris. He wielded a big metal pogo stick that for us was a crossbow known simply as "the heavy." I was Jones, the guy whose life was spent tracking down Dr. Hinton. Dave was my trusty sidekick, Max. Dave was always the sidekick, always the lovable freak with the large white-boy Afro. He was fascinated by blood and guts and could often be found reading *Fangoria* magazine or hiding in his kitchen closet with large knives to scare his mother when she came home. But Dave was the gentlest kid out of all of us. We lived across the street from each other and were close friends. We played together almost every day, until he careened headfirst into a tree while skiing in Vermont and died at age twelve. Twelve years was precious little. Dave was supposed to walk away from a fall. We all were.

We played Dungeons and Dragons for hours on end. Every part of those dice-and-paper adventures was conjured in detail, written down, debated, and vicariously acted out. There were dazzling treasures and beasts, fortresses and caves, secret doors and passages, and maps, so many amazing maps. Kobolds to hack apart, gelatinous blobs that would try to suck you in, poisoned chests that would shoot darts into you when you greedily pried them open, cloaks and boots that allowed you to move with stealth, backstabbings, entire books full of monsters, magical weapons, gold and platinum for the taking. Everything went through the imagination, and you'd have to watch your players, your thieves, rangers, and clerics, as you would yourself, measuring their strength and how much they could carry. The game taught us a whole new vocabulary for the world, words like "initiative," "dexterity," "constitution."

Pops was into maps, and all manner of strange facts and knowledge—natural disasters, UFOs, esoteric teachings. The family stopped going to Mass at St. Francis, and Pops began leading us in meditation circles on the living room floor, with books on the psychic Edgar Cayce and extraterrestrial contacts from the Pleiades on the shelves around us. During our meditations Chris and I would make stupid faces when everyone's eyes were supposed to be closed. Our younger twin sisters, unable to resist opening their eyes, would look up, see us, and burst out laughing, destroying the solemnity Pops was trying to create. He would take Chris and me on what seemed like daring expeditions to Half Moon Beach in Sands Point, where we'd follow him on treks over swampland, with us occasionally falling into the murk or, in winter, on our bellies, crawling over fields of ice. He liked to tell us about malamutes, the hardiest dogs: "They can go the farthest, with the heaviest load, on the least amount of food." In the winter we went out on missions with him to collect wood for our stoves. We'd find abandoned pallets behind factories, take them home, and cut and pile the wood into neat stacks under our front porch.

To be the Jolly Marauder, that was the ideal my brother and I imagined, our name for it. If we had an archetype or a life model, the Jolly Marauder was it, a kind of half-pirate, half-noble adventurer. We saw him as resilient and scrappy, with tons of energy. There was a lot that was honest and unfettered in him, too. He might be wounded, but he'd keep coming; he didn't mind the odds against him. He might verbally desecrate your mother, but he'd win the day; able as all hell, he was on the fly. And the Marauder knew without saying that life was a vast opportunity, a huge, kaleidoscopic treasure, so the trick was to plunge forward with near abandon. There was too much to enjoy. He'd jump ditches, fight if he had to, save birds by beaning predatory cats with tennis balls on perfect strikes from across the street, laugh into enormous slices of watermelon, eating them like a famished lunatic while Grandmom told the story of Granddad's death from the other side of the table (amazingly, she took no offense); he'd help where he could and work hard and do what he wasn't supposed to—throw snowballs at cars and handfuls of candy against the sides of houses, creating the sound of suburban machine-gun fire. I can see something Irish in our Jolly Marauder, his scrappy toughness, his celebratory spirit. In Conrad's short story "Youth," the boat young Marlow is on is battered by heavy storms on its voyage to Bangkok. Marlow is forced to tie himself to the mast by a rope as he desperately tries to bail water from her. He's sure the boat is destined for the bottom, but he's suddenly hit by a wave of realization there on the deck. He feels intensely alive, and joy rips through him as he sees he's right in the middle of one hell of an adventure, "the endeavor, the test, the trial of life." It's an example of the finest marauding.

When I was in college I met a guy who'd made good money playing guitar on the streets in Taipei and who introduced me to Sir Richard Francis Burton—the British soldier who made a daring hajj to Mecca in the 1850s, sought the legendary source of the Nile, took a Somali spear through his face near Berbera on the Horn of Africa, learned more than two dozen languages, was one of the finer swordsmen of his day, was knighted for his multi-volume translation of *The Arabian Nights*. I was mesmerized. Burton was a marauder of the highest order. After reading about him I knew what I wanted to do.

The places, games, and stories over the years didn't pass without leaving a certain spirit in me. Wonder was everywhere you looked; and the harder you looked, the more of it you found. I didn't grow out of that; I kept on believing I could find something extraordinary out in the world, an adventure of my own.

# 5

I WENT TO South Korea in the summer of 1993 to teach English. I couldn't think of anything better. I was splitting time between my parents' house on Long Island and my friends' apartment in Manhattan. My friends and I were mostly drifting aimlessly, all of us playing at our passions, drawing and writing in turns in a large journal that Jamie had named *The Big Book of Dreams*. Through Jamie's illustrations, Matt's photographs, Erik's general madness, and my and Jon's writing, we were supposed to create a new land of the lotus-eaters, a creative utopia of inspired living. But we were lazy and easily distracted. We spent our days looking for women, scraping together money, and taking Jon's pit bull on walks to Washington Square Park, where we'd smoke and watch people. All of us had artistic pursuits but none of us had the required discipline. I dreamed of traveling, getting away from what I knew and what was quickly becoming stagnant. The idea gave me a feeling of purpose and direction, and there was no more time to waste. I thought of how Burton, at my age, had already ditched Oxford for India, where as a soldier he was mastering horsemanship and local dialects, delving into the jungles of the culture. I'd done nothing. I was unformed and untested.

My parents encouraged me to travel: in an older era a young person's education wasn't finished until he went out and saw the world to an extent, they told me. That was how you gained empirical knowledge, the best kind. As the travel writer Robert Byron told it, the British, for their part, had been such great explorers largely because of their strong empirical tradition; they were guided by the simple notion that in order to truly know the world at large, you had to go out and experience it for yourself. The semester I'd spent in London in 1991 had further infused me with that spirit. Since that time, the idea of another trip abroad had given me a little soul-stinging thrill unlike anything else.

I'd graduated from Binghamton University with a degree in English in the summer of 1992, then worked in New York City as a waiter at the Slaughtered Lamb pub, where I kept myself alive by giving free pints of Guinness to friends and stealing bottles of Samuel Smith's Taddy Porter and fine ales from the storage room. I felt dead in my jacket and tie behind a register at a Rizzoli bookstore on Long Island. None of that made me feel very good about myself, and so I held on to my plan. My prospects in New York weren't great—mostly as a result of my own lack of focus and effort—but I knew that with my degree I could teach English abroad. A trip, then, would satisfy my thirst for adventure and give me the beginnings of a career all at once.

I chose South Korea, but really it could have been anywhere. If I'd had leads on teaching jobs in Sri Lanka or Uruguay, I might have tried myself there. Anywhere was dazzling—unknown languages and ways, the wild, disparate contours of countries on maps. I didn't know a thing about Korea, North or South. There were hundreds of Korean students with me at Binghamton, but I'd never had a good conversation with any of them. I didn't know a word of the language, nothing about the country's history, not even the outline of a custom; and yet South Korea became my place of choice with the slow inexorability of fate.

Korea kept appearing in the classifieds of the *New York Times*. The bold black letters of the ads drew me in:

## TEACHERS—SOUTH KOREA

I excitedly wrote the information down. I went to Queens for an interview at one Korean family's apartment. They owned an institute back home and were recruiting instructors in New York. A baby boy rocked and peeled leaves from a cabbage head on the floor. I sat with his mother on the sofa, played with my résumé, smiled like an idiot. I sent faxes to some of the other schools in the Help Wanted ads. As part of the application process I wrote short essays about discovering new places, opening myself to the world.

Offers came back: a one-year contract teaching at an institute for children in Seoul, sixteen hundred dollars a month, thirty hours of teaching a week, airfare, housing, medical coverage; or a one-year contract with a high school in the provinces, fifteen hundred a month, one-way airfare, housing, two weeks' paid vacation. The one detail that kept bugging me was the one-year contract. I'd never signed one before, and as excited as I was to go, I wondered what would happen if I got there and it was terrible. What if I couldn't endure Korea? What if I wanted to leave after six months? I'd never thought in long terms, certainly not in units as long as years. I didn't like feeling beholden or tied down; I wanted to be mobile and light. I can see now that it was also the responsibility a contract entailed that I was afraid of and was hoping to avoid.

While trying to make a final decision, I heard that a friend from college was teaching English in South Korea. Tim had signed on for a year and had already been there for several months. The news galvanized me. I called his home in Syracuse, got his address in Seoul, and wrote him straightaway. "The institute where I teach needs more instructors," he wrote back. "You don't need to come on a contract. In fact, you'll make more money per class as a freelancer, an illegal," he said regretfully. I declined the contract offers. "Come and stay in my apartment. I'll set you up with work at our school," Tim offered. "Decide soon," he advised me. His will to stay in Korea was crumbling. Five months, six, he was harried, running out of endurance. "This isn't an easy place to be," he warned. "The culture is too different, you can't really communicate with anyone, the Koreans have mixed feelings about foreigners," he wrote. I was parking Mercedeses, BMWs, and Cadillacs at a country club in Port Washington, harvesting tips from doctors and lawyers who would stuff themselves with tasteless food on nights at the club after days of golf, then come outside with uncontrollable gas and toss me their car keys. With each handoff of a few dollars they helped fuel my plan.

Around that time one of my sisters passed me a large picture book on South Korea that she'd taken out of the local public library. It gave me my first look at the place. It showed a rugged land of low, rolling mountains, ranges in the east and the west, seas on three sides, strong little islands off the rocky coasts, fishing villages and picturesque farmlands, pine trees and rice fields, cherry blossoms and orchids, beautiful, withered old faces like the skin of fruit. On maps the Korean Peninsula looked to me like an epiglottis hanging out of China's mouth—there in the northeast, caught between the formidable dragons of China and Japan, a humble nub jutting into the sea. That geographic position reveals a lot about her history. On a hundred-year-old map I have—I don't know where exactly it was made, but definitely in the West—the Korean Peninsula isn't labeled the Chosun Kingdom, after the native dynasty of that time, or Corea, a variation of the current name, derived from the Koryo dynasty of a thousand years ago, but appears simply as a nameless side theater of the Chinese empire. No doubt Korea has been overlooked, overshadowed, and overrun by the imposing lands and peoples around her.

While I was living there, I thought about the Hermit Kingdom and its historical isolation. I thought about how close-knit the Koreans around me seemed, how many of them also seemed to know little about the world outside their country. Do you have apples in the United States? they asked me. Are there mountains? In prison I met men who had never seen a white man in person before. Some of them asked to touch my skin.

Due to governmental policies and financial limitations, before the 1990s most Koreans hadn't had the opportunity to travel. And ironically, I thought, despite her recent economic fortunes and much wider exposure to the world, South Korea is today a virtual island. With the peninsula cut in half at the 38th parallel, the most fortified border in the world, you can't enter or leave by land. The deranged Stalinist upper half, the unpredictable red-headed stepbrother of the South, is a closed door.

EIGHT MONTHS INTO his year Tim told his institute that he was breaking his contract. I knew he could be an invaluable ally for me, and he'd be there just one more month. I bought a one-way ticket to Seoul for seven hundred dollars from a discount travel agency in Greenwich Village. I called home from a pay phone on University and Eleventh and excitedly told my family that my die had been cast.

≡≡

MY SECOND DAY in Seoul was the Fourth of July, 1993. Tim took us by subway to Itaewon, a hilly section in Seoul next to a large U.S. Army base. Itaewon serviced the bored soldiers, their families, the army's attachments, and other foreigners sick for home. It was an expatriate escape full of bargain goods, souvenirs, Western fast food, and loud drinking. Later, Itaewon would be the place where we would go to buy dollars with the Korean money we earned from teaching. There was a black-market exchange in a little lingerie shop on a lane running next to the Hamilton Hotel. Itaewon felt seedy and bastardized; it was all grit and cheapness (although the stately homes of foreign diplomats were close by). There Korea still felt like a dissipated, occupied country.

Tim and I walked up from the main strip to the top of Hooker Hill, whose namesakes were raffish Korean girls in miniskirts standing beside doorways or sitting inside the open bars. They flirted with the GIs. Guns N' Roses and Nirvana thumped in the background. Fireworks celebrating America's independence shot up over the hills into view and colored the smoggy sky. I wondered where in God's name I was. There was an odor of chemicals and apocalypse. The twenty-year-old soldiers in jeans and T-shirts rumbled from bar to bar, drank on the streets in packs. "Kettle" was popular: Korea's cheap, vodkalike alcohol, called *soju,* mixed with orange soda in teapots or kettles. Some soldiers engaged the prostitutes; others broke out in drunken fights with Koreans on the hill. It was a rare sort of Korean who frequented Itaewon—Korean girls looking to meet foreigners; *kyopos,* ethnic Korean kids who'd grown up in the States; or others who sought something more diverse than what the rest of Korea offered. And it was a rare U.S. soldier who spent much time outside of it. There were districts like Itaewon around U.S. Army bases in several places around the country. For many Koreans these areas were a disgrace: if these districts were an example of a more cosmopolitan society, it's no wonder they rejected the idea.

I remember a sweltering and humid summer in Seoul. The monsoon season came in July and August, bringing with it almost daily showers or sporadic torrents. Koreans avoided the rain; they said it was polluted. Some warned me that if my head got rained on in Seoul, my hair would fall out.

I wandered through enormous apartment complexes—mazes of concrete blocks, one identical building after another. They were distinguished from one another only by large colored numbers painted high up on their sides. Seoul had a lot of makeshift businesses, back alleys, hidden stores, tiny unmarked family restaurants, singing rooms, and bars jumbled together in clusters in nondescript spots, sprawling arcades and undefined markets, stalls on the sidewalks. Squat, jolly older women with short curly hair behind counters or crouching by their wares: the *ajummas.* They'd smile at you and cackle when you didn't understand, give you an extra portion of salted intestines, saying, "Service." Ajummas often looked like they could pull cars or go to war, carry a family of eight on their backs; they were favorites. Fashionable young women heavily made up and filling the streets in a profusion of tiny skirts, covering their mouths when they laughed, speaking with cute girly voices: the *agashee*s. Salarymen looking new to their suits, speeding through lunches, arms akimbo, cigarettes blazing: the *ajashee*s. Corps of identically uniformed secretaries and clerks. Giddy students in uniforms, arms intertwined. Mopeds with metal boxes of food buzzing up on the sidewalks. You could sometimes see the hills surrounding Seoul from down in the midst of this—I liked that—and sights of the restored palaces of the past. Not a city of great structural height; so much cement and soot. At night neon lit the way, marking everything in a bright, tawdry circus. Red neon crosses from hundreds of Christian churches stood up against the leaden sky.

I stayed with Tim and his roommate, Andy, in Chamshil, in one of those labyrinthine apartment complexes just south of the Han River in the eastern part of Seoul. Lee Sung Gae, the founder of the Chosun dynasty (1394–1910), made Seoul his capital in 1394 because geomancy, the Chinese idea of feng shui, wind and water—in Korean *poong soo*—recommended that a palace face south, have mountains behind and flowing water in front. Seoul was ideal. The Han was that propitious water. I often went there to sit on the terraced stone steps rising up from the wide, slow-moving river, to watch the lovers and families, the kites and bridges. The riverside at night was the only public place where I saw Korean lovers dare to kiss.

I started going to the saunas on Tim's recommendation. He'd been frequenting them, said they were immensely relaxing, aside from the unwanted attention his foreign genitals attracted. Koreans were intrigued, he warned me, because the vast majority had never seen a Westerner naked. He told me how he was once scandalized in a local sauna when a spirited old man walked up to him and, laughing, nonchalantly flicked Tim's penis with his hand.

Fathers and sons often washed each other in the showers. Naked, squatting, one over the other, the adolescent son dutiful, measurably devoted, scrubbing hard at the back of his father with a small cloth. Or the father, with his greater strength, scouring all of his boy, who would bear it stoically, and bend and shift as the father ordered. It was an odd sight for me, but also a poignant one. The bond that must be engendered through such family acts, those public ablutions performed for each other. One of the most affecting scenes I ever witnessed in Korea occurred in a sauna in the old Buddhist capital of Kyongju. It was a rainy, cold day and the sauna was a fine refuge. I'd been relaxing in hot water for a short while when in came a blind old man and a teenage boy. I watched as the boy led the man by his hand, sat him down, and then kindly, meticulously began to scrub the blind man's body. I thought I caught sight of something rare and beautiful then, through the vapors and liquid sounds of the bath.

Trucks laden with vegetables, fruits, and fish would drive slowly through our apartment complex while the men in them loudly announced their products through bullhorns. In the torrid summer, a noxious mosquito-spray vehicle also made regular visits. From tubular blowers the driver would let loose enormous clouds of repellent all over the outsides of the apartments. We would hear the drone of his blower as he approached, and would snap to and try to close our windows; we were on the first floor and were the hardest hit. The smoke would tumble into our kitchen in thick billows, then sit in the apartment awhile. It was acrid, made your head hurt, and left you retarded for a spell.

Before Tim happily left us, two friends of Andy's arrived from the States and came to live with us. We were five then, and cramped. Tim and Andy had their own small bedrooms. I had a small side room where I slept on a mattress on the floor. Willowy Craig took to the living room, and short Paul set up a makeshift camp on the constricted porch. They were hippies come to experience the East and earn the converted dollar. Paul played guitar and had lived in upstate New York in a self-styled nomad tent, said he hadn't paid taxes to the U.S. government in seven years. He was at least thirty-five. Craig was younger, skeletal, and droll. One night he sat on a stack of my clothes and farted. I never really liked him after that.

It was often easy not to like the other foreigners. I wondered how I'd fallen in with such a band of freaks. There were so many odd, wandering types—a host of bent Australians, warped British, tainted Canadians, tormented runaway Americans. (I considered myself fairly well balanced among this cast, but then look what became of me.) I'd expected it to a certain degree, but I was still surprised. Most of them seemed like misfits. Only a few seemed to transcend the impression of escape, anomie, and discontent. But all of us found teaching work with astounding ease. It didn't matter that, on the whole, we were ragged and suspect because the demand for English in Korea was so great that almost anyone was accepted.

THERE WERE A lot of Australians in Seoul, but their numbers seemed to be declining; their English wasn't the preferred form. Koreans wanted American English. They made this chauvinism obvious, stated it outright. The Australians, to some degree, resented this. Though the Canadians had a large contingent in Seoul, they also decried America's cultural and linguistic grip on Korea. But we worked together. Under different circumstances it never would have happened, but there were few of us, and so we instinctively attached to one another. What also linked us was a roughly similar spirit, a simple and unrefined one of travel and the pursuit of experience. That was the one thing that could always unite one's sympathies with the other foreigners, despite all the crooked and insurmountable differences. Koreans called us all foreigners, *weigookeen dool*, and in many ways treated us as a single category. We felt our differences from them acutely. Korea is one of the most homogeneous countries on earth, with few or no ethnic, cultural, or linguistic differences among her people. They often boasted of their racial purity—no matter that history quickly proves this to be a myth. Some histories state that Koreans descended from or mixed with various Mongol and northern Chinese tribes that migrated onto the peninsula more than two thousand years ago. Like the Japanese, Koreans still talk of being born with the Mongol birthmark, a bluish circle of skin, usually found on the butt, which fades after a few years.

The locals were coarse and kind to us at the same time. On the subways and streets, at the tiny food stalls, they would try out their English on us, asking bluntly, sometimes provocatively, why we'd come to their country. Where from? How old? This last question was paramount, came at us from all sides: in Korea's Confucian order, age most often dictates what mold of relationship is required. And were we married? Did we have children? Were we educated? How much money did we earn a month? And we came to Korea for that, right? These exchanges occurred often. Many of the foreigners found them intrusive. But for the Koreans it was an instinctive way of sizing us up and relieving the intrigue. Tim was right; it wasn't an easy place to be. But I'd wanted a new world, and Seoul was certainly that. I was excited to be there.

# 6

THREE DAYS AFTER arriving in Seoul, I went to work. Tim's institute asked me to step right in. It was in the Taechi neighborhood of Kangnam District, former farmland on the south side of the Han River that had been sold for a fortune. It had made many Koreans wealthy and was now full of clothing stores, modern malls, and shops carrying luxury items. Koreans called the privileged young people from Kangnam the Orangee Tribe—apparently, the inspiration for the name was a fad during the early 1990s that had men in their cars giving oranges to young ladies on the street who caught their eye. Our institute was one of the many ECCs in Seoul run by the largest English-teaching company in Korea at the time, Si-sa-young-o-sa. ECC stood for English Children Center, a screwed-up title that seemed to announce a place for British kids.

The school was above a Wendy's restaurant on the second floor of a faux-brick building. I walked into the reception area and was greeted by two smiling and polite Korean girls in extremely short skirts. Surrounded by children and their mothers and all the happy-colored walls and furniture, these secretaries, raised up on high heels like comic-book fantasies, gave the place an incongruous edge. One of the school's young administrators put me through a brief interview in an empty classroom. I gave her my résumé and a copy of my college diploma. She asked if I had a work visa. When I told her I didn't, she said, "Well, you cannot legally work in Korea . . . But it should be okay. Our company has an agreement with the government." Other schools were periodically raided, and occasionally one would hear of foreigners being fined and deported for teaching illegally. But the Si-sa institutes had everything well oiled. As an American with a degree in English and a relatively clear voice, I had an odd, almost accidental power. I was a viable business, in wide demand simply because of my voice and the syllables it could command.

So I taught illegally—teaching English, then, was my first crime in Korea. In my classes at the Taechi-dong ECC, tiny children cried and slept as mothers watched from the window, and I, desperately trying to keep the children happy and awake, repeated the names of animals and colors, pointed at pictures, told them to be quiet, carried in games, toys, blocks—and a soft red ball that I would throw against their heads from across the room to stop them from punching each other, tearing at each other's hair, urinating on the floor and trampling over the puddles in their socks. They never cried from those aerial attacks of mine, only suddenly grew quiet, looked around dazed while rubbing their eyes, then sat down again, chastened and calmer. I made sure the mothers never saw this.

I was given a tiny desk in the teachers' room. We had a selection of textbooks and toys against the wall, a prearranged curriculum for each age level. You had only to follow the folders that listed what topics and pages were to be covered each day. That was easy enough, and the money seemed almost free (about thirty dollars per hour, untaxed); but the series of forty-five-minute classes, each one on the heels of another, with only five or ten minutes of break time between them, wore down the mind just as physical labor wears down the body. I sometimes did nine-hour days, and by the fourth or fifth hour I was often in a catatonic state. *The ball is blue; the car is red . . . What is this? . . . How are you? . . . Repeat after me: This is a pig . . . Who is happy? . . . Who is in the kitchen? . . . I am a girl; he is a boy . . . Repeat after me . . .* There's only so much of that you can do in a day before your brain starts to atrophy.

In our desk drawers we had our folders and student-name lists, crayons, scissors, markers, and clips. It was elementary. We crafted and drew and cut out for the children; made copies of rhymes, puzzles, and pictures. We the teachers looked like a juvenile bunch, some overgrown civil army, big-kneed at our little desks, preparing our childish pedagogical tricks. The beginnings and ends of classes were marked by nursery-rhyme melodies that were broadcast through the halls. The cloying music would begin suddenly at the end of a class and into the faculty room we'd march, arms stacked with textbooks—*Hooray for English!* and *Side by Side*. After five minutes the children's Muzak would twinkle forth again and, arms laden anew, we'd march back out. The children would be scrambling through the halls, waiting for us, shouting, grabbing us as we passed. That music sometimes popped into my head out of nowhere as I lay on the floor of my cell years later. It always made me question my sanity.

It struck me that we were a kind of good-hearted asylum. There was something undeniably crazy about it all: our less-than-sterling foreign band; the vigilant, obsessive mothers telling us, or telling the director who would manage to translate their wishes to us, that they wanted their precious son Won Suk or their darling daughter Min Jung to learn three to five new sentences in English that week. There was a lot of pressure on the children. They had to be at our institute every afternoon and evening after full days of regular school—on Saturdays, too. I admired the Korean esteem for education and the kids for their diligence. I tried to imagine myself at five being led by my mother to classes in Russian or French. I might have been the kid peeing on the floor. Apparently, one day at nursery school, with all the kids' moms, including mine, in attendance, I volunteered to stand and recite a nursery rhyme in front of the class. I was a good and well-behaved student, but the little cretin in me seized the moment, and I proudly declaimed, "Jack and Jill went up the hill to fetch a pail of urine, Jack passed gas, blew out his ass, and knocked Jill down the hill"—a little gem I'd learned from my older cousins. When I'd finished my performance, all the other adults in the room turned to look at Mom. The things I've put that good woman through!

I MOVED ON to teaching adults. Like the children, they had a great deal of respect for learning, the classroom, and teachers. It meant that we were accorded a good deal more respect and deference than we had a right to expect. The students did sometimes challenge us, though. I remember a chubby kid in his mid-twenties who came to my evening class at the English Language School, or ELS, a well-known institute for university students, businessmen, housewives, and other adults, located in the heart of downtown Chongno. Breathing heavily, he took a seat in the front row on my right. He sat there in what appeared to be severe discomfort, his eyes strangely excited and his face red with tension. About halfway through the class, he blurted out in an aggressive voice, "What does 'of' mean in that sentence? What's the meaning of 'of'?" What a jackass, I thought. From time to time this happened: seeing that the instructor was young, a student would grow emboldened and decide to put a little test to him. I sometimes guessed that the students already knew the answers to their questions and were simply checking to see if I did. But they were good to push us. I realized that I had to know English grammar well to be able to stand before a class and conduct it with any authority.

While the students knew English grammar better than many Americans, in terms of speaking the language they were like Sisyphus, rolling the words from their brains through their mouths to the tips of their tongues, straining, nearing the final push, only to have the words roll back in their throats and back toward their brains in a tangled heap. Every day the same things came up; the work was never done, and the tedium of it began to weigh on me. Part of what made English a difficult subject for Korean students was the lack of a more active principle in their learning. They were accustomed to receiving, recording, and memorizing. That's the Confucian mode. As a student, you're not supposed to question a teacher; you should avoid asking for explanations because that might reveal a lack of knowledge, which can be seen as an insult to the teacher's efforts. You don't have an open, free exchange with teachers as we often have here in the West. And further, under this design, a student doesn't do much in the way of improvisation or interpretation. This approach might work well for some pursuits, may even be preferred—indeed, I was often amazed by the way Koreans learned crafts and skills, everything from basketball to calligraphy, for example, by methodically studying and reproducing a defined set of steps (a BBC report explained how the North Korean leader Kim Jong Il had his minions rigorously study the pizza-making techniques used by Italian chefs so that he could get a good pie at home, even as thousands of his subjects starved)—but foreign-language learning, the actual speaking component most of all, has to be more spontaneous and less rigid. We all saw this played out before our eyes and quickly discerned the problem. A student cannot hope to sit in a class and have a language handed over to him on sheets of paper.

Even as I was trying to help my students, I was at the same time facing many of the same challenges they were. My senses were being pricked, and my understanding of the world was being ruptured and rearranged. When we left the classrooms, our roles would flip; we'd step back onto the streets of Chongno, and it was I who was being humbled by a different language, trying to learn as a child does how to say "please" and "thank you," how to express the most basic emotions, how to get what I needed. I was trying to make room for it all in my mind: the Korean words, the new systems of right and good and well-mannered. I couldn't have guessed how much more intense these challenges would become.

# 7

SEVERAL DAYS AFTER I was arrested, I was summoned from the detention house and brought to the Seoul Prosecutors' Office building. Shin was waiting for me in his office on the twelfth floor. On his big polished desk was a picture of him and his wife, with her standing behind him. A white woman I'd never seen before stood up and offered me her hand. She was tall and big-boned, with short red hair and glasses. Her briefcase was on the floor next to her.

"Hi, Cullen. I'm Meredith Wilson from the U.S. embassy." A consul from the American Citizen Services department.

"So, Mr. Thomas, it looks like you're in a bit of trouble," she said. The cardboard box was on the table.

Shin sat calmly in his chair with his legs crossed. He seemed less threatening with Meredith there, even cowed somehow. The United States was with me now; I had the entire, favorably biased mother country right there in the seat next to me. In that moment Shin seemed to embody all of aggrieved Korea. He would teach the offending foreigner a lesson for all of them. Before I was just a common criminal, if a rare foreign one; now I was a peg between nations.

"Mr. Thomas was found with package of hashishee in the post office. He sent it from Philippines," Shin explained for Meredith's sake. My students had a bad habit of putting that same irritating *ee* at the end of their spoken *h*'s. It seemed like a cruel joke—the irony that the man who was intent on putting me away for years for this pronounced the word in such a goofy way. This time I'd have to live with the mistake.

"Well, wait a minute, you don't know that yet," Meredith said without hesitation. I was amazed to hear someone contradicting Shin.

"Why were you picking up the package?" Meredith asked me, gesturing toward the now empty box.

"His story is ridiculous," Shin interrupted before I could answer her.

"Now would you just hold on, you don't know that." Each time Meredith countered him I grew fonder of her, ignoring Shin and turning my body toward her the way a child instinctively moves closer to the sympathetic parent. I wanted to root her on, get her to challenge everything. For the moment mother America was far more forgiving than father Korea.

"You can see his writing is on the box," Shin said without emotion.

"It's not my writing, I swear," I blurted out. I could refute what he was saying now, because he was wrong about this detail, if not about the overall story. I'd had Rocket write the addresses on the box. Where was she now? I worried. What had I done? For all I knew Shin had her in the room next to us. The thought sickened me.

Meredith looked at the names and addresses in black ink on the top of the box. I wanted to prove Shin wrong in front of her and seize the chance to weaken his argument. I leaned forward.

"I'll write 'Jay Gallagher' right now and you can compare the handwriting."

Shin calmly gave me a pen and paper, and I printed the name. The two hands were obviously different; we didn't need a graphologist to tell us that. Meredith and Shin scrutinized the writing on the paper and the box, the Korean man of rectitude and that red-haired American proxy, swiveling their heads back and forth between the two like line judges at a tennis match.

"You see they are same," Shin quickly and smugly concluded. "The *y* and *a* are same."

"They are not the same, Mr. Shin; you can see clearly they're different," Meredith barked back.

My head slumped. I hated all of this; it was tedious and excruciating. Who really gives a damn? I thought. Why am I so important, my penmanship such a cause? What damn difference does a kilo of hashish moved from one place to another really make in the grand scheme of things? Can't we just let it go?

"The minimum sentence for this kind of crime is seven years. You should confess." Shin sounded like a machine again. "It will be better for you; the judge can give mercy only if a confession is made."

"You should contact your family as soon as you can," Meredith advised me. "If they call, we'll tell them we've seen you and let them know what's happening. We can receive mail and money for you and then forward it to you wherever they have you. We'll follow the case and the trial. There's a list of lawyers that I'll get to you, and it'll also tell you what the embassy can and cannot do for you, okay?"

She collected her things and rose to go.

"Are you all right?" she asked, seeing the look on my face.

"It feels like I'm drowning," I told her in a weak voice. I didn't want her to leave. Meredith let out a sympathetic *ooohh* and put the palm of her hand gently against the side of my face.

"Hang in there," she told me.

Shin watched us from the door with a look of disgust.

≡≡

BECAUSE OF THE distance, my family had little knowledge of what was going on and were desperately doing their best to find out where the case stood. They were quickly in touch with Meredith and the embassy in Seoul. They were scrambling to find a good Korean criminal lawyer, one who could speak English and explain the charges, the possible sentence, whether or not probation or parole was possible, whether I could leave Korea if either occurred, whether the time I was already serving would be applied against an eventual sentence.

Several Korean law offices in Seoul were recommended to my parents, and a flurry of fax exchanges ensued.

From the offices of Sohn, Min & Chang, June 9, 1994:

Re: Criminal Case 94 Hyungje 51383
Charges against Mr. Thomas:

As you may know, your son has been indicted already as of June 3, 1994. We contacted the Seoul Prosecutors' Office on June 8th and found out that the following four charges have been made against him:

(1) Importation of hash—Life imprisonment or minimum seven-year imprisonment

(2) Possession of hash—Maximum ten-year imprisonment or fine up to 5,000,000 won

(3) Use of hash—Maximum ten-year imprisonment or fine up to 5,000,000 won

(4) Forfeiture of hash

From the offices of Bae, Kim & Lee, June 11, 1994:

Thank you for contacting us yesterday. Please find enclosed the result of our preliminary analysis on this matter.

The relevant Korean law mandates a minimum sentence of 10 years in prison if one manufactures, exports/imports, purchases/sells or otherwise handles illegal substances such as drugs, for purposes of making profits or on a habitual basis. If one does so but without the intent of making profits or not on a habitual basis, one is subject to a minimum sentence of 7 years in prison.

Please note that each of 10 year or 7 year sentence may normally be reduced to a maximum of one-half (i.e., 10 years to 5 years and 7 years to 3 years and 6 months), depending on the judge's discretion.

Under Korean criminal law, a probation is only applicable for a sentence of three years or less. Consequently, unless special circumstances were shown, a probation will not be possible. Also, a parole is normally granted after serving one-third (⅓) of the actual sentence.

Therefore our prediction based on our experience involving matters of this nature is that Mr. Thomas may have to serve a minimum of one year in jail, out of the usual minimum sentence of 3 years and 6 months, and be consequently evicted from Korea.

The prosecutor I spoke with informed me that Mr. Thomas told the prosecutor that he did not wish to be represented by any legal counsel. Mr. Thomas appears to consider that his family is not rich enough to afford the attorney's fees. We, however, feel that he should have legal counsel to represent his interest, and most likely to reduce his likely sentence.

The last thing I wanted at that point was to burden my family further, adding to the anguish and upheaval I'd already caused them. My parents were not rich, and my twin sisters were on their way to college. I didn't want them to spend their money on me for this; the idea of it was shameful. I was sure that acting like a man, like the responsible adult I'd not yet become, meant getting myself through what I'd gotten myself into, and it had to start with my taking this one on my own and not asking the family to remortgage the house. My parents, however, felt it was no time to play cowboy and refuse a legal defense. This was my life we were talking about, not a game. How many years do we get, after all? Freedom was too precious to be cheap about it, and one couldn't put a value on the time. But that was the essence of what we were trying to figure out. From my cell I was considering whether it was worth it to spend tens of thousands of dollars to help me avoid several years in prison. What was a year worth? We assign monetary value to time in so many different ways, but I couldn't manage the calculation. Of course I wanted to be free, but the money wasn't mine, and I wasn't going to have anyone else pay for my stupidity.

IN THE FIRST month after my arrest I was visited by two different lawyers, each calling on me once at the detention house. The first, Mr. Lee, wore a neat cream-colored suit and glasses; his face was smooth and pudgy like a frog's. My friend Roy from New Zealand, a well-traveled fellow teacher in Seoul, had contacted Mr. Lee and come up with the four hundred thousand won (five hundred dollars) to pay for his initial visit. Roy and I had known each other only two months, but he was a loyal and steadfast friend. He'd thrown in his own money and collected the rest from other foreign teachers in Seoul. I imagined them sliding the bills out of the thick brown envelopes full of Korean cash that we received at the end of each month. I felt humbled by their effort.

Lawyer Lee's English was good. He started off by telling me that three and a half years was the best he could get me under the circumstances. That was a mandatory minimum for smuggling, the most serious charge. Nothing could alter that. I drew back from the table in the visiting room when he explained this to me. I hadn't fully considered until that very moment that I'd probably serve several years. There was little doubt about it now, I was sure. My mind was trying to stare the words and the concept down, to assess and bring it into focus. Like a small dog at the foot of a large sidewalk curb, I tried to make the mental leap over that 3.5, to grab the top ledge and crawl over. But like the animal, I couldn't leap high enough; my mind didn't have the legs or the elastic. That's more than three years I lose, I told myself, turning the horror over in my mind. The truth of it felt like death—nothing permanent, but a death just the same.

I'd listened eagerly to a couple of friendly guards on our floor in the detention house when they told me I might get lucky. I was American, after all, they said, and the judges knew that hashish was no problem in the States. I'd probably be deported. From the other foreign inmates I'd already heard some wild stories. In one, two guys from Thailand caught smuggling more than twenty kilos of marijuana into Korea in the late 1980s were supposedly given suspended sentences and deported after serving just a couple of months. I held on to that tale as though it were the creation story of a new faith I'd joined. I was a whore of false hope, thrown from one voice to another, desperate for impossibilities.

THERE WERE FEWER than a dozen of us foreigners on the third floor of block 13, a soulless hall of gray bars and faded white cement— Pakistani killers, Peruvian thieves, Korean-American drug dealers. Our only time outside the cells was our one hour of exercise each day, when we were let out and taken down three flights of stairs to a thick metal door that opened onto the dirt space between the blocks and the high outer wall. We could talk then, and in our hall as we were locked back into our cells when exercise was over. Sometimes we lingered too long in the corridor, squeezing in a few last moments of relative freedom, until the guard would get angry and yell *"Bang-e turo ga!"*—Get in your cells!—or push us toward the doors.

Guessing at the court's decisions was a common sport among us. It gave us a taste of authority where none existed. Each foreigner in turn offered up his case so that the others could savor the serious and satisfying pauses, the predicting that followed. Almost everyone played this guessing game. For the guys listening to a new arrival's story, the predicting was casual; it was so easy to throw out numbers from that side. "What did you do, Suppra? . . . You got caught using counterfeit hundred-dollar bills, really? How many did they catch you with? . . . Whoa . . . You'll probably get at least seven to start." "A couple of grams of methamphetamine? Let me see . . ." "You kidnapped a Korean girl from a room salon in Taegu? . . . I know, it's supposed to have the prettiest girls. But, man, you're looking at—I don't know, they might ask for ten."

There was a true thrill in trying to predict the course of other people's lives; it made you feel more powerful, involved in the outcomes, even though they were, in reality, painfully far out of your hands. Most of all, it allowed you a few blissful moments in which to put aside your own plight, to get out of your own wounded head and appraise someone else's. That was always a welcome escape. But being on the receiving side of this game could be brutal. Desperate to know what was to become of you, you listened way too closely to others who didn't know, and their words fell like hammers. I'd made a decision early on to try to distance myself from these exchanges, so that I might find some calm and not hang my hopes and fears on what other people said. I felt the upsetting seesawing intensely and could see that the prison demanded neither fear nor hope but the surgical removal of them both, to be replaced by what a good Korean Buddhist might practice and recommend: brutal and exact honesty. I didn't want to be an off-balance rag doll. I've got to stare my reality in the face, I told myself, not drift off to either side. There'd be less pain in accepting three and a half years than in dreaming of home or dreading something more. And through it all Shin's promises of punishment kept flashing through my mind like an unhurried runner, taking his sweet time, knowing he would win.

LAWYER LEE WANTED to get on with things, but I was staring off, on the verge of both crying and flying into a rage. Up I kept jumping, trying to clear the mental shock, and down I fell each time at the foot of it, growing more and more desperate with each failed attempt. The price for taking my case was five thousand dollars, Mr. Lee said. Then there was his "success fee," which would be three thousand dollars more if my sentence was four years or less. I don't doubt that, knowing the law and similar cases, he was pretty certain already that I was looking at less than four. He knew I had no prior criminal record and that I'd come to Korea as a teacher. Also, he must have safely figured that in light of the ample evidence against me I would be a fool not to confess and fall on the judges' mercy. The judges would most probably halve the seven-year sentence, and a lawyer wouldn't be able to do anything about the mandatory minimum. Mr. Lee wouldn't have to do much to achieve the "success" he was talking about.

"Do you want to retain my services?" he asked me from his side of the table.

"It's my father's decision. I don't have the money," I told him.

A few days later I desperately wrote Meredith at the embassy, asking her to call my father in New York to tell him that he shouldn't retain Mr. Lee.

THE SECOND LAWYER proved the greater test.

Just before entering the small counseling room to meet with him, I sat among a dozen Korean inmates waiting to talk with their attorneys. It was a hope-filled waiting room, except for the meaty young Korean sitting directly across from me: his skin was badly broken out and his eyes were horribly dark. His last name was Park; he was twenty, maybe, and at the time he was one of the most infamous criminals in Korea. I'd read about his case in one of the English-language papers we could receive in the detention house. Instead of mingling with Korea's best and brightest, I'd taken a seat next to some of her most scandalous and sordid. (They may have been no less compelling.)

From a wealthy family, Park had been sent off to America to be educated, but he ended up spending most of his time gambling in Las Vegas, running up huge debts, dissipating himself with alcohol and drugs. After returning to his homeland of devout respect for parents, troubled Park murdered his. One of the worst crimes imaginable, what Park had done was like stabbing centuries of Confucian life right in the eye. Seems he'd knifed them to death at home, then burned the whole house down to try to cover it. In the aghast self-examinations that followed, many Koreans blamed the crime on a corrupting, unprincipled America. It was American life, they said, its cheap values, its colossal greed and pleasure seeking that had polluted the young Korean's mind and made him crazy enough to kill his own mother and father.

Now Park sat plump and pitiable in front of me, with long shackles on his wrists—some kind of young demon. They were aiming to kill him. But he didn't look as though he was scared of his fate, not defiant or remorseful, either. Rather, he looked almost calm—not menacingly still, just not bothered by too much. The worst might be past him now, I thought, as he turned his head and looked straight at me. I wondered what he thought of me and whether I reminded him of his time in the States, whether there might be anger there in his memory, or wistfulness. His cards had been played, and that was it for his hand—they don't always turn out well, do they?—twenty wasteful, bloody, shitty years.

"*Sam chil chil ku!*" My number, 3779, was called, and I quickly found myself at a table facing the second lawyer. He was a thin thief who left me with the distinct impression that despite his business card and appropriate suit, he belonged where I was. His head was small and lean. He wore glasses. His hands were so smooth and clean that it looked as though the lines had been polished right off them. It was readily apparent that he knew hardly anything about my case. He put some files and papers onto the table, but I could see from what was written on the front of them that they had nothing to do with me. He spoke much too loudly from the start, in fair English. Worried about others overhearing us, I put a finger up to my lips to signal him to speak more softly. It only pissed him off.

"You will be sentenced to three and a half years and sent away to a prison! Where are your charge papers?" he asked me sternly.

"I didn't bring them; they're back in my cell."

"You should go back and bring them to me. I need to take a look. For me to help you, you have to give your thumbprint on your indictment."

My father had already transferred five thousand dollars to this guy, so all he needed was my thumbprint to give him power of attorney and in that instant the money would be his. His hunger for it wasn't well disguised. To show me the ease of the missing action, he even pantomimed it for me several times with his own thumb. I think what he saw was a naïve kid in a desperate situation far from home, a kid desperate enough maybe to enlist the aid of a charlatan. Regardless of my situation, I thought this guy was an ass, and in the end it was a kind of naïve idealism that helped me.

"Look, I just don't feel like you're on my side," I told him. "I thought a defense attorney is supposed to have his client's interests at heart. I don't feel that from you. I don't think you care at all about what happens to me. Tell my father that the next time you speak with him, please."

"I see," he said. "But you know you will be sent away to prison. And maybe I can still help you. If the president of the United States visits Korea, I can have you specially released."

Of all the wild things I'd heard, this took the cake. I was sure it was ridiculous, and I laughed at him. He quickly blurted out, "Okay, okay!" and waved his hands back and forth in the air as though he could erase what he'd just said.

Years later I learned that the guy billed my parents for six hours of work—when he did that work, and on what, I have no idea. Our meeting lasted all of fifteen minutes. Maybe he'd walked the considerable distance from his office in Seoul to the detention center to meet me and had counted that as service rendered. He took twelve hundred dollars.

BACK ON OUR floor I was shaken up as I told one of the Peruvian thieves that a lawyer had just gotten strange with me. There was no mercy and no grace anywhere I turned; everyone was out for a piece, it seemed. The world, I was coming to realize, wasn't necessarily going to play sweet and nice with me simply because I needed it to, simply because I'd messed up and was now hoping for a reprieve. No, the world might not give a damn. It was a heavy thought to bear at that moment, and the little rock of youth crumbled a bit more.

# 8

AFTER LIVING IN Tim's apartment for several months, I moved into the Moonwha Yogwan, or Cultural Inn. It was in the north of Seoul, in an old neighborhood of narrow cobblestone lanes, low, tile-roofed houses, and family restaurants serving dog stew and snake. Most Koreans thought of the yogwans as love motels, cheap places for vagrants, young lovers, men looking to bed their dates or their short-time prostitutes, husbands their mistresses. That kind of stuff couldn't go on in the family homes, where in many cases three generations still lived under the same roof, as at the Moonwha, where the slippers and sandals of the two rascal kids, their mother, and the grandmother and grandfather who owned the inn sat jumbled together in one multigenerational heap outside their room.

I could see the negative reaction in their faces when I told Koreans that I lived in a yogwan. That was one of my first lessons in the culture's robust stratification: where you lived, what you wore, where you went to school, and where you worked carried enormous weight. That is the Confucian way, a kind of tyranny of appearances instilled through hundreds of years of parochial village life. I'd have to lie, a Korean headhunter who found me teaching work in Seoul informed me. No way a company would accept me as their teacher if they knew where I lived. So I began telling people I lived in the district of Anguk, without specifying exactly where. In doing so I was continuing a long tradition, one that during the Chosun dynasty saw many Koreans, through forgeries, bribes, and other duplicitous means, falsely claim to be part of the noble class.

The old man of the Moonwha shuffled around smoking cigarettes, saying nothing to anyone, not even his wife, the grand-mother. We called her *Ajumoni,* a title of respect and affection that conveyed something like "dear old woman." She was weath-ered and scrappy, with a sweet face, and she carried the weight of the inn's work on her bent back. The Moonwha's charm—its spirit of an older Korea, the clay-tile roofs, the sliding wood doors, its peace won from adversity—flowed directly from Ajumoni. And once you'd stepped over the inn's raised threshold, you'd entered another realm; you'd left behind Korea's modern industrial surge and returned to a simpler life, one close to the ground and the seasons.

IT WAS LATE winter, early in 1994. I was sitting on the heated floor of our room in the Moonwha, poring over a map of Luzon. Rocket was next to me. She'd come from New York to stay with me for a few months, but now we needed to renew our three-month tour-ist visas. The timing was ideal, because Korea's winter was cold and endlessly gray. We were going to the Philippines—a month or two there on the money we'd saved teaching, then we'd return to Seoul. I was fascinated by the Philippines' thousands of islands scattered over the sea, its equatorial heat. We were going to ex-plore Manila, go scuba diving in the south, and venture down to Mindanao, an island full of intrigue. As adventurous as all that might have been, I was also planning something riskier, some-thing I'd never before considered. This poor choice was all mine, but I can see how the particular environment of Seoul at that time affected my decisions.

Whereas in New York I felt as though I had few good options and saw few inviting prospects, in Seoul somehow almost every-thing and anything seemed possible. In the early to mid-1990s South Korea became the eleventh-largest economy in the world. Freed from the destruction and poverty that resulted from the Korean War (1950–1953), and from the decades of military dictatorships that followed it, the country was waking to a new dawn. Seoul was exploding with energy, and you could feel a wild entrepreneurial fervor on the streets. There was this sense that things were unrestricted, without clear rules, there for the taking. There was a lot of money to be made, and if you were bold and aggressive, you could get in on it early. Even though most of us foreigners— unable to speak Korean, having no roots or strong connections to the society at large—were on the outside looking in, we still felt this frenzy, because of our English. There were English-teaching opportunities everywhere. We were approached and offered jobs while walking down the street. At twenty-three, for the first time in my life, I was earning good money and had some savings at my disposal. I could come and go from the country as I pleased, it seemed. I could work there illegally without question. Somehow it was all too easy, and I allowed myself to feel a false sense of empowerment, as though I was, to borrow a Korean saying, eating the pheasant *and* its eggs.

Like many of the other foreigners, I fooled myself into thinking that I could operate alongside Korean society and yet not have to answer to it. After all, we were strangers. We could barely speak to each other. Her rules didn't apply to me, it seemed. This impression wasn't so clear and explicit for me at the time, but I can see how the idea was creeping insidiously into my actions. It was a dangerous and arrogant frame of mind, but I wasn't wise or aware enough then to correct it.

At the same time, many of the foreigners, including me, felt intensely pent up and confined by the culture: the predictable social interactions, the uninspiring entertainments, the odd smells, the sameness of everything. We often escaped our feelings of disorientation by gathering together to trade complaints. We were drinking a lot, looking for other ways to make our alienation bearable. In some ways we were weak, buckling under the challenge that we ourselves had chosen.

During my first week in Seoul my friend Tim, whom I'd thought of as a pretty levelheaded and cautious guy, received an envelope in his name at our children's school. He'd mailed it to himself while on vacation in Thailand. It contained several grams of marijuana. Worn down from its journey, the envelope was nearly torn open in one corner. Tim and I both laughed at how crazy he was to have done this. We smoked every night after work for a week, decompressing in our apartment in Chamshil. Several months later, at the Moonwha, I met two smart and outgoing American girls from Montana. They were in their mid-twenties and like the rest of us had come to Seoul to teach. Not long after I met them, they told me that a friend of theirs was in the Philippines and that he was soon to mail them a surprise package. They kept the story vague, but the day they picked up the package at the post office they invited me back to their room to watch them open it. Inside an unremarkable square brown box, sent by someone calling himself Tocqueville, was a mess of white styrofoam squiggles and two large tins of cocoa. I watched in amazement as the two girls, giddy with excitement, stuck their hands into the cocoa in each can and pulled from under the powder thick slabs of dark hashish.

Several weeks later, Tocqueville returned from the Philippines and came to stay in the Moonwha. He was a charismatic thirty-year-old American, and he gradually began to tell me about his trip, about the wide-open nature of the Philippines, about the cheap and plentiful hashish he'd gotten in a small village up in the mountains of Luzon. He leaned in and whispered the name to me: Sagada. It stuck in my head. There, Tocqueville said, for about three hundred U.S. dollars you can get a kilo of great stuff that in South Korea is worth more than ten thousand. He and the two girls were selling it off to other foreigners.

I was impressed by what I saw as Tocqueville's cunning and daring, by the kind of money he and his friends were making. He seemed to embody all of our foreign, restless energies in Seoul, to have stretched out and seized some of the potential all around us, there for the taking at the edge of Asia. To me, the risks and danger involved in what he'd done were like distant noise, faint and invisible, as though they existed only as props to ratchet up the element of adventure.

The first time I smoked pot I was twenty years old and a junior in college. I'd gone to a rigorous all-boys Catholic high school and had been a disciplined student. I spent my time studying or playing basketball. I wasn't part of any social group, never went to parties or drank. Looking back on it, I think that lack of social experience, experience with drugs and alcohol, was a factor in why, scarcely three years after having first tried marijuana, I was plotting to smuggle a large quantity of it across international borders. Relatively new to it, I was too fascinated by it. I hadn't gotten the allure or the thrill of it out of my system. And, in my own misguided way, I was ambitious. Bored by teaching, I wanted to be my own boss. I wanted to escape the tedium of pronunciation drills and the parts of speech, those long days of listening to English stagger in its infancy. I wanted to be a pirate, to do something daring, like Tintin or Burton, something befitting the Jolly Marauder. I'm as smart as Tocqueville, I thought. I can pull off what he did. I can make that money. In my mind I had made the decision: while in the Philippines I was going to find my way to Sagada, get some hashish, bring it back to Korea, and become another entrepreneur. My small and foolish plan gave me a feeling of purpose.

I WAS MAKING Rocket nervous. My trusty Bartholomew mini world atlas didn't show Sagada, but I could guess its general position. I knew we had to go to Baguio, the start of the Cordillera, the high chain of tropical mountains that runs through the Philippines' northernmost island. We'd find our way into the Mountain Province from there.

We were bumped up to first class on the flight to Manila.

"It's a good sign, Rocket," I said excitedly. "You see, what a great start!"

Rocket couldn't complain. We ate cheese and crackers and drank champagne, smiling like kids at how the world was opening to us.

I read Thoreau's essay "Life Without Principle" while sitting on a stone wall looking out over Manila Bay. The palms stretched overhead like regal parasols; below me were piles of human feces on the sea-scarred rocks. Why should a man waste his life earning a living through senseless toil? Thoreau asked. Why should he? I silently agreed—why work always for someone else's dream?

We took a bus six hours north to Baguio, the summer capital. Sagada, written by hand in chalk high on the board in the city's bus station, stood out among the names of other remote villages in the hills. She was the secret that waited for me, that knew me personally, and I hung my gift of fate around her syllables.

Six hours up from Baguio, snaking into the Cordillera, I made the mistake of eating runny eggs for breakfast next door to the bus station before we left. I found myself booting out the bus window onto the fringe of the jungle, my mouth dripping open as we shunted from side to side, curving our way to six thousand feet. An older white man with a straw hat glanced back at me as if to say, "Well, you'll learn this way." I learn pretty fast, I thought defiantly as I vomited up more yolk, after making good mistakes.

The mountainsides were carved into emerald stairs. The bus dropped us in the Mountain Province capital of Bontoc. From there a converted army truck took us along high dirt roads through jungle, till we bounced into Sagada, once home of the New People's Army, a communist insurgency that had been battling the government for years in Luzon. A Filipino told us that not too long before, some NPA had waited on the hillside above the bend in the road we'd just come in on and had ambushed a group of government soldiers just as they'd arrived. The place was a glorious snare, set in a remote perch from which it looked far down into a valley that tumbled away. The air was a rich blend of vegetation, smoke, cock, pig, dog, and goat. I stopped to read a handwritten sign on the wall of the small post office:

> Reward: For any information that helps to solve the
> murder in February of a British national in Sagada.

And nobody in this small place knows? I thought. Impossible. A Filipino in the post office told us the man had been shot in the hand. And he died from that? I wondered. That isn't the story, can't be. It probably had to do with the drug trade; or maybe he'd crossed the rebels—and was that the same thing? I wondered. There was an immediate unspoken feeling that Sagada was united in some secret, or multiple secrets. It was almost too pretty. I couldn't say whether she was collectively involved in rebellion or the drug trade or whether the latter financed the rebels or whether both forces were exaggerated and it was merely a good little tourist town with a slightly lawless character. Those questions and that energy shifted under the surface, but nothing was fully revealed. Sagada cleverly cultivated shadows right under the light of the blazing sun.

On our first day Rocket and I sat in the Shamrock Café on the main dirt track. I had no idea where to find what I'd come for. We drank San Miguel beer at one of the wood tables. A group of young Filipinos played cards in the corner. All but two got up and left. One leaned toward us.

"Do you smoke?" the young Filipino asked quietly. I said yes and he told me to stay cool, pointing past me through the open front door of the café at a jeep full of government soldiers up the hill in the little cobblestone square, their M16s standing up between their legs.

"You know there's a curfew here. After nine p.m. you should

not be out," he said. He and his friend introduced themselves as Jim and Brent. They had smooth skin and jumbled teeth, sparse wispy tufts of facial hair: the wild, natural look of provincial mountain boys. Making sure we were the only ones who could see, Brent took out of his pocket a square brown slab wrapped in tight clear plastic.

"Many foreigners come here for hashish," he whispered to us. He turned and gestured with his chin in the direction of a well-groomed white-haired man in his fifties. He was enjoying a cup of tea and reading a book with one leg crossed over the other.

"He comes a few times a year for our stuff and goes back to Japan," Jim explained quietly. "He puts bags of it in his ass."

"Come with us to smoke; we'll show you a nice place," Brent said.

Rocket and I followed them past the old stone church on the hillside to a bluff overlooking a steep gorge of limestone cliffs. Hawks flew above us. Brent rolled a joint with hashish and tobacco, and we sat on rocks at the edge of the three-hundred-foot drop and smoked in turns.

"Look across," Jim said, pointing to the cliff wall opposite. "You see the coffins. It's Ifugao tradition."

Several small coffins were stuck into craggy niches high in the rock face. The wood was old and rotted, and I thought I could see the white of bones inside.

"Can you get me a kilo?" I asked them.

"No problem," Jim said. "Give us some time." Then he mused out loud that it would be great if I could smuggle them in some handguns. Rocket, high like me, though perhaps more grounded, shot me an incredulous look.

WE SAW JIM and Brent every day. We'd find them idle in the late mornings, smoking on hillsides in the sun. We had to keep them happy, because they were bringing me what I'd come for, and, more important, because we were, in the end, at their mercy and that of their friends in those mountains. The bond was forced and superficial. It seemed no women between the ages of twelve and thirty lived in Sagada; there were only prepubescent girls or older women with children. All the girls of prime age were off in Manila or the Visayas, making money on tourism, many in the sex trade. Wandering around drinking beer and gin, Sagada's two dozen young males seemed bored and heartsick.

With an oil lamp, Jim and Brent took us on a picnic into a deep cave just outside town. Japanese soldiers had hidden in it during World War II, Brent said. There was treasure down there somewhere, and in other caves nearby. We ate *pancit*, a traditional noodle dish, by lamplight on top of a bulbous rock at the very bottom of the cave, bats blanketing the walls around us.

Two days later Jim and Brent found us on a hillside, and then back in my room Brent took out of his knapsack four pieces of brown hashish wrapped loosely in newspaper, each about the size and thickness of a large hand laid open—pieces of dense soil broken off the edge of a secret island. I gave him the 10,000 pesos we'd agreed on. At the exchange rate then, the kilo cost me roughly $375. For them it was a substantial chunk of money; for me it was a steal, and I did my best to conceal my pleasure over the inequity.

"You have to be careful taking it down to Manila," Brent said. "You shouldn't smoke while you carry it. Eyes give you away." His were bleary. "Where're you going from the Philippines?" he asked.

"I've gotta go back to Korea to teach."

"How much money do they give you?"

Again I thought of the disparity, why I was there in front of him. I didn't want to talk about money. I put the pieces into my bag at the side of the bed, and we walked back outside together.

The next day I made up my mind to get more.

"Yes, but you have to wait a few days; we have to bring it from the mountains," they said. The fields were higher up, beautiful. We'll take you to see them, they told me.

Rocket and I waited and took walks in the hills and along the dirt paths. Rocket swam in the rocky pool of a river below the farm hamlet of Fedlesan. We covered our faces with the soft clay of the riverbank, imagining that it was healing our skin, transforming us.

We took a jeep to Bontoc to exchange more dollars at its sleepy post office. I was concerned about exchanging several hundred dollars—too conspicuous, I worried. One didn't need much money in that province. The heavyset Filipino woman at the desk asked no questions.

We waited. Jim and Brent seemed to be purposefully delaying. We grew tense wondering why. So that we'd spend more time and more money? Or was it something worse?

"We don't have it here; we have to bring it from another place," Jim kept saying calmly. Something didn't feel right.

But the next evening he had it. Back in my room again to make the exchange, Brent asked for a few hundred pesos more than the price we'd agreed on. The sounds of insects boomed in the humid air outside.

"Be careful going down to Manila," Brent warned me again after I'd given him the money. "We'll see you. Don't forget Sagada."

AT DAWN THE next morning we boarded a rickety bus. As we snaked our way back down the Cordillera, I couldn't stop glancing up at our packs in the overhead rack—I felt as if all the organs of my body were tied to their contents.

≡≡

IT WAS AMAZING how Manila didn't know a damn thing about our plan—and why should it have? But that was the naïve thrill: the glory and gamble were all ours. The Filipinos didn't seem to care whether we hanged ourselves or made a bundle. Their hot lives went on around us, and out of the thousands of other choices, ours had been quietly made, the direction greedily decided, and we alone were cradling its substance in our hands.

I stored the kilos in my black backpack and put it in the storage room of the family pension where we were staying, on a shelf below a bare lightbulb and a calendar with Filipino girls in their bathing suits smiling innocently. It was so humid in the house that upon returning on several occasions I thought I could smell the hashish permeating the air of those back rooms, its pungent odor being steam-released and wafting up from the depths of my tightly packed bag—the telltale hash, dead but pulsing, filling the air like a phantom.

We would deal with the bricks when we came back from the south. We were off to the Visayas and edgy Mindanao, to island-hop, scuba dive, trace the Sulu Archipelago, find the Moros—with any luck some pirates—and see what other jaws we could get our heads into. This is the Jolly Marauder, I thought. Still feeling it a week later, I wrote a poem as our ferry drifted out of the scrappy Cebu City port, not far from the very spot where Magellan, in 1521, had come ashore to plant the flag and cross. I couldn't help myself; I was slightly overcome.

> *The Visayan Sea*
> *spreads blue green before me*
> *and everything says, Well done!*

Later, I learned that Magellan had been cut down in the shallows of those same waters.

From our boat we'd watched the beautiful green islands pass slowly by, their jungles hanging over the coasts, their humps lush and seducing. The Filipinos ate boiled eggs and played cards. The sun burned down ferociously. Rocket threw oil onto her skin with abandon.

It was late when Rocket and I finally got back to Manila. Back in the pension, it was strange to see the wrapped slabs of hashish hidden in my dirty clothes just as I'd left them. I'd somehow imagined that something so ripe and concentrated wouldn't sit still, wouldn't stand for anonymity like that, stuffed ignominiously into a pack—that it would somehow get itself up and out, that it was too important to be sitting around waiting, like fat amounts of cash quietly tucked away and forgotten in boxes and drawers. There's so much potential in certain things that they pulse and live beyond their static forms, are animated by that potential—so much so that at times I half expected to see the hashish stand up and walk around on its own.

I thought that I should just take it with me through the airport.

"You're crazy! I swear I won't go with you if you do that," Rocket protested.

We had to do something, hide it, box it, ship it. There was no more time; our return flight was the following day. The hashish pulled all our energies to it, its weight immeasurable now, a vortex. We could have thrown the stuff out right then and there, stopped the plan dead in its tracks; and yet it seemed as though our control over the course of it was slipping away inexorably.

# 9

BACK IN SEOUL, Rocket was anxious.

"When are we going to get it?" she asked me impatiently, her mouth slightly open, the top row of her teeth visible. "We might as well get it over with." She wanted some movement, anything but the limbo I was settling into. I'd made no move toward the post office. I was taking my time, smoking during the day, going out at night with Zack, an American friend and fellow teacher, and waiting on the arrival of my box. I was sliding toward something ugly. Rocket had gone out in the few days we'd been back and had already set up a load of teaching work for herself. She wondered what the hell I was up to.

"You can use yourself better than this, you know; there are other things you can do. Why don't you write at least? You always talk about it," she said disappointedly.

"I'll write when I feel like I've got something to share," I replied, feeling good about the answer. But Rocket was right, and I wasn't seeing things clearly. I was in no hurry to go find teaching work. About two weeks before, at one of Seoul's main post offices, Zack had picked up the first package I'd sent from the Philippines, which contained one of the two kilos I'd bought. It had gone off without a hitch, just as it had for Tocqueville before us. Just as Korean airport customs seemed not to bother much with searching foreigners, the Korean authorities didn't seem to be too interested in or suspicious of our mail, either.

Zack had been selling the hash. We were splitting the money. And soon I'd have the second box and the money that would bring. I had considered this plan a onetime deal, and I wasn't thinking beyond it. But looking back at myself, I can see that I might have done it again had I not been caught. And I got caught because I wasn't a good drug runner, really, wasn't cut out for it. I was an amateur in over my head. As my mother would tell people about me with resignation while I was serving my term, "He's just not very clever."

ON THE CHOSEN day, Rocket and I stepped out of Zack's apartment. The Korean spring was fresh—light air and a soft sun. The fine weather and my nearly accomplished plan together produced a feeling of great possibility, and I thought I saw it sparkling there before me.

On the way to the post office, watching the Koreans on the subway, I began to think again about what I was doing in their country, about how I'd never done anything like this at home. So why here? Well, the rules were different. And Koreans don't know about marijuana, I thought, it's not part of their consciousness. This was something I'd discussed before with other foreigners. The locals seemed to be a pretty simple and moral people. I'd never seen a Korean smoking pot, had never smelled it on the street or from a room in Seoul, had never even heard the word mentioned (*tae ma cho*—but then I wouldn't have understood it if I had). I'd reassured myself that even if the authorities did discover my contraband, they wouldn't know exactly what it was, and I'd be fine. (An agrarian society that doesn't know a famous plant? It really was a stupid bet.) Based on what we saw out in the conservative Confucian society, many foreigners guessed that, on the whole, there probably wasn't even much crime in Korea. It's still a surprisingly common misperception in regard to Korea and Japan. It makes me laugh, how myopic and wrong we were, how effective Confucian appearances can be, how it took my going to prison for me to learn this.

What better place to do this, then, I thought, as the subway raced forward. They really don't mind and need not be bothered.

I can bring this thing of my world to theirs and yet keep it safely beyond them.

We got off at Ulchiro and began to walk the big, crowded blocks south to the post office. I was walking with my hands in my pockets, thinking of the fun ahead that weekend. No work on the horizon for me, and this sun and good sky. Korea's bleak winter was over.

About a hundred yards from the post office, Rocket, scooting along to my right, suddenly grabbed my arm and stopped.

"Cull, what if we're walking right into a trap? What if we're walking to our demise?" I thought of an old Korean saying: "Running into the tiger's cave"—as in throwing oneself headlong into danger. I laughed at her use of the word "demise." I liked Rocket's drama, her well-chosen words, but the thought seemed absurd; demise wasn't part of the plan.

"Is that what we're doing, Rocket? Come on; it's gonna be fine," I said. "We'll just go in and get it; it's gonna be all right." And though not truly convinced, Rocket let go of my arm and we continued on our way.

Just south of the traffic circle at City Hall, past the colorful front gate and outer walls of Toksu Palace, we reached the post office.

"Do you want me to come in with you?" Rocket asked. Customarily I wouldn't have thought anything of it; I would have just let her come along. But without thinking I asked her to wait outside. I wasn't protecting her, because I saw no threat. But I knew inside that this was my affair and that I should be the one to see it through.

I took a deep breath on my way in. Life had never cheated me, not as I saw it, and I thought the Jolly Marauder held a bit of fortune's fancy.

It was darker and cooler inside; the air-conditioning was on.

The sun was blunted and softened by the windows, and it diffused around me as I walked through the double doors. To my right was the main room, with a high ceiling and a row of neat counters and lines of Koreans waiting. It was 3:15 p.m., a Friday. This, and then the weekend, I thought again. Good things ahead.

Young female Korean postal workers were dressed in neat blue blouses and skirts, the men in uniform pants and shirts. They carried on their business with the expected Korean public courtesy.

*"Neh, neh. Ta-oom boon im ni da. Annyong ha shim ni ka . . ."* Yes, yes, next person, please. How are you?

The businessmen in the room were arrayed in their suits, and as usual they were reading newspapers and drinking coffee as they rested on the chairs and benches along the walls. There was nothing unexpected in that post office. It was the farthest thing from the setting for a demise.

I walked past the lines in the main room but couldn't seem to find the poste-restante counter for packages. I went around to the far corner, doubled back, then again. I'd come so far, and now it seemed funny that on the verge of completion I just couldn't locate the damn counter I needed. I thought about just giving up and coming back another day, but finally I asked a young woman behind one of the counters for help. Smiling at the novelty of using her English, she told me to go upstairs.

ROCKET COULDN'T BELIEVE I was taking so long. She was standing by the front steps amid all the activity of the day, with the sun on her, reading the copy of *Moby-Dick* she'd brought along. She grew bored and went over to several vendors' tables on the sidewalk. She tried to talk to an old man who was selling back scratchers, smooth wooden sticks with small carved hands with splayed fingers at one end. Next to him stood a table with a fetid pot piled high with hot silkworm larvae. A group of funny old men and women with weathered faces and warm eyes gathered to observe Rocket. She looked up at the post office doors and waited.

The sun was hitting the windows on the second floor, giving the room a pleasant mood and light. When I walked in, something made me stop. On the couches below the windows were a cluster of businessmen, a common sight, but my intuition didn't seem to like it. What if they're police? I asked myself. I mean, they could be Korean police in disguise, dissimulating in their suit jackets, hiding behind newspapers, waiting for somebody in particular to turn up. I turned slowly and walked over to the windows. I paused there in front of the huge glass looking out on Myoung-dong and the busy streets below. I'd been in Korea for a total of seven months, but she looked strange again, as if I were seeing her for the first time. My time in the Philippines made Korea seem more developed, more organized, more modern than I had remembered, and I was dimly observing the post office and the streets outside with this renewed interest. I was fond of Korea and all the things she'd shown me. I'd had good jobs teaching, earned good money, set up a little life abroad for myself. These were precedents for me, and I was proud of them. Korea felt like a part of me, a part that was innocent, if strange, and beyond all else, benign.

What if they *are* police, then? I thought again about the men on the couches. I could just turn and walk out of here. I could have someone else come get it. No, you've come too far just to give up now, another voice inside me protested. I threw my intuition aside.

I walked over to the farthest counter. A Korean man in a collared shirt with thinning hair and a mess of pens in his pocket was behind it. On the counter was a clipboard with a list of all the packages held there: name of recipient, name of sender, the relevant dates, place of origin, and a postal code consisting of numbers and letters. There was no one waiting when I got to the counter, so I picked up the clipboard and looked for Jay Gallagher and the Philippines.

On one of the first few pages I found "Gerald," the box that Zack had picked up weeks before. Then on the fifth page I found my box. I read the entry across the line; it had arrived two days before. Everything looked fine, except unlike the rest of the entry, the office code for my box was written in red. I didn't quite like it. I checked to see if there were other postal codes written in red, and there were, but only two or three besides mine in the pages of listings. I didn't know what to make of it, but as before, I just swept my doubt aside.

"Hi, how are you? Can I have this one, please?" I asked the clerk, holding up the list with my index finger placed just below the name Jay Gallagher. He squinted, and when his eyes reached my finger he said, "Oh," jerked his head up a bit, and took a half-step back. I tried to study him, but there was no time for any more doubt or intuition. I was insensate; only the plan mattered.

The man collected himself. "One moment, please," he said, and disappeared into the storage room behind him.

He came back around the corner with the box, but he was gripping it roughly and awkwardly with one hand. And then I saw that the box looked weak and damaged, as if the top had been sat on. Why the fuck is he handling it like that? I wondered. But he had already reached me and put the box in front of me on the counter.

"Can I see your ID?" he asked.

"I'm not Jay Gallagher," I said, taking out my wallet. "I'm picking this up for him."

"Can you sign, then? Because you are not person on box. And put address and telephone, please." He gave me a sheet of paper and a pen.

Without thinking of what might be wisest in the situation, I wrote my name, the address of the Moonwha, and Zack's phone number at the top of the page. I thought for a moment that it would be smart to give a fake number, but then that seemed unnecessary, because this was going off without incident.

"This is not my package. I am picking it up as a favor to Jay Gallagher," I wrote, then signed it.

I slid the paper over to the man and took hold of my box. As I moved it to the edge of the counter, it knocked my wallet onto the floor. One of the businessmen behind me comfortably sidled up, bent down before I could, picked up my wallet, and placed it on top of the box for me. I turned and thanked him. He was a foot away, leaning against the counter now with one hand on his hip, and I saw that he was a man in his forties with a soft, friendly face, but he was smiling smugly, insinuatingly. But never mind; Koreans could be very odd.

I put my wallet in my pocket, picked up the box, and turned and walked away toward the doors. I looked down at the box's worn brown cardboard, Rocket's pen work. The weight inside felt unbalanced. I took about ten strides, going slowly enough, trusting that I was on my way out. I was two steps from the doors to the stairs when a voice behind me yelled out "Korean police!" and I felt a pair of hands clamp down on my shoulders. I knew right then it was done, and all the strength in my body seemed to leave me. Something sank in my bowels, an inner tension and suspense that extinguished itself and collapsed in a heap. Rocket's words and all the signs along the way flashed through my head in an instant. The sounds around me, the hands on me, my own hands against the cardboard—all these stimuli were smeared and slowed down now. The action seemed to be happening through a thick gauze, or through something that slows us like water does, like the tropical sun, as though the world were sedated and everything a game, a slow, queer carnival in which, suddenly, I was center ring, in a role that surprised me.

"Korean police!"

I let the hands take me. They steered me away from the doors, toward the massive clear panes of glass looking down on the street. Four or five other suited agents were right up on me then. Maybe they expected someone larger, maybe a hardened group; but it was just me. One man faced me and took the package out of my hands. The one who'd grabbed me from behind pressed my arms against my back and slapped handcuffs on me.

"What's wrong? What's the problem?" I asked.

"There's something very wrong with this box," one of them answered tersely. Their cheap suits revolved around me, their intensity overwhelming any emotion I could muster.

Down the stairs and out of Myoung-dong's post office we went, into the bright, soft sun of late May. I had six agents pulling me by the arms, guarding my sides. I was property now; I could feel that, if nothing else. I was scared, trying to keep my head up and my mind alert, trying to think of what to say and how to hide the damning things and people they didn't know yet. Like Rocket, who when I'd last left her, was leaning against the front steps.

*Pray they don't see her, pray she doesn't give away a sign. You can't look at her. You can't look to the right when they bring you out. They'll see you look at her; they'll see the connection between you; it'll be impossible to hide. So look left, man, look left!*

I followed that voice now, though I wanted to look at Rocket and to somehow tell her that I was sorry, that she had to get the hell out of there. But a taste of shame made me ambivalent, made it okay for me not to see her, because there I was, her supposed clever man and hero, stooped and coiled in failure.

You've seen pictures of the captured with shame on their faces, the sheer weight of opprobrium causing their heads to drop, their eyes to turn away. It's a classic and unmistakable moment. Well, when I walked out into the light and looked left, away from where Rocket was watching the scene play out, I recalled in a flash all those pictures and news pieces I'd seen of captured criminals dripping with squalor, triviality, arrogance, malice. I couldn't believe it was me this time. But there was no denying it. Even the requisite audience was there. When we plowed out the doors and onto the sidewalk, about two dozen Koreans caught sight of the spectacle and turned to watch. *What in God's name did the foreigner do?* I tried to keep my head at a decent height; I hadn't given up entirely. Not smugly high, but not abjectly low, either. I don't know how I fared. It's a hard balance to come by.

THE DETECTIVES LED me to the post office parking lot. Now everything seemed to be happening at a rapid pace, as though the outside light had kicked everything back into speed. They pushed me into a silver minivan, and I saw a couple of them hustle back toward the front of the post office. The agents had me share the backseat with a tough, middle-aged detective on my left, who put his arm around my shoulder. They'd brought along a young American I'd said hello to upstairs before I was grabbed, putting him in the seat in front of me. He looked dumbfounded.

Suddenly a tall, wiry detective with bony shoulders came hustling back to the van. He leaned in through the open sliding door and asked me sharply in English, "Who did you come with?"

"Nobody. I'm alone."

"Who came with you? The American girl with shorts, she was waiting for you in front, wasn't she?"

"No, I came here alone. Nobody was with me," I said again quickly, my heart in my mouth. Please don't let them get Rocket, I thought. The skinny agent seemed to give up, but he didn't get in the van. The other agents jumped in and we sped off.

The two closest to me were leaning in toward my face and asking me where I lived. I knew it would kill us if they went to Zack's apartment, where we'd stayed since coming back from the Philippines. Take them to the inn, I thought. That's what I'd written down as my place of residence anyway. No other solution. My key to Zack's apartment was in the right front pocket of my pants.

"I'm staying in the Moonwha Yogwan," I said.

"Where?"

"In Anguk-dong, near Chongno."

We drove furiously. We got there fast and pulled up in the narrow lane in front of the inn. They charged out of the minivan. It was a lightning strike, a slam-bang bust.

They stormed into the Moonwha, pulling me by the arm behind them. The old grandfather was there in the courtyard with his daughter, and they wheeled around. I was ashamed of being dragged in there as a captive and criminal, handcuffed before these kind people in whose place I'd lived for months without incident. I didn't want them to see me like this, didn't want them to be tainted by it. Korean shame has a way of seeping into others.

The detectives aggressively asked the old man a flurry of questions. They gestured toward me. I thought I was finished, because, of course, the old man knew I wasn't staying at the inn anymore and that I hadn't stayed there in more than two months.

"Where are your possessions?" the men asked me.

The place was reeling. The detectives spread out like dogs in the courtyard.

"I've got some things in storage," I told them weakly.

Suddenly I was gripped by an urgent pressure to bolt, to try to escape right then and get away before I sank. *Get out of here,* the voice said loud and clear. *Run through the passage to the back courtyard, up the stone block to the tile-topped wall of the inn, you remember the place, then drop the eight feet into the lane, no matter that your arms and hands are useless, run, run, run . . .*

"Can I use the bathroom?" I asked. The bathroom was off that corridor. *You got to do it, man, bolt, go, you can do it!* Everything seemed in an uproar.

The agent next to me said I could go, but he followed at my side and held my arm. The fantasy crumbled.

Back in the courtyard the agents were dispersing. The old man looked meek. I felt I'd disappointed him by bringing this trouble to his place, but I didn't think that they'd gotten much out of him. The agents pulled me back out through the sliding front door.

*"Ka-ja, ka-ja!"*—Let's go, let's go! they shouted. Back out to the street and into the van. If we went north and they pressed me for where I'd really been staying, we'd be in it deep—I was terrified. But they didn't ask me why my things weren't at the inn, hadn't looked in my pockets and found the key.

We turned south. I didn't know where they were taking me, but I knew it wasn't to Zack's apartment. The other American, still watching his innocent trip to the post office play out ludicrously, was quiet and unmoving. I could feel the agents' energy subside. Their conversation died out; they opened their jackets, put their arms over the sides of the seats, and stared out the windows. The quick rush was over.

≡≡

ROCKET ISN'T SURE whether she ever saw me come out. Maybe the bodies of the police had hidden me from her sight, but I don't see how she could have missed me. She doesn't remember it clearly, not because of the passage of time and the blurring of memory, but because of the confusion and strange malaise of that moment. She swears I was inside for nearly an hour.

A young Canadian girl who knew us from the Moonwha came up to Rocket as she was waiting on the front steps and told her that the police had just grabbed me inside. The blow had struck, but now Rocket had fair warning. I was already gone. She knew she had to escape, so she turned and walked quickly away in the direction we'd come, back over the very spot where she'd spoken of demise, and then broke into a run. Rocket was a good runner.

She ran north, back up to Chongno, through the thin girls with high boots and the bespectacled, black-haired men, to ELS, and pulled Zack from a class to warn him. I've tried to imagine the mixture of emotions she felt—anger seasoned with shock and panic, *because, damn it, how many times did I tell that fucking idiot to do something else with himself? Now he's dragged me into this; he's done, I'm in danger, everything's fucked!* We'd been from Binghamton to Barcelona to Basilan together. We were going to travel the world—Vietnam, then India, East Africa, the Middle East. All of it gone.

Rocket ran out of ELS and hustled west down Chongno, then north to the U.S. embassy. She had to hand over her passport to get inside and was terrified as she did so. Automatic doors slid shut behind her, and she feared she'd just given herself up and might be captured now, too. She went in shaking. At American Citizens Services she told a consul that her boyfriend had just been arrested and she didn't know why. She asked them to help me if there was any way they could.

That night she called my house in New York from a street phone near the Moonwha. It was 7 a.m. of the same day in New York. My brother, having just returned home from the overnight shift, was drifting off to sleep on the living room floor in a sunbeam, still wearing his United Parcel Service uniform. Rocket's call woke him.

She fled the country the next day. She realized on the ride to Kimpo airport that she had too much Korean currency left and unloaded it all on the cabdriver, the equivalent of a hundred-dollar tip. When the plane was off the ground she breathed easier. She returned to New York in shambles and spent the next six months shielded by lawyers. Not knowing what else to do, she went to live with family friends, took care of their children, tried to make sense of what had happened in Seoul. She was forbidden by her lawyers to contact my family or me.

# 10

"THREE-SEVEN-SEVEN-NINE, Colleen Tomasuh, tomorrow, prosecutor." The guard stood in front of my cell and read to me off a strip of paper. The thought of Shin didn't help me sleep any better. Dreams were disturbed and the fluorescent lights that glared down into the cell twenty-four hours a day burned the eyes and prevented deep sleep. The lights struck me as a touch of slow torture. Some guys had been sentenced to life or decades—why the need to torment their sleep as well? It seemed perverse. Sleep was one of the last escapes left to us. Maybe that's exactly why they attacked it. Or maybe the prison feared the dark's seductive powers. Maybe what the guards and the Korean government feared most was the vision of dozens of inmates secretly fornicating in the shadows of their cells.

At 8:30 the next morning I was escorted downstairs to an empty room that served as a human loading dock. Coils of different-colored ropes and sets of handcuffs waited for us in neat piles on the gray stone floor.

"Why did you come to Korea?" a guard asked me as he wrapped handcuffs around my wrists.

"I was teaching English."

"What kind of teacher are you?" he said snidely as he tied me with a yellow rope. Yellow for drug cases; black for murderers; blue for the liars, cheats, and business frauds; white for the common lot. He tied the yellow rope tight around my wrists, across my back, around and under my arms.

"Bong?" he wanted to know. Methamphetamine.

"No."

"Heroin?"

"Hashish." I really didn't want to answer him. I knew what the reaction was going to be; it was always the same: a kind of knee-jerk moral nursery rhyme:

*You're wrong you're wrong you're wrong,*
*Stop! Don't do it again.*
*You're bad you're bad you're bad,*
*Stop! Don't do it again.*

He sent a low scratchy growl hissing through his throat, a common sound of Korean displeasure. "In America okay. In Korea no good. You understand?" he said, tightening the knot against my back.

I boarded the detention-house bus with Korean prisoners, all of us tied together under the arms by another rope like a long necklace of broken shells. I was one of only about a dozen foreigners out of thirty-five hundred men in the Seoul Detention Center, and I was the youngest. I grew accustomed to Koreans staring and jockeying for position around me. It was as if I didn't belong, as though I were only an actor who'd stumbled onto the wrong set and had taken to aping the motions of the true residents. But this was a tricky illusion, because I *did* belong, and the unwanted reality was mine as much as theirs.

I watched the faces of Koreans in their cars as we passed them. They must realize what we are, I thought, even though we're higher up than they are and they can't see our cuffs or ropes clearly. But they must've seen our uniforms, the blue of each man's shoulders. Some people in the cars around our bus stared questioningly at me; others did wild double takes. But most of the time people looked away, and the guards told us not to attract attention. I looked for expressions of judgment or revulsion from the free citizens. They seemed so damn lucky. I envied them their decent lives, their modest jobs, their families to return to. What before would have seemed to me stunted and vapid—the cheap suits, the economical little Hyundai and Daewoo family sedans, the same drive every day to join the well-behaved workforce, the conformed, common, safe life—seemed beautiful to me then, and my heart ached for it.

I'd been down for little more than a week, but I couldn't get my mind around what I was seeing; the outside world was no longer the familiar arena of common life. Now it was a hallucination. I stared at the open doors of the shops and cafés; Korean kids skipping around in groups, happy to be out of school for the day; bands of climbers with high striped socks and backpacks gathering to scale the mountains around Seoul; friends waiting for one another at the entrances to parks. The movements seemed strange. There were endless possibilities out there, a million different directions one could choose. I thought about what I'd chosen, and like an insatiable voyeur devoured everything I saw, each little moving picture of the outside world giving me a kind of paint-fume high.

"GET AGAINST THE wall," a guard at the Seoul Prosecutors' Office building ordered us. We squatted in a line against the side of the hall opposite the holding cells. The guard called off our names one by one from a clipboard.

"Tomasuh. What is this?" He stumbled through the foreign pronunciation and looked up to see who I was.

"Yeh," I replied from my squat with the Korean affirmative.

The Koreans squatting near me tried to get a look and whispered to me or to one another if they were too far down the line: "Are you American?" "Is he American?"

"Be quiet!" the guard shouted.

"Why did you come here?" the Korean suspects asked me in whispers. "What's your crime?" in other words; that was equivalent to "hello." They gave me little conspiratorial smiles, seemed happy as hell to have me with them. I wondered whether the guards would hit us, wondered what strange, unforeseen Korean practices—of punishment or penance—I might suddenly have to endure. I wasn't as used to squatting as the Koreans seemed to be, and I felt my knees stiffening. But I didn't want to draw any further attention to myself. I struggled against the pain and waited tensely to see what would happen.

EACH HOLDING CELL was the same: a dirty urinal trough set in cement in the back; a hardwood floor; white stone walls colored with blood and other stains, etched with names and defiant exclamations in Korean; draining fluorescent lights; a square opening near the floor where food and water could be passed; and a barred window about the size of a fat human head in the center of the door. The corners of the walls just inside the cell doors were scraped and chipped where Korean prisoners had tried to pry off their cuffs by pressing the small metal teeth of the mechanism into the hard concrete, then snapping their arms hard in the opposite direction, so that the teeth shifted, the hole widened, and a hand could be slipped out. Doing this bruised and bloodied their wrists, but I saw them pull it off pretty easily. They would smile proudly, then usually lock the free hand back in: they couldn't allow the guards to see them like that, but the trick did something for them—a little spark of independence.

I spent about a dozen afternoons sitting or lying on those hard floors, back to the wall, anxiously considering my case and Shin's strategy, fighting back memories.

*Where could Rocket be? Is she safe? Maybe he's got her upstairs. Should I tell Shin what I did? Damn it, I can't. Does he know about Zack? If he does, we're all screwed. I can't fucking believe this. Is he just trying to scare me, talking about ten years? How can I get out of this? What can I tell him? Why won't he let this go? There have got to be more serious things for them to deal with. I never hurt anyone. Why do they hate me for this? They've got no idea who I am. I've got to show Shin I'm sorry for disrespecting Korea. I wonder what he's doing upstairs. Does everyone back home know? Man, I fucked up. Why did I do this—why'd I get so fucking greedy? How many guys have been in here? Should I get up and pee? Maybe I'll try and sleep; I'm drained. How close to lunch is it?*

It felt as if I'd drowned, and the deep water around me had altered my hearing, the speed and nature of my thoughts, the movements of my body. But I could do nothing but wait in it. I sat there in the strangeness and let it creep all around me while my mind pivoted and ran nuts from side to side, like a crazed dog after its tail, driven on by regret, sadness, fear, suffocating boredom. Regret, so late and so irrelevant, but I couldn't help feeling it anyway, because of the bleakness of what was before me; piercing sadness for all I'd lost, how far away it was; and fear of the sentence, of how long, and whether or not I'd be able to survive mentally. That was a constant concern, spurred on by something deep in me, near the very instinct to survive. The fear it produced rose dreadfully in my mind and made me ask myself, not really whether I'd live or not—though there were moments of that— but whether I'd be anything close to the same person, as sane, as capable of happiness, whether my soul would be scarred.

Urinating became an ally, an activity to anticipate, plan, execute, and recover from: right there a full five or ten minutes of absorbed time. It's not that difficult to pee with handcuffs on. Once, waiting in absolute boredom, I decided to masturbate in my holding cell for the defiant thrill of it, for five precious minutes of pleasure, with my back to the door, standing above the trough at the back of the cell, thinking of Rocket's little body. Despite the handcuffs, that wasn't so difficult, either.

They passed food to us through the little opening near the

floor: soup with seaweed or sprouts, bowls of rice, pieces of fish, and kimchi, the ubiquitous fermented red-peppered cabbage eaten with every meal—Korea's unofficial national symbol. Kimchi is fiery, bold, and abrupt; it can be amazingly satisfying or give you gas and diarrhea.

I WAS USUALLY isolated in my own holding cell, but on a few occasions I found myself with Korean suspects.

"Yaa, American. You're American?" a man in baggy white pants and a jacket that tied at the sternum asked me. It was a traditional Korean *hanbok*, only prison style. The Korean prisoners took their appearance very seriously—I could see that from the start. Despite the limitations, they strove to maintain good hygiene and dress as neatly as possible. That cultural trait, the Confucian emphasis on appearance, definitely added to the overall order of the country's prisons. If they could afford a prison hanbok, they would wear it with pride. Another inmate, wearing a Buddhist bracelet, a loop of little polished wood balls, was sitting with his back to the wall with his eyes closed. A third guy cursed periodically and bounced his forehead off the wall.

"America and Korea are friends. America helped us in Korean War," the guy in the hanbok said to me. "America number one." His head was a leathery block. He stood up with a sigh and began to pace with his cuffed hands dangling in front of him.

"What's crime?"

I didn't want to say anything to him, because some of these guys also had Shin as their prosecutor, and I didn't really like these exchanges. Having to continually repeat my crime brought the disappointment and failure of it home for me time and again. That was a form of collateral punishment the authorities didn't directly impose: a kind of penal bonus for them.

It's almost impossible to ignore someone with you in a closet, so I finally answered the guy. He pantomimed the smoking of a joint.

"So you like happy smoke, eh? I used to have a lot," he said. "Army?"

"No."

"How old are you?"

"Twenty-three."

"Do you know why I'm here?" He made a fist and smashed it into his other hand. "Gang. I am cap, boss," he said proudly, jabbing a finger into his chest. "Mr. Eee. You can call me older brother, all right? Older brother, eh?"

The prisoner who'd been yelling out curses (*"Sheebal seki dool! Kae seki dool!"*—The fuckers! Sons of bitches!) was up on his feet now and pacing. Watching him, I was reminded of the lions and tigers I'd seen a month before in the Manila Zoo, pacing desperately in their pens in the tropical heat.

"Yaaaa, you're handsome, mask good," Mr. Eee told me, running his hand over his own face. "You have Korean girlfriend?"

"No."

"You're lying!"

"Korean women are pretty, but I don't have a girlfriend." This was both the truth and the much safer answer.

"Your *chajee* is big?" he asked, making another fist. "Americans are big size. You have American girlfriend?"

"Yes."

"She waits for you?"

"I don't know," I said, considering this for the first time. I missed Rocket.

"She should wait for you. Korean girls will wait; they are loyal. What do you think of Korea?"

"I like it."

He seemed relieved, and proud.

"Tomasuh, good!" he said, smiling, giving me a thumbs-up.

I WAITED WITH these guys the entire day. They came and went and wondered why I hadn't been called. Waiting in sometimes excruciating doubt in the box was a full-time job for me that day, from nine in the morning until six that night. I'd missed our hour of exercise back at the detention house. The guards took me out only once, and that was to retie me with rope. Was Shin busy, or was he intentionally letting me stew? I wondered.

ANOTHER DAY I waited for five hours in holding before Shin summoned me upstairs. When I entered his office, he was sitting stoically at his imposing desk, gently cradling a Korean-English dictionary in both hands.

"Sit down," he told me. He stretched back in his chair with a pillow behind him and casually admired his superiority in the situation.

"What is a clapboard house? How does it look?" he asked me suddenly.

For a second I tried to think of how clapboard might be related to my case. He had me bewildered.

"They're old colonial houses, made of wood planks," I answered him after a moment, hoping I was getting it right.

"I am reading a book. Perhaps you can translate the title for me. There is one word and 'Heights.'"

"'Wuthering,'" I guessed correctly, though I'd never read it. I felt like I'd scored a point. Maybe I could win Shin over to mercy with English lessons.

"What does 'Wuthering' mean?" he wanted to know.

It was a good question really; I didn't know the answer myself. I told him that it was an uncommon word that meant something like stormy or turbulent. He went into his dictionary.

"How do you pronounce 'clothes'?" he asked.

I spoke the word for him.

"Hhhmm, how it is different from 'close'?"

"How do you pronounce 'perfect'?" For Koreans, "perfect" was often impossible.

"How do you pronounce 'refrigerator'?"

Not a word about my case, and then, as abruptly as he had begun, Shin ended the session and left the room. I had to wait for my guard to come back to escort me downstairs, so I had a moment. I turned and saw Shin's secretary. She didn't answer when I said hello, and I could tell that she knew she shouldn't talk to me.

Though I'd been in jail only a few weeks, I'd begun to grasp the importance of the rare opportunities one got as a prisoner. Billy, a Colombian on our floor in the detention house, had stressed that to me: *"No llora, no mami,"* he would say. It meant that if you don't cry, Mother won't come to comfort you. In other words, you've got to speak up and fight for what you need. No one really gave a damn about us; we had to do it by ourselves. You had to be quick and sure about those moments, to speak up and gain what you could to make life better. I didn't always behave that way, because I saw it as scrounging; it seemed too opportunistic, desperate, petty. I didn't want to live so small, scavenging for an extra slice of bread, battling for a bit more water—being reduced to that was part of how the prison broke us all. I saw self-sufficiency as a nobler way, not needing anything more than I had, however little it was. Better to keep one's peace than continually fight for something more, I reasoned. But that thinking sometimes worked against me, and I could feel myself adapting. With Shin out of the office, I decided to take a chance.

"I'm sorry to bother you, but can I please have a cup of coffee?" I asked the secretary. There were packets of instant and hot water right next to her. Coffee wasn't allowed in the detention house, and we almost never got our hands on it. It had become forbidden, brown-powdered gold, and we lusted after it nearly as much as we daydreamed of women.

She looked up for a moment, paused, and finally said yes. I couldn't believe my luck. And when she handed the clean white cup to me, I felt the warmth generated by her little act of kindness. It was beautiful to still be considered worthy of a little.

# 11

Again sadness has boarded me.

My life is an old house where only memories live.

I look like an old man, with a fallen beard and dead years,

Without illusions, without laments.

My eyes fix upon a forgotten port; without sea, nothing.

I forgot what day it is today, and I don't know the time. Nor do I remember
my name.

My heart scratches like a beggar's rags, beating without desire.

The birds have stopped singing, and they've flown far away.

But of course, if there wasn't even one piece of grain for them.

Nothing. Only sand that moves with the weight of my body,

And stones that hurt my bare feet with each of my steps.

This is all I find.

My life is an old house, lost and forgotten.
                    —*Billy the Kid, 1991*

ONE DAY DURING my first week in the detention house, I was walking laps by myself, skirting the base of the high outer wall and our cell block with my head down. It was a hot, sunny day. In the beginning there were no games—later we would buy volleyballs from the detention center's *koo may,* its list of purchasable goods, and use them to play soccer in the small dirt space. I didn't know any of the other dozen or so foreign inmates. I was seeing most of them up close for the first time, all of us in blue prison pants and white T-shirts. In Korea at that time, even those not yet convicted were made to wear the same blue uniforms that convicts wore:

a violation of international conventions. The guiding principle seemed to be a presumption of guilt until one's innocence could be proven. The U.S. embassy agreed with that assessment; during one visit an embassy consul told us that more than 90 percent of all criminal cases brought to trial in Korea ended in conviction. (Not all those convicted are necessarily sent to prison; many are given suspended sentences.)

As I walked quickly around the yard, a young guy sidled up to me and introduced himself. He looked like someone I might have known on the outside. Just a few years older than me, he was about five foot nine, with short dark hair, light skin, and a good-looking face. He looked a bit like a pit bull, compact, with a pronounced chest and muscular arms.

"Hey, you can call me Billy," he said. The Colombian Billy the Kid. His English was slightly accented. "What are you in for?"

I got a good feeling from him immediately; something in his face seemed genuine. I was desperate to speak to someone, to release some of the internal weight I was carrying. We talked in Spanish and English as we walked side by side, the dry dust of the ground billowing up in little clouds as we went along. A Korean soldier with an M16 resting on his shoulder looked down on us from the tower forty feet above our heads.

"You got to tell him it was yours for personal use. They'll convict you anyway, believe it," Billy urged me after listening to a brief outline of my story. "My case had no evidence against me, just a witness who lied, but in Korea it doesn't matter. Listen to me. Selling and trafficking is at least five, what I got. You can get less than that. Tell him you smoke always; give them numbers, Koreans like numbers. Tell the prosecutor you smoked like twenty grams a day. Tell him you're addicted."

As crazy as it seemed at the time, what Billy was telling me was sound—and a better strategy than the one suggested to me the next day during exercise by an older Korean-American man who'd gotten fouled up in a shady business deal. Tall, with glasses, this guy seemed to look down with a smug superiority on the riffraff he'd been put with. The only reason he was willing to speak with me, it seemed, was that I was an educated, middle-class American. He told me to lie, to deny to the end that the package was mine.

In the end Billy's idea worked, and I remember marveling that he had been more attuned to the ways of Korean justice than the older Korean man. I eventually told Prosecutor Shin that I smoked twenty grams a day, rolling dozens of cigarettes with tobacco and hashish for my friends and me. This was an absurd amount, an outright lie, as was my story for why I'd tested positive. I told Shin that on the day before I was arrested I'd crumbled twelve grams of hashish into a cup of coffee that I'd enjoyed outdoors in Pagoda Park. I *had* flavored my coffee in the park—it was one of my favorite spots in Seoul, a refuge where I'd go to sit and watch the old men play *paduk,* or Go, the pigeons flying up near the Korean flags blowing at the four brightly painted wooden gates—but with nowhere close to twelve grams, which would have knocked me unconscious, I think. The number made it a ridiculous story, but it satisfied Shin. Maybe he knew it was nonsense, but what it did was give him a pretext for not hitting me with a selling charge. Shin never did, sparing me an additional year and a half at least.

BACK BELOW THE WALLS, I was about to ask Billy why he was giving me advice, but having already read the question in my face, he said in Spanish with a playful swagger, "I'm the lawyer of the poor."

Billy had apparently been a cocaine and emerald smuggler. He told me about the media attention his case had attracted. In the early 1990s a kilo of any drug in Korea was a big story. After Billy had been caught, articles in Korean magazines had shown policemen standing proudly next to a tableful of gleaming green emeralds and bagfuls of white powder—all of it from the faraway valleys and mines of South America. He'd somehow gotten ahold of one of the magazine pictures, and he kept it in his cell. When he showed it to me, he revealed the same kind of brute pride I saw in almost all the guys, the law that for them governed survival and business. I may be as good as dead and buried here, they said, but look at what I did before I was taken out. Look at me then, on top of the world, working above fools and authority. I may have failed in the end, but while it lasted I was something.

But a flip side of that mean pride stemmed from a purer instinct. You looked back on your deeds, the criminal ones included, as proof that you were alive, that you'd done things, regardless of their merit, cut a swath across the field of life. That didn't mean that you couldn't also regret those same actions or wish that you'd done things differently, but the record seemed to have been sealed and frozen, and what it contained was your life, and that was something to hold on to.

BILLY HAD BEEN a hotshot, no doubt. An older, wealthy Colombian man who owned several mines had put Billy in charge of one of them; he was entitled to a part of the profits he made from selling the gems the mine produced. He'd done real well. In a poor country Billy had been connected to power. He'd been involved with the strongman's daughter, and I felt for him when he spoke of her, how he'd lost her, told her to live her life and forget about him because he'd be gone for five years. That made me think of Rocket, and each time I did I felt my chest go hollow. As we talked to each other through the bars of our cells—Billy's was right next to mine—projecting our voices out into the hall while not being able to see each other, he would tell me that I'd been responsible for Rocket and that I'd endangered her life. That was wrong, he said, dead wrong. I'd been reckless. He made me look hard at that, and at the fact that I'd have to let her go. The last time he said that to me I ended the conversation and stepped away from the bars, deeper into my cell, because he'd broken something in me. Before I knew it I was crying hard, though I didn't let Billy hear me. I had endangered the life of someone I loved, and that was horribly wrong. I accepted that then, along with the pain and humiliation it carried.

The days were excruciating. I was dreading a long sentence, drifting restlessly in my cage through the hours of boredom, looking back sadly and angrily at the track record of my life, bleeding inside for the loss of everything I'd squandered, everything good and clean and free in the world, my family, the United States, Rocket. Billy stepped into that with a directness that disturbed me, but it helped keep me from fantasies. "You'll probably be here a few years," he told me before my trial, and I hated him for it. He said he refused to "give candy."

When I met him, Billy had already been down for four years. His lawyer-of-the-poor persona really existed, as he often gave advice to the other foreigners, translated for them. He could speak Korean better than any of us, and because of the complexity of his case and the time he'd already spent, he knew Korean law and her prisons better, too. His discipline and sheer energy quickly became apparent. I learned that he'd written a seventy-page letter in his defense to the appeals court judges, helping prove to them that the Korean woman who'd incriminated him had lied about several things. I wondered if the judges had been impressed simply by the extent of his effort, the seventy pages. They lowered his sentence from seven years to five. Billy sometimes told me that he was innocent of the crime, and that was my biggest problem with him, though I kept it to myself. It was a common escape; maybe it was true for some guys, but it always sounded pathetic to me. Our failures were often too heavy to accept, as was the authorities' right to judge us. The general attitude was: What I did is not what they say it was, and I reject their version.

Billy had fought to reopen his case, and the Korean justice ministry had made the rare concession of finally doing so. That was why he'd been sent from Taejon Prison, where I would later end up, back to the detention center in Seoul. Billy told me that while in Taejon he'd fought for the opportunity to join the prison band, a choice appointment that allowed him to study the saxophone and trumpet. He'd earned the equivalent of eighty dollars for two years of musical service. In Taejon he'd also made himself proficient in English and Korean. In the Seoul Detention Center, before I checked in, he'd cut his wrists in order to win better food for the foreigners. That was why in the mornings we got two slices of American cheese, four slices of white bread, a hard-boiled egg, and juice, in addition to the option of the Korean food—rice, kimchi, and soup. He showed me the scars on his arms. Part of me thought Billy was a crazy bastard; some of the guards did, too. But I wasn't the only one who also respected him for that same intensity, his commitment. While so many inmates were droopy, passive sacks, helpless and doomed, Billy was like lightning. You knew he'd never go down without a fight, that the Kid was going to come at you with guns blazing. It might be easy to dismiss him as a two-bit narcotrafficker, but of all the people I've met in my life, he was one of the very few who blazed like a force of nature. There in a truly shitty place, Billy had reached down in himself and found an emerald made of iron, a backbone of strength that only death would break. My man held his head up and urged us to do the same.

I was surprised to find someone like him there. He was the opposite of the somewhat hackneyed image I'd had of the typical convict: seedy, polluted, bizarre, a loser in life. Billy brought sanity and discipline. He framed the experience in words and thoughts

I could understand. He was curious, searching for truths in our experience, and the time had in no way deadened his mind. I could see that if I held my head up as he did, accepted the circumstances and made myself hard to them, if I stayed steady and worked at keeping myself moving forward by doing the little I could—reading, studying, exercising, and staying positive—I wouldn't lose my mind. I could do the time. Billy was proof.

That state of mind wasn't easily earned, as I later found out for myself. Billy was twenty-two when he was caught in Korea. Depressed, he tried to sleep all the time, he told me, and he ate too much while sitting in his cell doing nothing. That was just where I was.

"I got fat and lazy, and this can happen, so watch out," he warned me in my first weeks. "You gotta use the time, young gun. Don't let it use you."

I awoke many mornings to the sound of his breathing, as he always began his day with one or two hours of exercise in his cell. I tried to copy him. Despite not having a lot of formal education, he devoured the books my mom sent me, returning each one to me quickly only to ask for more. We read Nietzsche, Ayn Rand, Lao-tzu's *Tao Te Ching*, James Baldwin, Hemingway, passing the books to each other using Billy's *mensajero*, a little black bag he'd tied to the end of a string, which he'd cast sidelong through his bars and into the hallway, where I'd catch it in front of my cell. After we'd both read Tolstoy's *The Death of Ivan Ilyich*, Billy pointed out to me the lines at the end where Ilyich, an ex-judge on his deathbed, finally sees his life clearly:

> As though I had been going steadily downhill while I imagined I was climbing up. And that is really how it was. In public opinion I was going up, and all the time my life was sliding away from under my feet . . .

In a sense Ilyich's story was the exact opposite of ours, Billy noted. He was a respected and wealthy judge, a man of high social standing, but internally he was bankrupt, having cared most about status and reputation and never having sought a deeper meaning to his life. We inmates, on the other hand, were considered the lowest and basest of all groups. In public opinion we could sink no lower. But internally we could still climb up, Billy and I figured; with the right effort and the right thinking we could make ourselves better, form finer characters.

When the nightly music in the hall made our conversations difficult, Billy and I would retire to the small back windows of our bathrooms, where we'd continue to talk through the bars and watch the sun fade behind the mountains. We would count the first stars as they appeared diffidently in the twilight over Anyang. During the summer he would sometimes charm the guards and I would dart over to his cell to share lunch and a game of chess. On one of those occasions I saw something I'll never forget. Billy was talking about the time he'd done and his sick mother at home in Bogotá. He told me that the years had been difficult to bear; he needed to get back to Colombia to see his mom before she died. He didn't cry, but for a moment I thought I saw clearly in his eyes the wound in his heart, the deepest point of the cut that carries the greatest pain, and from which emanates the greatest compassion. His eyes spoke of what awaited me, and I knew it.

# 12

I CONTINUED MY hundred paces in the cell—from the foot of the bed, where the blue bucket for hot water was, five purposeful steps across the wood floor, a duck of the head as I entered the tiny bathroom, to the sink, then a turn, and five or six steps back to the water bucket. The pacing was necessary to combat my slowing metabolism. Too much rice, not enough movement.

*"Payshik!"* the *so-jees,* or hall workers, would yell from the top of the corridor as they rolled large plastic buckets on a flat cart, stopping at the food hole of each cell in turn. The unchanging repetition of breakfast, lunch, and dinner was often the only action in a day. You had to put your white plastic bowls into the food slot before the so-jees got to your cell or else they would assume you weren't going to eat and would pass you by. I became pretty skilled with my justice-ministry-issue white-plastic chopsticks.

With each and every meal came white rice and kimchi. I was taught that the rice could double as an adhesive; some guys used matted clumps of it to glue their number patches to their uniforms, instead of taking the time to sew them on as we were supposed to. That made me question what large quantities of rice did in my stomach. Chicken twice a week; a lot of soup, fish, seaweed, radishes, hot peppers sometimes—brought around specially, a few for each man, divided up at each cell—and lettuce also on occasion. Once a week a bit of pork, also Korean vegetables, sprouts, cucumbers, all of them made better by sauces: the potent, burning *dwen-jang,* a soybean paste that came only rarely and was spooned out at our cells if we wanted it; or the famous and ubiquitous *ko choo jang,* or red pepper paste. (It was a constant supply of red-peppered and spicy food; one logically questioned whether this wasn't the cause of the high incidence of stomach cancer among Koreans.) We were being punished, but not by starvation. The authorities seemed to want us relatively well nourished for our appointed suffering. I'd grown to love Korean food on the outside, and so I had few complaints about our payshik, despite the fact that it was served to us out of buckets and lacked variety.

*Ramyun,* the little plastic bowls of instant noodle soup, saved us from the monotony of what we were fed. When the thought of the rice and kimchi gave you no appetite, you could grab a ramyun, and you felt saved somehow because you had that option. We bought them from the detention house's shopping list: about twenty-five cents for one; twenty-four of them in a box. Each inmate had an account, a money bank—if he had any money to put in it, that is. The thousand dollars I had on me when I was arrested was put into my account, so I was able to buy things. I lived on that one thousand dollars for about three years. We never saw the actual currency, of course, and it was amazing to live for years without seeing money, without having it be a part of your life in any physical sense.

Into the ramyun noodles we added the spicy powder packets, then our own raw garlic and sesame oil from the shopping list, maybe an egg, either boiled or raw, a slice of cheese, green pepper, chopped, if we had it. Add hot water from our blue bucket, which I learned to wrap with one of my blankets in order to insulate it and keep the heat in longer. It was best to take a ramyun when the water was hottest. So immediately after the hall worker thrust scoopfuls of boiled water through our wood hole, turning his wrist to dump each scoop into our bucket, we pounced. That was the ramyun hour. Most of the inmates seemed to love ramyun. The plastic bowls were stacked proudly in guys' cells, spoken of, bragged about, borrowed, bought by the box, bartered, and savored. In Taejon Prison the so-jees would make special passes through the cell block with hot water meant exclusively for ramyun. We made their call of *"Ramyun mool!"* into a running joke and used to shout it out at inappropriate times—like at night when the block was completely silent—just to be idiots. I still yell it out sometimes just for the hell of it, though no one understands what I'm saying. And I still eat ramyun, especially in the fall and winter. When I do, though, the red traces of old boils and rashes I had in Korea seem to reappear on my face. It's as if the ramyun triggers my entire biology, bringing it back to that time in prison by some feat of alimentary recidivism.

ONE EVENING IN late June the guard strode down the hall, stopped in front of my cell, which I'd had to myself for about a month, opened the door, and sent in a tall and fleshy Peruvian. More foreigners had arrived recently, and I knew it was only a matter of time before I got a cellmate. I was hoping that they wouldn't lock me in with a freak. I watched him intently from my side of the cell as he ducked his head and entered. He had a helmet of thick dark hair set on his massive head and scars across his forearms. He introduced himself as José Luis. That first night he stood on his bed and with a pen he wasn't supposed to have wrote two words in large block letters on the wall: RIMAC, his barrio in Lima, where his wife and children were at home waiting for him; and TECHI, the name of a pretty young girl who lived there. Trying to get a sense of what kind of man he was, I sat and watched him, asked him questions. That was the evening's entertainment. He told me how he'd wanted Techi for a long time and had just gone one day and taken her, leading her away to an empty house. From the way he told it in Spanish, I wasn't sure if this was his idea of romance or a tale of rape.

When I asked him about his crime, he told me, "We're *choros finos*. Do you understand what that means? Thieves of quality."

He and his fellow thieves traveled the world in business suits, stealing suitcases in airports and hotels. They often worked in teams; while one man distracted the intended victim, another would make off with his belongings. His favorite victims were Japanese businessmen, he said. An associate once plucked an Arab's attaché case that had eighty thousand dollars in cash inside. José said that at home he had a supply of cameras, passports, cell phones, and laptops.

"In my neighborhood people don't judge me for what I do, because I don't steal from them. I go abroad. Everybody is friendly with me; they greet me in the street, ask me about my travels."

When I told him about my smuggling hashish, he asked if I'd ever seen the movie *Midnight Express*. He told me that in Peru he got into smoking the paste made from coca leaves; he'd always go sit on the toilet with the stuff and take his first hit there because the physiological reaction to the thought of the imminent high would otherwise have him dumping in his pants. We talked about the Peruvian novelist Mario Vargas Llosa, about rumors of treasure troves of gold hidden in the mountains in Peru. He told me how he'd discovered the little barbershops in Seoul where you could get a shave, then a massage, then sex, all in the same chair. You just have to look for the spiraling red, blue, and white of the barber poles outside the storefronts, he told me happily. I remembered seeing those everywhere.

We took turns at night waking up to comb the walls for mosquitoes, smacking them with pleasure into the stone before they could drain more of our blood. Dozens of them flew through the flimsy blue netting on our windows; we were sitting meat for them in our little closet. I would sometimes kill them as they tried to fly into our cell from the hallway, and I'd wonder which fellow inmate's blood it was that was now smeared on my hand. José and I also took turns getting up at night to reach through the bars— a long arm could do it—and flick the fluorescent light switch.

Those damn lights were easily among the most hated things. Of course we weren't supposed to touch the switch, but by doing so we were at least able to fall back asleep in the peace of darkness. The inevitable flip side was that the guard would eventually make his way down to our cell on one of his stroll-throughs. He'd turn the light back on and scream at us: *"Ya! An-day. Bool man-ji-ji-ma!"* Don't touch the light! His yelling would wake us and we'd have to try to fall back asleep with the lights on again. Everything seemed to function in perverse little cycles.

José told me that when he was eighteen, he and a friend accidentally killed a visiting priest from Spain while robbing him in the street in Lima. He said his friend shot the man in the stomach. They were caught, and José and his friend were given the death penalty before having their sentences commuted to twenty-five years, to be served in Sepa, a notorious prison camp buried deep in the remote jungles of eastern Peru. José told me about how he escaped from there after several years, on a wild adventure through the virgin jungle. He and two other convicts wandered lost, hungry, and wet for weeks. One of them, a bullying murderer who was older than José, began threatening and hitting José as they snaked their way through the dense undergrowth. José felt sure the man was going to kill him out there. So one night, when the man fell asleep at the base of a tree by their fire, he crept up and with one downward stroke lodged an axe in the man's head.

José had to swim rivers in which he felt large creatures under the water against his legs. I felt myself there next to him, filled with terror, risking everything to be free. His story transported me out of the detention house, back out into the world at large. And as he recounted his experience, I could feel myself instinctively rooting him on, hoping he would make it out of the jungle to freedom. He did, and then fled Peru.

José struck me as a survivor, and I admired him for it. He'd had a sordid life, had been soiled by it, but it seemed to give him an almost healthy glow of resilience. He was the first killer I'd ever knowingly shared a room with, but I didn't see anything malicious or bitter in him. I spoke some Spanish, and we shared a Western sensibility that was made more palpable in Confucian Korea. At the very least I trusted that José wasn't going to try to kill me in my sleep. Here was a killer and a lifelong criminal, and yet he was all right. It reassured me. Maybe the other inmates wouldn't be as bad as I might have imagined.

In his years abroad José had learned a lot about other countries' prisons, and so he was a wide and colorful source of information. Since I knew only a little bit of our Far Eastern pen, it was fascinating to hear about Western punishments and corrections. That kind of comparing and contrasting seemed to interest all of us: to know what our situation would be like in other countries; how we had it better in Korea's can; how we were damned with it worse. But what seemed true was that many of the fundamental elements of organized punishment were universal—the fact that regardless of country or culture, as a lawbreaker you almost invariably would be locked away, have your freedom of movement and communication severely curtailed, and be denied a long list of things. And this was strangely reassuring, because we knew then that the grass wouldn't really be much greener elsewhere. Some of the details might be different, but the big ugly picture would be more or less the same.

There were José's two years in a Belgian jail, from which he says he wrote the queen and actually won a bit of royal sympathy with a maudlin recounting of his family's life of poverty and misery in Peru. All the robbing was for his family, he pleaded. She sent a vassal to the jail to meet him. He was eventually released early from his sentence. Italian dungeons with a sharper edge:

pornography late at night on televisions in the cells; wine and beer sold to inmates; narcotics if you wanted them; the inmates burning their beds when they protested. No rebellions here in the Seoul DC, I noted, and certainly no televisions or narcotics to help while away the time.

In Greece once, before his appeal, José was given a long sentence to scare him. He'd been caught stealing briefcases again. In the Greek jail he befriended a shrewd, vicious Moroccan who traveled about with powerful tablets and slipped them into women's drinks to knock them out, then crept into their hotel rooms. Scandinavian prisons were good, José recalled (something about an attempted bank robbery in Stockholm): good food and decent treatment. Geneva's jail was so fine that José didn't want to leave it. He said he couldn't believe the selection and quality of the food—just like a restaurant, he swore. The keepers wore regular clothes, not uniforms, and they spoke politely to the inmates. When they came around the cells to count the men, they made sure not to disturb them in any way. There was a well-kept grass field for soccer. Visits were easy and open. I was curious to hear if this different approach to correction had an effect on José, because it was ridiculously clear that nothing else had. For him, an alternative to his criminal lifestyle was an absurdity—someone else's life, not his. Well, he said, after thinking about my question, he respected the country and in the end left it without any malice or contempt; maybe he would refrain from robbing the Swiss in the future, he decided.

José revealed that he'd been involved in a shooting in Italy and was still wanted on serious charges, so when his court date in Seoul was suddenly pushed back, he got jumpy, paced from one side of the cell to the other. He asked me if I thought Korean police and prosecutors were sophisticated enough to contact Interpol. He feared that was the reason for the delay. I watched how the mind played wild tricks in the cell; I could see it in José's face, the wheels churning but in absolute uselessness. Not knowing how much time I was looking at, I could feel my mind doing the same. Delusions, paranoia—the brain was sent reeling from constant thoughts about what was going on outside our maddeningly tiny world. Things have gone so wrong that you wondered what other shoes were going to drop. As I sat there on my cot frozen, terrified by thoughts of Shin rooting through the record of my life, José kissed his fingertips, marked a sign of the cross on his body, and exclaimed *"Ojala!"*—that, God willing, he might be called to court quickly, with no more delay; that the Korean police would fail to uncover the outstanding warrant in Europe for his arrest; that he might receive a suspended sentence.

So far Korean jail wasn't winning José over. He really wasn't enjoying the Seoul *koo chi so,* the twenty-three hours a day locked down, the mediocre food, the shortage of water, the lack of any facilities or activities whatsoever, the disdain of some of the guards. "You know, *puta madre,* I'm gonna target them," he said with a sneer, "steal their money, and throw away their passports." And we laughed together over inane thoughts of revenge.

JOSÉ SAID HIS thieving was pretty easy and that he made a good living from it. He encouraged me to smuggle drugs again when I got out. I might have used up South Korea, he said, half joking, but there were so many other countries I could try. After all, he said, "You need money; without it you have no power." Now he was completely serious, and it got me thinking. At its core what I did was for money, and it seemed that the crimes of almost everyone with us revolved around the same. You could trace them all back: cash was the common denominator, greed the broad category. And yet I still felt separate from the others—with the exception of Billy—morally superior to them, even. I didn't belong there in the same way that they did. They were more criminal than I was. I'd simply made a mistake. But the truth is that I might have been worse than them, because I'd had the advantages of growing up middle-class in the United States. I'd been educated. I'd had other options open to me, and my crime wasn't for someone else's sake. It was for my own satisfaction and gain. Conversely, the tiny fifty-year-old Indonesian, for example, who was caught stealing in Seoul and lived as quietly as a bird in the cell next to me for two months, had acted partly out of the need to support his family, as a response to his poverty. I would say that he was more justified in his greed than I was. Fact was, I still hadn't accepted who I'd become, that I was no better than any of them.

JOSÉ ASKED ME if I wanted to join him when we were out. If my handwriting was good, he could use me to forge signatures on the many traveler's checks he found inside the suitcases, attaché cases, and bags he stole. I'd have to sign dozens of them, he warned me, in front of bank tellers. But they did it all the time and he'd give me a good percentage, he said. For a moment I thought about what it would be like if I joined the *choros finos* as their penman, though I knew it was an absurdity, and in the same category as my last criminal adventure. But the conversation got me thinking about what I was going to do for money when I got out. For the most part that pressure was suspended in prison, but it still sometimes crept into your sober head and made itself a nagging, unsettling concern. Even though it might be years away, the pressure of survival on the outside still made itself felt. How was I going to start over with nothing? What was I going to do?

Without funds in your *young chigum* you could get by—the Korean government would still give you your cell floor to sleep on, your three meals a day—but you couldn't buy ramyun or the big green bars of laundry soap (we scrubbed clothes on the stone floors of the little bathrooms in our cells); you couldn't be the man to purchase the next volleyball so that everyone could play soccer during exercise; you couldn't get sesame oil or raw garlic; and you couldn't buy white T-shirts or socks when you needed them. You were also at risk of being labeled a *yangachee* by the Korean inmates, a fake gangster, a kind of parasitic bum, one of the worst insults there was. It often seemed that being poor was considered a more terrible crime than murder.

LOOT HAD GUIDED Mr. Sha from Bombay into illegally importing diamonds into Korea. If you skirted the legal way, which involved paying taxes on the gems, you could make larger profits, of course. He and his son, Sandir, were arrested together. Mr. Sha had a large nose, a head of rich black hair, and a belly that stuck out well beyond his feet. Waddling when he walked, he was a goofy yet painfully serious character. Sandir, tall and in his mid-twenties, was a quiet, almost timid kid, doing his best to help his dad and keep him calm. Mr. Sha was just a few cells to my right, and Sandir was down the line in one of the first cells on the hall. Mr. Sha would frequently call down the corridor to his son in a desperate, worried voice, the last syllable of the name rising like a question: "San-*dir*? San-*dir*?" We laughed hard whenever we heard it and would sometimes try to imitate it out loud.

After Sandir answered his father, hot flurried conversations in Hindustani would ensue, disturbing all of us: Mr. Sha rattling things off; Sandir repeating dutifully after each volley, *"A-cha, a-cha-hey."* Some of the other foreigners would yell at them to shut up; after giving them a couple of moments the guard would yell, too. But father and son would ignore everyone as best they could.

Mr. Sha raged about his situation every day. "What do you think?" he barked back at me once when I asked if he was doing all right. "My wife and daughters are outside alone; my son and I cannot be there taking care of them; they have no man to watch over them. It is unbelievable what they have done. They must let us go immediately; we have done no crime!" He cursed at the guards, threatened revenge on Korea and her damned people: "They are crazy people to do this!" He preached furiously about an anti-Korea campaign he would launch as soon as he got out, to discourage would-be visitors to the country. He was going to make critical posters and advertisements. "I will put them in airports, I swear!" he yelled, his face flush, spit flying out of his mouth. "I will tell my country what animals they are. Look how they keep us!"

I got the feeling with Mr. Sha that it could have been anywhere; he wanted to fight. I had a vision of him haggling viciously with buyers over his precious stones.

The one thing Mr. Sha had going for him was that he had money, apparently, and in Korea, as is true everywhere, it made things happen. He'd become ill and needed to move around outside his cell more. Somehow he'd arranged it so that he was allowed to walk in our hallway for a short time each evening. It was a pretty radical privilege, but he looked beaten and bitter as he passed back and forth on the other side of the bars. He finally gained his release to await his trial on the outside, and just like that the only father-son team I would see on the inside left without ceremony one day, hurrying down the hall and out of our world.

Before he moved into his own cell next to mine, Billy had shared one with the Pakistani Mohammed, who'd received a death sentence in 1992. He'd been part of a Pakistani group in Seoul that ran what they call a "manpower" business, a kind of human trafficking that entailed forging visas for immigrants from poor countries—mostly Sri Lankans, Bengalis, and fellow Pakistanis—bribing immigration and customs officials, and smuggling the people into more developed nations. Once there, the poor immigrants could get menial jobs that paid better than anything available to them back home. For their services Mohammed and his crew charged five thousand dollars or more a head. They made a lot of money. Mohammed's crew eventually fought with a rival Pakistani group who'd moved into their territory in Seoul. Three Pakistanis had been murdered, I'd heard. One was found dead in Itaewon early one morning with stab wounds in his chest and crotch. The bodies of the other two were found buried in a field outside Seoul. Their heads had been cut off.

The case was a bloody mess: about a dozen Pakistanis had been convicted in it, receiving sentences ranging from three years to death. They'd been beaten, stripped naked, doused with water, and shocked with cattle prods, including in the genitals. I believed Mohammed when he told me this because I'd seen the cattle prod myself. If the Korean police were willing to shock an American to get a confession, I could only imagine what they felt entitled to do to suspects from poor countries with no power in Korea. Unfortunately, that kind of cold thinking was apparent in the Korean mind-set, in things the guards often said, in the subtle differences between my life in prison and the lives of the non-American foreign inmates. I was seeing vividly for the first time how the wealth and power of a man's home country could become just another crude measure used to place him into another hierarchy of inequality. It seemed so random and fortunate that I'd been born into a country of privilege and power—the great initial accident that would always figure prominently in my fate.

Contradictory confessions had been coerced from some of the Pakistanis. Mohammed and his friend Jamil, who was also jailed on our floor, had been singled out somewhat arbitrarily as the leaders behind the murders and stuck with the death penalty. They both said that they hadn't done it; Mohammed was vehement in his protests, Jamil less so. They'd been down going on three years. Billy and I guessed that Korea wouldn't execute a foreigner, especially when the case seemed so unclear and involved claims of police abuse. I guessed that no foreigner had been executed for many decades, and that one would have to go back to the time of the Korean War, or even farther back to the arrival of Christian missionaries in the country during the Chosun dynasty, to find a state-sponsored execution of a foreigner. None of that slowed the maelstrom in Mohammed. When I first met him, he said to me casually, though full of disagreement, "They gave me the death sentence, these crazy people," shaking his head at the thought.

Physically, Mohammed was a beautiful man, tall and elegant, his movements fluid. His head was perfectly bald and his smile broad and bright white against his smooth dark skin. He could be cheerful, but then there were many times when you could see a deep hollowness in his eyes, and he often had the faraway, intense look of a madman. He unnerved me. I looked at him and tried to fathom how he could get up in the morning, what kept him going, how he could laugh or ever take things lightly. I knew how my sentence felt, like a weight, a heavy one that—just when you might feel a tug of hope or carelessness, a thought about something good in life—would lean on you from above, reminding you with a heavy hand that it was there. What about his, then? Mohammed's and Jamil's presence constantly reminded me that the game was all too real, that life and death were at stake. Yet at the same time they lightened my burden, because they showed me that shit could have been far worse. My situation was nothing compared with theirs, and that was a necessary and saving perspective. When I was pitying myself and my thoughts fell on them, it was like an instant kick in the head. How can you sit here and cry like a baby for nothing? my conscience would lay into me. Look at them. Imagine *that* fate. What if I'd been caught in the Philippines and been given a death sentence? That could have happened. It was a disgrace to pity oneself in the face of others' suffering, and yet it was inevitable. As the Nazi concentration-camp survivor Viktor Frankl told it in his amazing book *Man's Search for Meaning,* which I'd read for a class in high school, suffering in a man is like gas in an enclosed space; regardless of the volume of gas, a little or a lot, it will spread out to fill the space evenly. I have no doubt that each man with me there, regardless of how his fate matched up with the rest, felt his pain fully and intensely.

Mohammed's friend Jamil seemed quiet and harmless. For months after I'd arrived I never heard them speak to each other. It made me think that they were hiding a terrible secret, that they *had* butchered those men. How can everyone here be innocent, for Christ's sake? I wasn't convinced, and I didn't want to get involved. I wished for their sakes that they were innocent. Hell, I wished *I* were innocent. But I was mostly selfish, removed, neutral. I didn't know their case, really, or their past. I could do little except pity them.

The death sentence freed Mohammed in a sense. Nothing worse could come to him, so he had no qualms about arguing with the guards, pretending to hang himself in his cell at night when the guards walked by, refusing to eat for days. On Billy's advice he and Jamil went on a hunger strike, which definitely got the attention of the higher officers. They tried to force-feed Mohammed and Jamil intravenously. They pleaded with them, brought pastors and other religious men into the detention house to try to talk them out of it. On Mohammed and Jamil's behalf Billy and I wrote letters to Amnesty International, the United Nations, Korea's justice ministry, and the South Korean president, Kim Young Sam. We wrote that Mohammed and Jamil had been tortured, their confessions coerced, that the case should be reopened. Whether they were murderers or not, I knew them personally now, and killing them simply seemed cruel and unnecessary.

Concerned that condemned men would hide rope or blades with which to kill themselves, and would, in general, be more desperate and intractable than other inmates, the guards concentrated on Mohammed's cell during their regular searches. They drove the neat man into a frenzy by tearing his room apart: blankets shaken up and thrown on the floor, boxes moved, their contents spilled out, books scattered, papers strewn around the cell. In protest Mohammed finally left it all like that, rather than straightening and arranging everything anew only to have it torn apart again a week later while he looked on from the hall. I thought he was right to do that and admired his will to fight back, but I couldn't help laughing whenever I saw him in his ransacked cell, stepping around things, living defiantly in that state of cartoon chaos.

I remember him at my cell some evenings at dinnertime when he was in good with the guard and had been granted a few minutes in the hall with the so-jees. Mohammed would spit and curse and denounce Korea and its laws and her people in the best angry English he could muster. "I will fuck them! Really no good, these bastards." Then he would catch himself, telling me through the bars that it was a holy time, as he'd just said his evening prayers at sundown. "No, no, no cursing. I don't use foul language or think bad thoughts at such a time," he assured me, as though he hadn't just done so. He would collect himself, rub his bald head, hold his big, beautiful hands together, and solemnly begin to talk about something else. A moment later he would stare up the hall toward the guard, his eyes blazing, and more verbal savagery would pour out of him: "The motherfuckers! They cheat you; they don't know good manner!"

Then he would immediately deny it again, collect himself, and reaffirm the holy hour.

There were moments when the third floor of block 13 did feel strangely sacred, with Mohammed and the others forming a kind of museum exhibit of human frailty. Each of us framed in his square cell, one after another in a line along the white wall—a gallery of pathetic struggle almost artfully frozen in time.

## 13

*Hamlet:* What's the news?

*Rosencrantz:* None, my lord, but that the world's grown honest.

*Hamlet:* Then is doomsday near: but your news is not true. Let me question
    more in particular: what have you, my good friends, deserved at the
    hands of fortune, that she sends you to prison hither?

*Guildenstern:* Prison, my lord!

*Hamlet:* Denmark's a prison.

*Rosencrantz:* Then the world is one.

*Hamlet:* A goodly one; in which there are many confines, wards and
    dungeons, Denmark being one o' the worst.

*Rosencrantz:* We think it not so, my lord.

*Hamlet:* Why then, 'tis none to you; for there is nothing good or bad but
    thinking makes it so: to me it is a prison.


THIS SCENE CAME to me. One of my high-school English teachers
made us examine and discuss it at length in class as we worked
our way through *Hamlet*. I spent hours turning my memories of it
over in my head, trying to apply Hamlet's meaning in reverse: this
existence may be tough, I told myself, but to endure it you can't
think of it like that. If Denmark was green and lush and yet Hamlet saw it as a prison, then maybe by the same feat I could see the
Seoul Detention House as a good place. I was trying to convince
myself of what was basically a delusion. Anyway, it didn't work.

As the shock of incarceration wore off, it revealed below it an
ugly primordial layer of fear, anger, and self-hate. But it wasn't
just depression and anger; it was *prison* depression, *prison* anger.
Those customary and natural states were amplified in intensity,

beaten to a fever pitch against the walls. They were nothing I'd ever felt before, strange new species, deeper and darker variations on old themes. The cell pitted me against myself. The fresh stain of failure, of having cried in front of Shin, of having nearly crapped my pants when they brought me in; the stupidity and the luckless pall that covered me. You're still good, buddy, I feebly tried to reassure myself. But without waiting a second for that to take effect, the warring side would hit home: Come on, man, who are you kidding? You're in prison, in Korea! You've fucked yourself completely!

Other prisoners left with suspended sentences and I could feel myself turn bitter and envious. Those guys, it seemed, regardless of who they were or what they'd done, were better than me. I struggled to feel glad for them. As they walked out of their cells and down the hall out of sight, I was screaming inside, *I can do that, too! I can throw my feet forward, smile big, and walk the hell out of here!* Two Iranians, Fasel and Mansur, who'd been working in Korea in a factory for low wages, were brought to trial for stealing a Korean man's wallet. They told me they'd taken a chocolate bar. They received suspended sentences and were set free, and as they were at my cell shaking my hand through the bars I could feel that awkward ambivalence rise up in my smile. And after the sounds of their departure emptied out of the hall, I sat right back down again on my seat of misery. I was so small in my defeat.

As I waited for my trial, nothing physical was happening—suns and moons through the window—but it seemed that so much was being decided internally. I desperately wanted to know what might become of me and scrambled for something to hold on to as my image of myself kept shifting. I saw myself variously as an idiot and a clown, then an alchemist who might turn isolation into strength, then a cipher, a shut-out. Sometimes I rose in the mornings like a lion. And often in my head I was simply a prisoner, one story buried among thousands. I knew I had to keep fighting, to hold that thread of reason and see where it would lead. Out of the shifting mess something would remain.

I learned the Korean word for "exception," because I desperately needed to be one. I wrote it several times on the wall by my head. Let Shin accept me as that, I prayed. A praying mantis hung on the screen of my window for several days. Koreans told me that was good luck and a good sign. I made the poor mantis my ticket out and was devastated when he left without me. My friend Eric wrote me from New York and, fueled by some rage from his own life, told me that I should throw semen and feces at the guards. That brought me back and helped me through another day.

NATURALLY, WE SEARCHED for ways to vicariously escape. There was no contraband, but we had a few tricks, all of which were new to me. One week the detention center sold us bananas. Billy told me to leave the peels out on my windowsill until they were black and brittle. I then broke the dried peels into pieces, dropping them into a cup of hot water. This weak banana tea had a slightly euphoric effect. Small bags of peanuts were for sale. Billy and others swore that smoking the peanut skins got you high. Guys also occasionally made alcohol using small plastic containers, juice, and bread: pour the juice into the container (if they wanted to get fancy, they would throw in pieces of fruit); then wrap a small ball of bread in a piece of the mesh taken from our windows and dangle it from the top of the container into the juice; seal the container and wait. You had to remember to open the container every so often to let out the pressure from the fermentation, otherwise the thing would blow. You'd have to clean the mess in the cell and hope the guards wouldn't catch you. If all went well, after about a week or two you'd have some weak booze. Once or twice I had a few small cups from these infrequent experiments and felt that familiar tilt, if only ever so slightly. I wasn't drunk, and the buzz only gave me an excuse to escape again into sleep.

I dreamed I was in my wheelchair, Pop my pilot, as we tore through hospital halls. I'd contracted Guillain-Barré syndrome, a rare neurological disease, when I was five, and spent more than two months in the hospital, paralyzed and looking like I might die. Only years later did my parents explain that there was a time when the prognosis wasn't good, when the doctors couldn't figure out what was wrong with me. I was too young to realize the danger I was in. In my dream came eggnog and the hospital's pork chops, and the nurses who magically appeared when I pressed the red button at the side of my bed. I dreamed of Grandmom Gertrude, my mom's mother, who'd passed away. She came to me like a gentle specter, with martinis in her hands, dancing sweetly while asking me why so many of the posters in my room at home were of black sports stars. I dreamed once of stepping on a train track's third rail, feeling the electricity surge through my body, my heart slowing toward a stop, then beating back to life.

JOSÉ AND I would sometimes fall back asleep after the morning horns. We'd still be sleeping when the *tamdang,* the lowest level of guard, often young guys who enjoyed their power over us, and the *kaejang,* a higher officer in charge of an entire block, would come by for the first count. They'd kick our door and yell into the cell. José and I would rise like livestock pricked from sleep. Swallow and accept the day's difficulties if you can, take them smooth or recover quick. Let the guards do as they will. Let the prison decide for you, or else see tricks in everything. Each new denial or change could seem to be hiding an experiment: What are they trying to make us feel? Are they tampering with our food? Is the sentimental-sounding Muzak at night meant to work on us psychologically? Are these tests or thoughtless punishments?

One day we were told the kitchen had decided that the foreigners should receive only one slice of cheese in the mornings,
not two. Apparently two was excessive. It was just enough to show
us who's in command. They could take away what they wanted;
nothing was guaranteed. But swallow that one cheese.

The guards finally objected to the soccer games we played during
our exercise time. It was too dangerous; such leg use was not permitted, they told us out in the dirt one day. We told them that no
one had ever gotten hurt. Two young guards tried to grab the ball
from us, but Billy picked it up and ran away, tossing it to Hong Kong
Rico when the guards were almost on him, then Rico to someone
else. It was the most satisfying game of keep-away I've ever played.
The excitement of watching the guards flail at us, reacting to our
feints like puppets; it was just thirty seconds, but it was worth so
much. The next day, when we played again and someone rock-
eted the too-light volleyball over the enclosing wall of our exercise
pen and into the main yard, the guards refused to open the gate
so that we could retrieve it. And the day after that, we were told
that we couldn't buy any more volleyballs. Kiss our only game good-
bye, and though that burned, we had to swallow it and let it go.

My friend Roy told me in a letter that he had tried several
times to visit me during the summer, but he'd been turned away
on every occasion. The guards had told him that because he didn't
speak Korean and hadn't brought a translator, they weren't going
to allow the visits. Seven thousand miles from home and they
won't grant me the visit, I thought. If the prison is so concerned
with what we might say, then why don't they supply the fucking
translator? Like so much else, there was no help for it, and I
yanked myself back.

Saturday mornings were for haircuts and shaves. A troupe of
eight Korean prisoners in long white coats would swing into our
hall. They looked like malpracticing doctors or mad scientists escaped from some prison lab. The shaves and haircuts were done

right there in the narrow corridor. The Koreans asked us questions, teased us as they pressed their one electric shaver hard into our faces. I was stupid to let them shave me like that after they'd done six or seven guys before me: they were rubbing into me all the dirt, blood, and oil from the faces that went before me. Soon after, I was visited by monstrous boils in my chin and near my mouth that came and went and marked me for years.

On the one Saturday that Rico was anxiously awaiting a haircut—he was desperate to look as clean-cut as possible for the judges in court in three days—the cutting crew never came. Now Rico's small hope was lost, along with his will to let it go. For the next several hours we listened to him go berserk in his cell, cursing, smashing things, throwing hot water on the so-jee.

As the weather cooled, a little coal stove was placed at the front of our hall. November came and our breath was visible in the cells, but no one lit the stove. Every day for weeks we requested heat, both politely and angrily, yet the little stove continued to sit there, insolent and unused.

In late November one of the high officials of the jail came by on a surprise inspection. He walked ponderously down the line, pausing in front of each cell, only continuing on to the next after receiving a sufficient show of respect from each of us: we were supposed to sit on the floor—to make ourselves low—and bow our heads to him. A small group of nervous subordinates followed behind him, looking at what he looked at, stopping when he stopped, speaking when he spoke. If he got upset, they would become furious; if he was pleased with something, they would be overjoyed. When the high officer got to my cell, he stopped and exploded—something about shoes. I looked down at my cheap blue canvas prison slippers.

"Take off your shoes! You don't wear shoes inside the room!" He was screaming at José and me. It was snowing outside. The cell was chilly. The windows, full of gaps and cracks, were covered only with thin plastic. His prison had provided no heat. Our feet were freezing.

Stop and take it smooth.

*But I'm right!* I raged silently. *This is crazy!* Didn't matter. The point was moot, and there was no way for me to make it in the high man's language anyway. Koreans, in prison or not, always remove their shoes before entering the living space. José and I hadn't done so. That was all the high man saw, all he could see.

"Hurry up! Shut up! No talking! Quickly, get in!" the guards often commanded, pushing us toward our cells. Many of them told me not to speak English; they felt threatened when they didn't know what I was saying, because my words were outside their control. "You are in Korea, speak Korean!" they commanded. That got to me more than most things. Do you think I can just decide to speak Korean? I fumed inside. Are you going to tell me how to speak even? Why don't you cut out my fucking tongue! I found it painful to surrender to men whose careers consisted of sitting around, reading newspapers, slamming and locking doors, counting heads, and enforcing punishments without thought. Yet there were moments when I saw them as prisoners, too, but of a different kind, and some of them treated us decently. So I swallowed their power over me as best I could.

THAT POWER ENCOMPASSED what we could see and read and touch. My father, my aunt, and my friends made reference in their letters to things they'd sent me: poems, pictures, books. But I hadn't seen any of it. This way I learned more prison rules. That was how it happened: I became aware of specific sanctions only as they were one by one applied against me.

*No prisoner shall possess more than five photographs at a time. Photocopies and writing materials (blank paper, notebooks, diaries, pens, etc.) are prohibited.*

The picture rule tested José, as his wife had mailed him a pack of thirty-four. He'd have to apply for five, wait a few days to a week, enjoy them, then apply to exchange them for five others from the batch. At least this drew out the time.

To discover the fate of my things, I filed a meeting-request form and waited. Three days later I was escorted by a tamdang to the education department, where they dealt with the mail. The walk down the three flights of stairs and through the halls was a thrill in itself—it felt like I was really getting somewhere. When we got to the office, I was put in a chair in front of the elderly captain's desk. He was listening to headphones and skimming a newspaper. He looked up for a moment with an attitude of "Who are *you* to request a meeting with *me*?" I was fascinated by the civil servants at work in the office. These were the hidden operators, I marveled, the wizards behind the curtain of our lives, part of everything we couldn't see.

After making me wait in silence for a few minutes, the captain asked me what I wanted. I said I was certain that I'd received some things in the past few months that I hadn't been given and wondered where they might be. The captain called out an order and a small stack, tied with string, was brought from a storage room and laid in my lap. The inadmissible items consisted of two sturdy gray notebooks, a book of crossword puzzles, pages of typed poems, pictures from magazines, letters of recommendation. As I sat there looking down at these things, they were transformed into little mirrors in which I could suddenly see myself, the guy I was before this, the world from which I came. Aunt Patty's poems about her mother, Grandmom Gertrude, and those about her sister, my mom, and the baby who died just outside of Mom's womb a few years after I was born. I'd never heard Mom talk about it, but there it was in Aunt Patty's words. Mom was sure that the little girl, rather than entering life without her soul mate, had stepped back in order to wait. The twins were born two years later.

From the other side of the desk, the captain was watching me pick through the pile. I looked up and started to try to explain to him what each item was, but he couldn't understand. A few of the others in the office were looking at me now, too, seeming to wonder when the captain would snap at me and end my self-indulgence, others trying to understand. I wanted to tell them all what was human and personal in this, in me, that there was heart and pain and secrets at work, because they would understand that, I thought for sure. They would see I'm not so different.

I knew there'd be a fight if I asked to take the items with me. I'd have to pull hard; it might ruin the old captain's day. It was enough just to look through the things there at his desk, to read what my family and teachers saw in me or thought they saw; to see pictures of Manhattan, the furious little island; those gray notebooks calling on me to write. The Korean voices around me seemed to fade and I felt myself lift beyond the office. Nothing is lost, the forbidden items whispered to me, just held outside your reach for now. Everything is waiting. I stood up, bowed, and thanked the captain sincerely, and for several relatively peaceful days felt like I could wait, too.

# 14

WE WERE NOT allowed to have our own pens in our cells, but
the so-jee came around every day with cheap ballpoint pens in a
little wood box. If we wanted to write a letter, we were allowed to
take one. But after just a few hours, on the orders of the guard,
the so-jee would come back down the hall and collect the pens,
counting them to make sure none was missing. Having a pen in
your cell could mean two months in solitary. We were prohibited
from writing anything about our cases or the prison, but I had
to; it was helping to keep me sane. I wrote on the unused backs
of letters I'd received and slid them back into their envelopes.
Because those letters had already been inspected, the envelopes
bore the education office's stamp. I had a growing bagful. When
the guards inspected my cell, or went through my things during
transfers between prisons, they never once looked inside those
old envelopes. When I was deported, the bag of letters was all I
took with me.

After several months of being allowed to send one single-page
aerogram a day, we were finally permitted to write letters on a
maximum of three sheets of regular looseleaf paper—if you wrote
on the backs you could get six sides out of them. I started using
parts of my letters home as a journal. I knew they'd be inspected
and that I had to somehow disguise what I was writing. I also
knew that the prison had hundreds of letters to inspect every day,
and that they struggled with English—on several occasions I
would be called down to the education offices in Uijongbu and
Taejon to be questioned about my writing. The officers assigned
to translation duties would often get help on my letters from

young Korean soldiers who were good in English. I'd be brought down to them. They'd be frustrated; too many tough words, they'd say. Invariably there would be a Korean-English dictionary on a desk next to a list they'd been keeping of the words that had stumped them. It gave me the pleasure of knowing that there were some things of mine that they couldn't claim.

To throw the translators off, I always began my letters with common pleasantries and small talk; then after about a page I would start in with the journal. Then I would leave off writing about the prison several lines before I got to the end of a letter, finishing with a common closing. I figured the guards might check just the beginning and the end (I'm sure they sometimes just stamped my letters and sent them through). I was right. The guards never caught on; every one of those letters got out, each one bringing the thrill of an escape.

> Dear Mom,
>
> How are you? Busy with school and the hospital no doubt. Keep going; I'm rooting you on. I know you're close to completing your studies. Congratulations on your new position at St. Francis. The nurse extender it is—I'm sure you're extending a lot of goodness and calm. It sounds like this new post involves more hands-on work with the patients. Do you still talk to Doctor Mary?
>
> You've really been doing this for quite a while. I remember writing home from a computer at our school in Seoul, asking you about your walks through the hospital halls.

The translating guard would be sufficiently bored at this point, and with no break in the text or sign of a change, I would start in on my secret Korean life.

> A new rule passed last week. No more pen in the room for a few hours during the day. Now we have only an hour a day with a pen

in a supervised room at the front of our hall, next to the guard's station. Saturday is a half-day for the weary pens; Sunday their day of rest.

This time, though, I was able to take matters into my own hands.

One by one we were called into the guard's little tollbooth office at the top of our hall. When it was my turn, Mr. Han, a Korean-American prisoner arrested for methamphetamines, was in the office with the tamdang. Mr. Han explained to me in English that the detention house had to record in each inmate's file a number of unique physical characteristics by which he could be identified.

The guard was curious about my crime. "Slicky boy?" he asked me in English, smiling impishly. I had no idea what he meant.

"He means a jul-do, a thief," Mr. Han explained.

*"Anni-yo. Tae ma cho,"* I corrected the tamdang.

He put two fingers up to his lips to imitate smoking. *"Eego?"*

I shook my head. He shook his harder in disapproval.

There are three ribs near the center of my chest that curve out in an odd manner. You couldn't see this, but you could feel it, and when I told the guard, he put his hand on my chest.

There is a long scar down my left knee. My brother and I, when we were about eleven and twelve, were playing capture-the-flag with our camp group in the woods. I was running fast and saw that I was coming up on a tree stump; I knew I had to jump it if I wanted to stay on the fly. I cleared the stump smoothly, but something under the leaves right after it took my leg out from under me as I landed, putting me down on my knees. I stood up, and when I looked down I saw that my left knee was cut clean open, from north to south, in a deep snaking S. I could see the white cap inside. I sat down in shock and tried to hold the two sides together. I'd cut more than 90 percent of my patella tendon. I can still feel it on rainy days, and the scar tissue in there is a bumpy, uneven range.

There were also two scars on my forehead—one from a radiator that my brother had accidentally thrown me into when we were very young, the other from a rusty tin can I fell on when I went with my mom once to an auto repair yard. Apparently the can was stuck in my head when I stood up.

With Mr. Han's help the guard wrote down what I'd shown him, then drew in my exact markings on the body diagrams on his report. It reminded me of the car rental forms with little drawings on which you have to mark the existing scratches and dents on a vehicle before you take it away, risking more. I wasn't thinking anymore about the contingency of the guards having to identify my corpse by these marks. I was still alive and was going to do my damnedest to keep it that way. Thinking that, and remembering the little battles I'd weathered, I felt a sense of pride come over me. I own these scars, I thought. I'm larger than they are.

The guard got up then and took Mr. Han back to his cell, leaving me alone in his booth. I looked down at his desk and saw a pen. I quickly grabbed it and slipped it into my pocket. There was some slicky boy in me after all. The guard came back and had me press my thumb into a pad of rubber dyed in bright red ink. He then took my hand and guided my thumb to the exact spot at the bottom of his report and pressed it down for me in several places. We must have done this hundreds of times over the years: thumb into the red ink, each time staining you. The prized visit forms, thin strips of light-as-a-feather paper that fluttered in the guards' hands like fragile birds; infirmary-visit forms; forms telling you that you'd received a package; forms listing the items you were buying from the prison commissary; inspection forms for books you received. There must have been a rather large record under my name, sheaves of dull gray paper bearing circles of smudged red. It would have shown so many of the pedestrian details of my life during those years, days made whole and endurable by a book or a letter.

*"Tes-so,"* that's it, the guard told me, handing me some toilet paper so I could wipe away the scarlet administrative deed.

Safely back in my cell, I brought out the pen. My own pen, I marveled, staring at it as though it were a rare jewel. Now I wrote when I wanted, sometimes at night seated on the toilet in the tiny bathroom. The door to it was transparent plastic, but José and I smeared it with green soap so that from the hall a guard could see if someone was in there but wouldn't be able to tell exactly what the figure was doing. The guard would probably think I was just relieving myself. In a way I was.

Each month one of the foreigners on our floor would order the *Korea Times,* an English-language daily, from the detention center's shopping list. Each day the paper would be passed from cell to cell by the so-jee as each guy finished with it. On the op-ed page there was a kind of public forum called "Thoughts of the *Times.*" I knew it well. When I was outside teaching in Seoul, I'd written several times for the column. Foreigners wrote in to discuss Confucianism, the moral and political philosophy imparted by the ancient Chinese teacher Confucius and contained in nine ancient texts; how these teachings entered Korea with the early Chinese incursions into the peninsula about two thousand years ago, came to dominate Korean society during the Chosun dynasty, and remain the pillars of Korean society today: ancestor worship; respect for elders; obedience to superiors; a preference for relatively frozen social hierarchies; the importance of ritual performance; and loyalty to family.

Others wrote about South Korea's miraculous rise from the destruction of the Korean War through rapid industrialization to her standing as the eleventh-largest economy in the world. They tried to examine *han,* the name Koreans have given to an integral part of their collective character, a kind of bitter, pained aspect that has been forged over the centuries of suffering the people have endured, most often at the hands of foreigners. Expats cried about the thick traffic and deadly driving in Seoul, the unapologetic pushing on the streets and subways, the spitting. Missionaries and religious workers contributed their humanitarian pleas for peace, brotherhood, and justice on the peninsula. Filipino and Bengali workers decried the unjust treatment they received in Korean factories at the hands of their nefarious bosses. They spoke of severed limbs, a hard life far from home, and the government's xenophobic policies.

The occasional Western businessman would pass through and add his impressions of the South Korean business climate, protocol concerning the exchange of gifts, differences in management and power structures. Teachers complained about the Korean attitude toward contracts, how the locals didn't seem to view them as binding but simply as words still subject to whims and shifting feelings. There were opinionated pieces on bribery (why was it such a common practice in Korea?), the government's malfeasance (why were there so many buildings and bridges falling down?), the behavior of South Koreans when they went abroad (everyone had heard of the Ugly American, but here was the new phenomenon of the Ugly Korean). Koreans would sometimes enter into this public fray to rebut the criticisms of the foreigners, or to discuss university life, trips to Europe, the profligacy of rich families, the presence of the U.S. Army in the country, the romanization of the Korean alphabet.

The eating of dog was a frequent topic, with outrage and defense from both sides. Korean men liked to eat dog because it heated up the blood, giving them sexual power and endurance, they said. The dogs for consumption were supposedly a special breed, a mountain dog, and their meat tasted best if the animals had adrenaline coursing through them just before they died. So the practice, as I'd heard, was to kill the dogs in a brutal way, such as lighting them on fire or beating them with clubs. This way the dogs went to their death fired up, raging, and their meat was suffused with this energy. (I never saw this carried out, but I think I heard the sounds of some such canine carnage once or twice, mad howling on the air at night over the streets of Chongno.) Before the 1988 Seoul Olympics, the Korean government had anticipated foreign sensitivities to the traditional practice of dog eating and had asked that it be stopped, or at least well concealed, while the world held a spotlight on the country.

In the paper there were plenty of feel-good pieces, too, on tae kwon do, the renowned Korean martial art, Korean Buddhism, excursions to the beautiful countryside, friendships between East and West. What developed in the *Korea Times*'s exchange of ideas, then, was a constant seesaw between praise and criticism of the country—a vivid outward display of the internal struggle going on in every foreigner in South Korea. Both foreigners and natives would respond to the negative articles by attacking those they saw as arrogant, presumptuous, and silly enough to publicly criticize a culture and a people they knew little or nothing about. (Yankee, go home! You came here—if you don't like it, then get the hell out!)

From my cell, all these arguments and opinions seemed so innocent now, as if they belonged to a different age, not to a time scarcely six months before but to a former life. I remembered how, after having been in Seoul about a month, I'd written an article for "Thoughts of the *Times*" on how the strongest impression Korea had made on me was one of confinement. I felt constrained by the culture, by Korea's homogeneity, by the specific rules of Confucian etiquette. Now I was in a ten-foot cell. How do you like your confinement and Confucian constraints now, kid? The irony was rich; and as distasteful as my situation was, it wasn't lost on me.

The innocence of those early days. It was the first time I'd ever been paid for my writing, twenty-eight thousand won per article, about thirty-five dollars at the time. And Mr. Kim, the managing editor, had been so welcoming when I met him in the offices of the government-owned Hankook Ilbo, the *Korea Times*'s publisher. We shook hands, and he asked in polished English what had brought me to South Korea. I told him that I'd come to teach and learn about the country. "It's exciting to be here," I said, and thanked him for publishing my article. He smiled, took a business card from his desk, and handed it to me. "The next time you write something, don't mail it in, just fax it to me directly."

Seoul was good. Korea, however strange and inscrutable to me, had seemed like such a benevolent place.

≡≡

ONE DAY AFTER lunch I was suddenly called to the prosecutor's office, and as the guard was coming down the hall to take me out, I had enough time only to stop my writing and toss my pen under the thin mattress of the bed. I usually hid it better. When I returned to the cell that evening—José Luis was gone by then: suspended sentence, and off he flew with a *puta madre* to continue his stealing—I found my mattress turned over and the blankets thrown around. The pen was gone. Billy had heard them from next door and knew from the excited voices that they'd found something. I could have gotten two months in solitary, but nothing happened.

Just before I was transferred out of the detention center, the justice ministry legalized pens. (Associations of Korean journalists, along with the likes of PEN International, had protested against the writing restrictions on inmates.) But only the new black pens they would sell were permissible, and only one per prisoner. Blue pens remained punishable by up to two months of solitary. Blue ink bad, black ink good. And like that the farcical side of our penal lives grew richer. Anything written in blue would be confiscated and destroyed, including the writing I'd done over the previous six months. The notebooks they began to sell us for twenty-five cents were the only place we were authorized to write. When these notebooks were filled up, we were supposed to turn them in to the guards, with no pages missing. They wouldn't be given back.

When the new pen rule first passed I was elated, imagining tension-free hours of writing with both eyes on the page instead of one nervously scanning the window for passing shapes. But any concession also meant a flood of new restrictions. We were immediately given new lists of rules and hot glue to paste them on our walls. We were reminded never to write about the prison or our cases. It struck me that the Ministry of Justice was indirectly paying us a compliment: fearing what we might write, they were tacitly acknowledging that our words had power. Through their opposition they lent me an imagined sense of importance. In my mind I could play the dissident writer. My lines were hunted, but they couldn't corral my English, couldn't handle the Anglo of it, fathom the French, light out the Latin. I was going to formulate my revolution on the toilet. I would rip them to pieces in my Korean-fried samizdat, scribbled pages full of fear, anger, and longing, hidden in envelopes dusted with the freedom that began, and resounded with an echo, on the other side of the high white walls.

15

THERE IS A Korean proverb that says there are only three times in a man's life when he should cry: at his birth, at his parents' death, and at his own death. Well, I've never seen men cry the way they did outside those courtrooms and on the detention-house buses after being sentenced to their years, one Korean man after another, grown men, some large and strong, most of them in their thirties and forties, with the marks of life already on them and visible in their faces; and yet this was something that broke them—tears for our own deaths.

I had confessed to Shin—the package was mine; the made-up twenty grams a day; the kilo of black Philippine hashish for personal use—while avoiding any mention of Rocket or Zack or the profits we'd hoped for. It was trial time, and it came quickly for me, in early July. I knew I was going to be convicted and down in this deep water for years. There was no way around it. In my head I kept hearing Shin's promises of punishment, and the truth of what Billy had said to me about being there for several years. I was handcuffed and tied again with yellow rope at the detention center and driven with a busload of Korean accused to the courts, in the same building that housed the prosecutors' offices and the headquarters of the narcotics division, where I'd been interrogated the day I was arrested.

After waiting several hours in ropes with twenty Korean prisoners, I was escorted into the courtroom by a bailiff in a black suit, a short Korean man in his sixties who smiled as though he didn't have a care in the world. The inner chamber reminded me of a church, and I half expected to smell incense. Three judges in black robes gazed down from a long table that was raised above us like a throne. In a section to my left waited the prosecutor—not Shin, though; Shin was either too big to sit through petty trials like mine or he had better things to do. To my right sat the public defender assigned to me; three days earlier I'd met him briefly at the detention house for the first and only time. About twenty people sat in the public gallery behind us—family members or victims of Korean defendants waiting to be tried after me. Just inside the door I was ordered to sit facing the judges. My palms were sweaty.

The prosecutor quickly recounted the details of the case and asked me only three or four questions. I responded by saying "Yes" or "That is correct." I could catch some of the numbers and phrases before they were translated for me. I heard "nine hundred and thirty grams." It wasn't a perfect kilo, then. The Filipinos had shortchanged me. It was the defense's turn to speak. As my public defender spoke to the court about my family background and education, I felt an affinity with the guy. He seemed to be the only friend I had in the world at that moment. The best that we could do was to convince the court that I was a fundamentally decent guy caught in a mistake rather than a true criminal captured in his practice. Regardless, just as Shin and the lawyers who'd visited me had said, there was no way around the mandatory minimum for the smuggling charge.

A week later, my heart heavy and numb, I returned for my sentencing. The judges performed without emotion, pause, or a second thought—those were reserved for me, along with a three-and-a-half-year term. It was written in some form of stone. I knew the Korean phrase for that block of time very well by then; it came to me on wings in my sleep. Rico, Mr. Park, and I—all three-and-a-halfers—had begun greeting each other and calling blindly down the hall using *sam yun yuk gae wall* as though it were a name we all shared, the time phrase a dart that pegged us and helped us find the absurdity in our sadness. Though the sentence came as no surprise, it sat its weight right on top of me just the same. It felt too long and covered everything, swallowing my life in one gulp. Out in the dirt the next day I walked by myself, full of hate and self-loathing, and threw the few rocks I could find as hard as I could against the outer wall, shattering them against its immovable face.

AFTER I WAS sentenced, Billy wanted to write my family to thank them for the books they'd sent and to reassure them of my health. I thought it was a good idea and wrote my home address on the aerogram for him.

August 12th, 1994

To the Thomas Family:

I hope this few lines find you all healthy. Cullen went to court and received the final judgment of 3.6 years. I guess, involuntarily, that every one of you may feel it too long and painful to be separated from him during this period of time, plus the doubts about his condition could make it harder for you to bear. Well, that's why I felt the impulse to write this letter. By the way I apologize if I'm being intrusive. My name is Billy. Like my good friend Cullen, I've two sisters, a brother, and good parents which love me and don't want to see me here, of course. But as the time went by we all realized that it wasn't really a tragedy as we thought at the beginning. I can never fully explain the changes this experience has brought to my life. Now I know and realize a lot of things that could have taken my whole life to learn, if learned at all.

It didn't take me too long to realize how blindly we all lead our lives while free. How many mistakes we commit once and again, and under how many illusions we live every single day. I don't have to convince anyone of the great value of the time spent by ourselves.

Yet, I would be lying if I say it's all pleasant and easy in here.

It has the same bitterness and hardships of life outside, plus the lack of freedom to go and come as we please, the spontaneous impulses of tiredness, the constant knowledge of powerlessness, makes living harder sometimes, but in the long run it's the essence and secret of the transformation that all discerning men will be at the end of any experience. Believe me: I've had several moments of complete bliss here, too hard to put into words.

As for Cullen, we've been together for several months. He is capable enough of facing any circumstance while making out the best of it. I believe he will be alright and I suggest that none of you should worry too much about his welfare. Just write often—letters make a great difference! He will be transferred to prison anytime soon, but as I said, he will be alright. I can assure that. He reminds me of myself four years ago, but with the difference that he is more prepared for the adventure right now than what I was back then. Well, I hope you will accept my gratitude for the wonderful books you sent to Cullen, from which I could feed my insatiable hunger of learning always something new.

Thanks for listening and please take care of yourselves.

With all my friendship and love,

Billy

≡≡

SHIN CALLED ME to his office more than a month after I'd been tried and sentenced. I was still in the detention house, awaiting my appeal of the first court's decision. There was no apparent reason for his summoning me, and so it played on my mind. What now? I dreaded. Just give me my damn bottom, nasty and low but firm, so that I can begin my crawl back out.

Sitting across his desk from me again, Shin smiled. "What happened in the first court?" he asked.

"Three and a half years," I said.

"I did that," he stated proudly. "I made sure you received minimum, the best results in Korea for your crime."

He got up and poured us each a glass of juice. I strained against the ropes and handcuffs to lift the glass to my mouth.

"What about my appeal?" I was still clinging to some slim hope.

"The judge would have to break the law to reduce your sentence," he said matter-of-factly as he sat back down. I hated his certainty, his cold manner. The last door had closed on me.

"Do not appeal to Supreme Court," he advised me. "They only decide guilty or innocent; if they find guilty, two months will be added to your sentence. And try to take care of yourself in prison. Teach English to the guards. It could help you." Then Shin surprised me by warning me not to make friends with Billy, whose appeal he had been handling. Shin knew the foreigners were grouped together in the detention house. Criminals like Billy are dangerous, he said, because they can never leave their professions.

On Shin's desk was a pile of certificates and character references sent by my family. All that effort had been utterly useless. I grimaced, imagining the desperate phone calls, my parents' embarrassment at having to ask people to write letters praising me now that I'd gotten myself into prison. Shin began to slowly leaf through the pages. He looked pleased, and handed them to me to read. There were letters from everyone in my family, judges back in New York who were friends of my parents, teachers from my high school, neighbors, priests, directors at the hospital where my mom worked, the local police station. I was a scholar, a natural teacher, a romantic poet, a sensitive and spiritual young man, honest, responsible, with much to offer the world, from an upstanding family, a Christian background, with no criminal record, of sound moral fiber. It was embarrassing; all of it sounded exaggerated and false. I wondered if that was what all eulogies were like. It was done in such good faith—and I was thankful that they'd tried—but it was somehow a mockery of a life. None of them had me quite right. Shin's version, the detention house's, the images from those back home: just angles and half-truths, never the whole picture.

Shin suddenly asked about Rocket. By then I knew, through letters from my family, that she had made it back to New York.

"Is she fat?" Shin asked me.

Bewildered, I told him she wasn't fat at all. He was getting strange again.

"Some of my men saw her get off the plane."

I couldn't follow him.

"You know I can charge her in the States. I have friends in the DEA. I can have her put on a plane to come back."

That Rocket had made it out was miraculous news, but now the nightmare just wouldn't stop. Shin had to be full of shit about dragging her back to Korea, but I really didn't know. Part of me was terrified. His reach seemed limitless.

South Korea and the United States had no extradition treaty in place at that time. But I learned much later that Shin actually did send two agents from the Drug Enforcement Administration to Rocket's parents' house in Brooklyn and my family's house in Port Washington. Rocket was living elsewhere. They found my mom at home, flashed badges at the door, and asked if she could answer a few questions. They wanted to know if Mom knew where her son was.

"Yes, he's in prison in Korea," Mom answered plainly, as though it were no stranger than having a kid away at college. She had nothing to hide but didn't want to show the agents any emotion, either. She invited them in. After they all took seats in the living room, Mom noticed that the men were gazing around the house, as though checking to see if there were a lot of expensive goods on the possibility that I was a millionaire trafficker with a well-cared-for family. Maybe they thought the Thomases were a cartel.

They asked Mom if she knew where Rocket was or if anyone in the family had been in touch with her. Rocket's lawyers had already advised her to cut off all contact with my family and me. She'd done so, except one day in the detention house, about five months after I was arrested, in the late afternoon, when letters were handed out, the so-jee left at my cell a plain white envelope with no return address. I'd been lying on the wood floor staring up at the ceiling. Inside was a photocopy of a lesson from one of the English books we'd taught from in Seoul. It was a drawing of a little girl with flowers in her curly hair, a little boy in shorts standing shyly next to her. At the top was a line written in Spanish: "I'm thinking of you."

Shin couldn't let it go: Rocket had escaped. It burned the man's ego, made his suspenders pull too tight. When the fright from his threats subsided and I knew Rocket was safe, the fact that she'd escaped was a huge consolation, a stick in Shin's eye, a gift I went back to over and over to lift my spirits.

BACK IN SHIN'S office, he and I looked through his windows down onto Seoul.

"There are a lot of people out there right now doing the same thing I did," I said, trying to convince him that I wasn't so bad. He stared back at me. "Neither side is going to convince the other," I added. Shin knew this was just talk; it had nothing to do with his job as a prosecutor or my fate as a felon. He saved his breath.

Suddenly the chief public prosecutor, a trim, handsome man in his forties, entered the office aggressively and registered my presence with a sharp glance. He spoke roughly to Shin, then turned and exited angrily. Shin stood up and immediately dismissed me. He must've gotten in trouble for squandering valuable time. My case was finished; I shouldn't have been there.

I was escorted by a guard onto the elevator. Just before the doors closed I saw Shin for the last time, spinning himself around in the hall with a troubled look on his face, searching frantically for his chief.

≡≡

MY APPEAL TO the high court in September was quick. The court-appointed translator this time was a Korean man in his fifties who stammered and bungled his English from the get-go. He seemed nervous. Resigned to the inevitable outcome of the proceedings, I felt bad for him and had the urge to speak up and help him through his rough patches. The faces of the three judges seemed to be slowly dropping as he hacked his way through clumps of words. The judges asked me to rise then and face the three of them to speak my final thoughts. As soon as I stood up I felt ridiculous. My words meant nothing. How was this supposed to be some kind of consolation to me? There were only one or two people in the courtroom who could even understand what I was saying. Just like the translator, I began to flub my words; they unraveled into gibberish. I've never felt myself to be more pathetic, compelled to be meek, penitent, holding my hands humbly, telling the court one last time, though the record had been sealed, that I wasn't a threat, that I had some good in me. I felt as if I was being forced to justify my soul to strangers, as though I'd offended them all personally. Regardless of my guilt, it was a sickening exercise.

"The sentence cannot be reduced or suspended," the speaking judge announced. "There is nothing this court can do for you." I thought that was an interesting choice of words; it sounded as though they really wanted to help, as though it were their hands that were tied.

Back in the waiting room there were a half-dozen guards, a couple of soldiers, and twenty prisoners waiting their turn. I could feel many of them watching me with curiosity as I came out of the courtroom, trying to read my fate in my face.

I joined the line of Koreans moving through the halls—an outgoing stream of men on one side of the passage flowing against the long incoming stream. Rounded shaved heads and rubber slippers, ropes over ill-fitting blue. I came back to the main waiting room and took a seat on one of the wooden benches next to a group of Koreans who had also just received their sentences. A tiny old guard came up, asked or told me something, then worked without me when I didn't reply, writing my number on the list on his clipboard.

On the bus back to the detention house I was in a seat next to a Korean man who looked about thirty years old. He was crying quietly with his face against the window; then he turned toward me and strained against his ropes to lift both hands enough to indicate to me that he'd just gotten ten years. Not knowing what he'd done, I felt for him, for all of us. At the gates to the detention house, soldiers lay down in the road to peek under the bus and between the wheels. In the holding dock we untied each other. Once the guards had given the order, you would set to work on the inmate in front of you: first undoing the knots and crisscrossing at his back, releasing his arms from his sides; then spinning him around to face you so you could untie the rope looped and knotted around his wrists. Your own ropes and handcuffs would hinder your work, but as you went about the pleasing task of freeing someone else, you were at the same time being freed by an unseen stranger behind you. I was always glad they made us do this ourselves—letting us undo what was done. You thanked the man behind you who undid your ropes—it was no small thing—and you received thanks from the prisoner in front. We had to squat in even rows, calling out the number of our row as we went down in unison, rubbing our wrists and whispering quick news about how we fared in court.

It was at this point in the procedure on that particular day that something new happened. A few other inmates and I were called out by number and sent to a room across the hall. Already this was odd. The dozen guys on wooden benches in there seemed cheerful. They were being allowed to talk freely and get up and move around as they wanted. The one guard even left the room for a time, closing the door behind him, leaving us alone. The feeling was intoxicating, but I was confused by what was happening. I was sitting next to a young Pakistani named Idris who was twirling his long hair. He told me he was going home; his sentence had been suspended. He'd be released in a few hours. And so would everyone else in that room, I slowly discovered. All of them had gotten suspended sentences in court that day. They turned to me and laughed at my confusion.

"You're going out today, too!" a couple of older Koreans practically sang in unison.

"No, there's been a mistake," I said.

More laughter.

I couldn't believe what was happening: no more than an hour after receiving final confirmation of my fate, just as I was laboring to hold together my fragile acceptance of it, here was something of a cruel tease to test me. Or was it a miracle in the making?

"Really, I got three and a half years," I managed in Korean. "Second court. Judge said no suspended sentence."

One guy turned around to face me. "Look, me, suspended sentence," he said, pointing; "this one, suspended sentence; him, suspended sentence—all of us go home. That's why they put you in this room!"

"Believe, you go home," Idris joined in. "They put you with us. Why you no believe it?"

"The judge didn't say that. I'm sure, three and a half," I asserted again. I couldn't believe I was arguing against getting out. For months I'd been hoping against everything for a suspended sentence—the glory of its grammar even, a fragment, a merciful clause. This has got to be a mistake, I thought. Mistake or not, I suddenly became aware that in those few minutes I'd already breathed in something I hadn't felt since my arrest. The air was lighter in this room. Even though the men around me still wore blue uniforms and were still inside the jail, they were already decidedly different. The guards trusted them. Judgment had been lifted from them. They were about to be set free. But the redemption was rubbing off on me, too. I could feel again what it was like not to be considered a problem, not to have the brutal weights of stigma and condemnation defining my existence. I tried to breathe in as much of the air in that room as I could, because I knew it wouldn't last.

A minute later the guard came back in. I stood up and went over to him.

"They made a mistake. My sentence wasn't suspended."

"No, no mistake. You're on the list. You don't want to go home?" He chuckled. "Just wait and see."

Ten minutes later a different list was consulted and the issue was straightened out. Number 3779 wasn't getting out with a gift; they weren't going to screw up and release me by mistake. It just depends on how they put me down in their logs, I marveled. That will decide me—not who I am but how they write me down!

# 16

ONE GRAY DAY in late October, I was sitting quietly in the cell, my thoughts floating like weeds over water. It must have been around noon. We were waiting to be let out for exercise. I could guess almost without fail when the guard or hall worker was about to yell *"Oondong!"* down the hall, even though the time varied from day to day. I could feel it in my bones, not unlike the way animals are said to sense earthquakes in advance. Our oondong was like an earthquake; it always shook my head up, allowed me to breathe better, made me feel saner. Just seeing the sky was a big part of it, not being in a box—well, we still were, but outside in the yard the dimensions of the box were bigger, the walls were pushed back, and there was no lid. In some ways the word "oondong" was sweeter than freedom even, because freedom waited in an unborn future, the immaterial promise of unformed forward time. Exercise time was real right then; the minutes actual, and you could run and feel your body respond. I'd be up pacing, sometimes a good hour before oondong was called. I would launch myself out of the cell when we were let out and run like mad around the small dirt pen, just like Billy, the two of us keeping track of our goals, trying our damnedest to win each game. Billy the Kid and Young Gun, lost in Asian space.

This particular day we waited. It had to be two or three, and still there was no sound of the guard's keys, no creaks from the first doors on our floor. Something was wrong. I could hear the other guys up, wondering aloud why we weren't being let out. Hong Kong Rico was cursing in Cantonese, and Mohammed yelled out for the guard. Soon the whole floor was angry.

Just then the so-jee, pudgy Mr. Che, down on a traffic violation, strolled down the hall, poking his glasses back onto his nose with his short fingers.

"Mr. Che, why aren't we being let out?" Billy asked him in Korean.

I studied Mr. Che's face as he answered. He turned around and headed back up the hall.

"What did he say?" I asked Billy.

"He said they're killing ten guys here today."

Mr. Che had spoken too quickly, too casually for that to be right, I thought.

Maybe he'd said the guards were attending one of their ceremonies or their periodic target practice—something more important than watching us outside. Or they just didn't feel like letting us out, which seemed to be the case some days. I asked Billy if he'd heard right.

"They're doing executions, that's what he told me."

Our floor quickly grew quiet, silenced more than pacified. We never were let outside that quiet Thursday, and the guards did execute ten men, hanging them somewhere in the detention center, a few hundred yards away in the maze. I remembered that earlier in the day the Koreans on the floor below us hadn't sung or made their usual noise at lunchtime. I hadn't heard their bowls being passed and shared, their rough banter and slurping, the men calling out to one another. Now I understood why it had been so strangely quiet: the Korean inmates had acknowledged their condemned brothers. They'd paid them the respect of silence, the only gesture they could offer. And for the first time I saw the Korean prisoners as my brothers, too. They became less of the abstraction they were in the hidden honeycombs around us, the bees in their native hive. They were on the same side of this awful equation, and in many ways they had it worse than us. I admired them for observing silence for the killers that were executed—though most didn't know those men at all—and by doing so seeming to withhold judgment on their lives even as the authority judged enough to kill them. I saw more grace in the inmates. In my mind I tried to leave my cell, to stretch around the corners of the halls and peer into the execution room. I wondered what it looked like, if it was the same as all the other rooms in the detention center. Had they been killed one by one or all at once? I felt ashamed for having been concerned with our hour outside when men had been going to their death right near us. I was angry for them.

The game is for real, it dawned on me as it hadn't before. The prison is serious. They'll deny us and hold us and kill us as prescribed, I thought. Even the young friendly guards are a part of this machine. Why are they still hanging people? Everything grew darker. My hatred rose like a wave and covered the walls. I hated every one of the guards, the prison, Shin and his righteousness, the false piety and morality of the whole fucking mess. The hatred stayed in me for a long time, buried in some new organ that was tucked in among the others.

Mohammed and Jamil were even quieter than the Koreans and remained subdued for weeks after the executions. I wondered what was going on in their heads. Mohammed walked slower during exercise the next day, his head down, darkness over him. He disappeared into himself for a long time after.

≡≡

ONE MORNING A week later they came for Billy, gave him ten minutes to prepare, and then hurried him down the hall. Shin had rejected his appeal and Billy was to be transferred to another prison. Knowing that his time with us was coming to an end, I'd written him a letter the week before, to thank him for his strength and his friendship. As he passed my cell that morning he barely had time to stop and shout. I jumped up and handed the letter to him through the bars.

"Don't let them take it from you," I shouted after him.

"They're not going to get it from me!" he yelled back.

They sent him to the prison in Kunsan, south of Seoul on the Yellow Sea. He had a year left. From there he wrote my mom, and she sent him books. He tried to calm her when she worried about me.

. . . I don't know the contain of Cullen's letter but I can well imagine what is it all about. I keep saying this a great opportunity, yet not an easy one. There is so much involved. Nobody thinks this is a place worthy of him. Then comes the rules, ignorance, system, new life, the acceptance of the sentence. But none of them is harder compared to the desolation left when our pal, our first and closest friend is taken away. As used as I am to it, I was particularly touched this time again. He surely needs a friend to rely upon and you are in the best spot to give him strength. Out of friendship I will do whatever I can to be helpful but please do not thank me, for the little I do is just a part of my duty.

A few months later:

. . . I got to accept that some kind of anxiety is taking hold. [He was suffering from what the Koreans called "release day disease."] The closer I get, the more I will it. Having tried— successfully at times—to keep cool, it keeps charging insistently with strength and joy. I did it! And more than that. Even in prison I became a free man. (What is the seal of attained freedom? No longer being ashamed in front of oneself—Nietzsche.)

He rode it out like that until the end. Three months after his release my mom received a postcard from Bogotá.

Dear Kathy,

I seem to be the most ungrateful guy of all, I'm sorry. I came out to find that the most beautiful of all things was the silence of my

life in Korea. Though life has been good to me so far, freedom seriously keeps me so busy with matters of secondary importance. I
seem to be fighting a great monster: incompetence, dependence,
greed, ignorance. I'm back on my emerald's business. I'm doing
good. I got my own apartment and car. My mother died the day
I returned. I couldn't see her. But I keep focused and strong.
Nothing hurts me. I seem to be heartless.

He'd stayed in Korea for a week after his release in order to set up
contacts with jewelers, hadn't gone straight back to see his ailing
mom. The irony was cruel. Or maybe just the knowledge that her
son was alive and had returned at last was enough to let her die
in peace.

On the postcard Billy had given us a couple of phone numbers.
Years later, when I was free, I tried them but couldn't get through.
We never heard from Billy again. I often wonder what became of
him, whether he'd held to what he'd promised himself in prison
(I know that I haven't; too much was promised then), or whether
the monster had gotten him in Colombia. I think he may have
deliberately cut the link between us. The experience had bound
us in spirit forever; but our time was Korea—that was our war and
our moment.

## 17

NOVEMBER 12, 1994: the strangest birthday I've ever had. I was struck by having come so far only to end up in another little womb, hemmed in tight, gestating, breathing a strange substance. Wanting to pass the day quietly, I didn't tell anyone about it. All of us had birthdays locked down. But about a week before, when a conversation about age came up—as it always does when Koreans are around—I slipped and mentioned that I'd be twenty-four on the twelfth. I didn't think anyone had paid attention, but sly and sensitive Rico had made a mental note.

On the morning of the twelfth, after the guard had finished his stroll and head count, I heard Rico call out to me. It was rare for anyone to speak in the hall so early. I cringed. Voices echoed hard in the emptiness, so I knew that if he said anything others would hear him.

"Happy birthday!" he yelled out, the words rounded and childlike in his Cantonese inflection. I crouched by the bars listening for ripples.

"Thanks, Rico," I called back.

Nothing more, and I thought that might be it. The rest of the morning passed without incident, but at lunchtime, when the hall workers opened Mohammed's door, he slipped into the hall, walked down to my cell, and while wishing me a happy birthday with a big smile presented me with two heated cheese sandwiches. From there it escalated. I was powerless to stop it, and by the end of the day I was moved by the warmth of our murderous, drug-scarred, thieving family. Most of us shared a general amity and encouragement even as we all desperately sought divorce; but this longing, shared equally by all of us, offended no one.

Ken, another American English teacher brought in two weeks before, sent down an apple and a Korean language lesson. Then, as the afternoon faded, Mr. Park, a lanky Korean American, passed along a sampling of the special rations he received each month from his former employer, the U.S. Army: tightly sealed spaghetti with meatballs, a delicious slab of cherry nut cake, and two single-serving packets of instant coffee. I held up the coffee and yelled thanks to him down the hall; I might have thanked our army, too. Mr. Park usually received two or three boxes of these rations at a time, but he always gave half, or at least one box, to the chief of our block as a kind of ransom or tribute. Why would a prison officer need sealed army rations? I wondered. It must have been the principle of the situation. *Sang boo sang jo:* You do for me and I'll do for you. The Koreans were well schooled in this. I wasn't yet, and didn't realize to what a large extent this principle actually dominated affairs.

Mr. Na, a dainty Korean who grew up in China—he was fond of wearing tight little shorts at exercise and moved with the grace of a well-bred girl—gave me ramyun and biscuits and asked why nobody had told him before about the occasion. Caught with a fake identification card—police had asked him to present his on the street one day—he spent a month with us. He was sad about being deported; back in Harbin he wouldn't be able to match the money he'd been making in Seoul. Mr. Na had worked in the hall for a time and tried to learn English from me at my cell and in the letter-writing room. He bought a new notebook and sat next to me enthusiastically. But his innocent determination could do nothing with the days of the week, which alone made a mess of the gentle airhead's mouth.

As the new so-jee finished up his tasks that evening, the last of which was always to roll a strip of green carpet down the length of the hall—to muffle the sounds of the guards' approach, so they could sneak up and catch us in our rawness—he deposited a new white T-shirt and a pack of biscuits at my window. Then he raised his thin arm like a saint bestowing salvation and exclaimed, "Alleluia!" We'd dubbed the guy Mr. Magoo because of his small, frail shape, his eyes squinting behind glasses, and his languid, lost movements. He wore a makeshift thread cross around his neck and chanted "Alleluia!" with zeal whether dishing out hot water or bidding us good night. Trying to imagine the pickpocketing he said he'd been charged with was a good source of entertainment. Apparently, the young girl Magoo tried to steal from on a bus foiled him and wrestled him to the ground herself.

Magoo was soon moved to the hospital ward; with his constant blessings he was a good fit there, I thought. He was followed in our hall by an anonymous clod who used to toss our breakfast bread on the floor if we were still resting in bed when he came by with his cart. The new Peruvians, *choros finos* just like José, wanted to kill him for that. Then came two baby-face twenty-year-old Koreans, Jehovah's Witnesses serving two-year terms for refusing to comply with South Korea's mandatory military service requirements. They refused to pick up a gun. There was a clean, innocent energy to them. They chose prison as a more acceptable alternative, and as willing entrants, the antithesis of nearly all the rest of us, they fascinated me. I wondered if other Koreans respected or mocked them. South Korea is a nationalistic, cold war–hardened country, and military service is a rite of passage. It must not have been easy for the Witnesses and their faith in paradise for a chosen few. One of them had lived in Toronto for two years, spoke good English, and insisted on being called Richard. He told me that his parents were Jehovah's Witnesses, too, and fully supported him. I wondered if over time the prison would break him, causing doubts and questions to creep in around his faith. Anyway, what he faced in prison—the discipline, the tower of rules, the subjugation of individuality, the rigid hierarchies—was probably surprisingly similar to what he would have faced in the military life he avoided.

CELL 12 HAD a lot of Arabic script on the walls and carved into the wood. As we returned from exercise one day I called Fasel over and he entered my cell to explain what was written. Much of it was in his native Farsi, and seeing it made him happy: *Allah first and only* emblazoned large upon the door, the script like wings spreading, repeated over the walls; *Mohammed the prophet second*. Jehovah, then, out in the hall; Allah watching from the door; and Jesus, not without representation, on the scene through a small picture, torn from a magazine and pasted to one of my walls by a former inmate. It showed Christ kneeling with his hands held together before a large rock, his illuminated head turned up, gentle light from the sky beaming down on his face. I guessed that it was the Garden of Gethsemane, where he's said to have prayed to his father for mercy. The thought of his imminent trial and pain grieved him; he wondered if there was some way around it. The scene, which I'd first heard about as a teenager, took on meaning for me then. This was a Christ I could understand. We all have our private Gethsemanes, I thought, little sanctuaries we flee to, seeking escape, praying for reprieve, though none can be.

I remembered sarcastic stories of vicious criminals suddenly finding God as they're being led away to execution or serving life. No such conversion gripped me. But in my desperation I did go looking for something transcendent. Lying in my cell at night, I often cast myself out into the universe, and there I found my kind of god. It was the whole blue-green Earth. I could see her in her entirety, powerful and beautiful, and I stared down at her and begged for her help.

I WANTED TO stay with the other foreigners, but now that my appeal was complete I knew my time to be transferred was overdue. My six months in the detention house, which counted toward my sentence, were coming to a close. A harsh Korean winter was coming, and I was to be sent out into it, into the unknown. The fear of that was tempered by a base desire to be on the move, regardless of the destination, just to be able to leave and look back and rearrange my world. I was starved for movement.

In the first week of December, returning from a trip to the infirmary one day, Mr. Park stopped at my cell and told me in a low voice through the bars, "They're going to move you soon."

"When?" I asked him, quickly getting up from the floor.

"Any day."

"Do you know where?"

"They said Uijongbu." A city north of Seoul. That's all Mr. Park or I knew about it or its prison. It was an advantage, I suppose, as many inmates were informed of transfers only a few minutes before the guards came to get them. But all I could do was wait for it, and anxiously wonder what waited for me there.

외 정 부

# 18

WE DROVE NORTH toward the DMZ and North Korea, out of the frying pan into the fire. Five Korean convicts and I were only being transferred to another prison, to officially begin our lives as convicts, but there was the undeniable sensation of change, wild movement, the small bus racing us forward into the unknown. I could indulge the false hope that things might be better where we were going. I was hoping there would be at least a few other foreigners in Uijongbu. I wondered if I would have much contact with the Korean inmates, what they would be like. I worried that it would be like the Seoul DC, with its twenty-three-hour days in the cell. Billy had said it would be harder. It was an overcast, gray day. I stared out the windows, searching desperately for signs of life: trees, houses, towns, farmland. The sights were infusions. The outside world still existed, but it was continuing in all its mundane ways without me. I thought of New York City and saw my friends going in and out of their apartments: the beautiful privilege of going out into the street, to leave when one wanted. Is Rocket going out on dates? Has she met other men? I wondered. What is everyone in the family doing? They were all impossibly far away, and I was losing precious time. They had life sprawling in front of them. I was a remedial thing, a backwoods creature and cave dweller shuttling north through scarred and bleak country.

In less than an hour we passed a U.S. Army base and entered the high white walls of a prison outside the town of Uijongbu. Out into the courtyard and down into a basement room. We stood on blue mats and were told to strip. Then we were each given a new blue uniform and a new number on a piece of cloth—these we'd have to sew onto our uniforms as before. I retired 3779 thinking he'd done all right, all things considered, and was given 1214. For transfers most inmates had only enough time to throw their possessions into a blanket, then pull the corners together like a fried dumpling. The guards were now searching through these Santa-like bundles. They called every item out, and a guard sitting at a desk listed everything in a log. I had only a box of books and a black bag filled with letters, my smuggled notes and pages tucked inside them. I was secretly thrilled when they gave me the bag. No need to look through letters that already had inspection stamps. And all that English: Korean civil servants didn't get paid enough to deal with it. The guards took my box of books from me; they'd have to be inspected and cleared before they'd be given back. I expected this, but every time it happened I felt a jolt of tension run through me. I needed my books. Also inside the box were my three balls of plastic wrap that I'd made and saved in the Seoul DC. Those looked suspicious to the guards and they asked me what they were for. Juggling, I said, pantomiming what I meant. They were puzzled. The guard at the desk told me to take the balls and demonstrate. When I got the three up and going, the guards and Korean inmates laughed and said, "Yaaaaaa!" in approval. Anything that pleased them was good for me. They let me keep the balls.

The head guard walked around us with his hands clasped behind his back and barked orders. My face had to be shaved, he demanded. That was always unpleasant news. My hair should be cut. I was led out by a guard and taken away from the other convicts. In one hall we passed a group of fifteen female prisoners walking in stiff rows the opposite way. I thought I saw a few of the women smile. They must have been surprised to see a white man. I was used to seeing young Korean women wearing makeup and fashionable clothes. In stark contrast, these women looked worn, their hair stiff and matted, their bodies shapeless in their uniforms. They were images reminiscent of the rough past, of women who'd survived the war, who worked fields, who carried their belongings on their heads, their babies on their backs. Seeing them was such a shock to me that I stared and turned my head after they'd passed to try to catch another glimpse. I never saw that spectral gang again.

My escort turned me into an empty cell block. Cells down the left side, all of them empty. We stopped before the second door. Above it hung a blue plastic sign with white Korean characters for *weigookeen:* foreigner. The guard locked me in. I put my bag of letters down. The cell was half the size of the one in Seoul—about ten feet long, five feet wide, and six and a half feet high. Also unlike Seoul, there was no toilet, no sink, no standing bed frame; just a thin green mat for sleeping, a couple of blankets, a hard blue square of plastic that was supposed to be a pillow, a porcelain trough in cement at the back, and a small window looking out at the high wall. The words "three years" jumped into my mind and then stayed there insistently until they were all I could hear or think. I kept looking around the cell as though searching for something I couldn't find. Three years in here? My brain was struggling to keep the thought down, to digest it into reason, but I was heaving against it, tossing it back up into the strata of fear and panic. The illusion of movement and change the trip had provided was gone. In that tiny cell the starkness of my reality was frightening, suffocating. I'd die of boredom, isolation. There was nothing to live on. And they hadn't given me my books. Three years here? Impossible. Vomited up again, reason cracked and I broke. I started throwing whatever I could get my hands on. I threw myself against the walls and the door. I screamed unintelligible things. Noise sounded good.

A moment later the cell door was thrown open. Staring in at me wide-eyed were five guards and the warden. He'd come by to meet the newly arrived American, the only foreigner currently in his joint. No doubt he'd been hoping for a more pleasant introduction. There I was, frozen in the middle of the cell, awkwardly tall in it, sweat and spit on my face, things in my hands to throw, the cell upturned. They must have thought they'd been delivered a lunatic.

"The *boan kwajang* is here!" two guards shouted at me, assuming I knew what that meant, knew how to respond, would respond the right way and snap instantly out of whatever fit I was in. The warden, a middle-aged man with glasses, said nothing.

"I can't do this," I said in Korean, though out of ignorance I left off the formal and respectful *yo* at the end. This caused the lower guards to bristle. No one talks to the chief like that, especially not the inmates. In Korean, how something is said is often more important than what is said. Though the warden himself didn't react, a young guard at his side puffed up and stepped forward. *"Yo!"* he barked, trying to teach me the lesson. "You say *yo,* fool, when you're addressing the security chief!"

"I don't know your language," I yelled back, half defiant, half sorry. I gestured around the cell. "There's nothing here!" The warden spoke to his men and one of them shut the door. The welcoming party was over.

Five minutes later a lone guard returned and escorted me to the warden's office. He was standing in front of his door and he waved the guard away. He told me to have a seat on his black leather couch, a bizarrely incongruous and modern amenity in the stone world he oversaw. The room was full of natural light; a potted orchid stood on a table. The warden asked me what was wrong, maybe thinking I had a specific problem, and that small kindness seemed to shatter me. Through tears I rambled: "New York . . . I didn't hurt anyone . . . so far away . . . my books . . ." It was the song of self-suffering we all sang and that played in our heads. I was still feeling my own pain too acutely to see that it was universal, to be relieved by that knowledge.

The warden fidgeted next to me like an uncomfortable father, hanging in there but powerless to help. I remember thinking that if this is what they want, to break us, to humble and degrade us, make us ill and infirm, then they'll get what they want from me. I'm too sensitive for this shit not to hit its mark. I'm too young to accommodate this with grace, too far from home to keep a stiff upper lip. It was unfortunate that the warden had chosen to be the one to do his humane best with the shattered results. He explained that I had to be there; there was no getting around that, so I had to make the best of it. He got up and brought us a plate of oranges. I kept letting my nerves and emotions pour out, only now with slices of orange wedged into the front of my mouth. When I'd calmed down and begun to regain my composure— maybe with the help of the vitamin C from the fruit—the warden slapped me on the knee like an uncle and said it was time to go back now. On our way out he told the officials in the education office to stamp all my books so they could be sent to me right away. They were brought to my cell later that afternoon.

THE SOUND OF rats scurrying through the hall, through the long tunnel they'd burrowed along the outside of my cell. I could hear them at night as they socialized. It was a form of company. One morning I found one frozen in time in the icy water of the stone washbasin across the hall from me, its limbs petrified in defiance, its face screaming. I could hear the Koreans upstairs—work detachments consisting of fifteen men to a room—hunting the rats with brooms. There would be hunts when one appeared and the crashing could sound like a riot. They'd corner the rodents—only so many places to hide, even for a rat, in a prison—and bludgeon them to death.

Uijongbu Prison was in Kosan-dong, a high mountain district. Above the outer wall on my side of the prison rose the sharp snowcapped peak of Surak Mountain. Without heat the winter was brutal. Frigid winds blew down from Siberia, freezing the water in the bucket at the back of my cell. I stayed under my blankets, fought to shake the icy grip from the middle of my hand so that I could hold a pen to write. Often my hand would be too stiff with cold, and the pen's ink too cold to flow.

Other times I could get my hand loose enough by keeping it under the covers for several minutes, pressing it into the warmth of my armpit, then taking it out and writing until, about a minute later, after a sentence or two, the fingers would lose their coordination and the sinews in the palm would tighten again. I'd give up and wait. Waiting was the answer for everything.

In those first weeks of December in Uijongbu, there were several times late at night when I sensed something moving out in the hall. As I was the only inmate on the ground floor, no guard was posted there. And there were certainly no prisoners around at that hour. It felt like a restless presence. I was afraid that if I looked up I might see some creature staring in at me through the barred window in the door. My hair stood on end and I kept my head under the covers. The cell felt safe then. If you believe in spirits or the possibility of ghosts, then I tell you they're in prisons. In some ways they're places with little else; what's there besides the present inmates is only the compressed, captive energy left behind by thousands of others. Vice, terror, longing, rage, sadness, memory with nowhere to go, locked in rooms so that they seep into floorboards and walls, permeate the air and hang. The stillborn, the unresolved. They're haunted places. After I'd returned from Korea, a friend took me to the old Stone Jail in his hometown of Mauch Chunk (renamed Jim Thorpe), in eastern Pennsylvania. Anthracite coal country, a place of hard luck and hard lives. In the late 1800s, more than a dozen poor Irish coal miners accused of being Molly Maguires, members of one of the earliest American labor unions who were convicted of murder and other violent crimes, were hanged on an old-fashioned wooden gallows in the center of the jail. It was a black and weary place, and as my friend and I walked around it, I instinctively felt for the men who'd been held and killed in it. To try to attract more visitors, the owners of the jail touted the story of an indelible handprint seared into the wall of one cell for eternity by one of the Irishmen shortly before he was hanged. I wasn't interested in the handprint even if it really was there. I didn't need to see it. I could feel its equivalent in every inch of the place, in the air that seemed filled with silent screams. Too much had been pressed out there.

# 19

SOUTH KOREA HAS between forty and fifty prisons. During my
term, there were between sixty thousand and sixty-five thousand
convicts in the country. Foreign inmates never numbered more
than one hundred, and many were ethnic Koreans from China
or the United States. Uijongbu was a medium-size facility that
held fifteen hundred men. You can walk to the DMZ and North
Korea from there; the 38th parallel is less than fifteen miles away.
Several months before I was transferred to Uijongbu, the North's
founder, the hypnotizing Great Leader Kim Il Sung, had died. I
always thought it was curious—especially since I never heard it
discussed in the press—that following a visit to the North shortly
before the Great Leader died, Jimmy Carter had specifically said
that he'd found him to be in fine health. Carter didn't give the
man a physical, obviously; and a heart attack, the reported cause
of his death, can sneak up on anyone, of course. But I can't help
wondering if there isn't more to the story of the dictator's death.
There are some sources, albeit ones of questionable legitimacy,
that claim the Great Leader died during an argument with his
son, Kim Jong Il, the self-styled Dear Leader, who took over the
helm of the nation after his father's death. These questionable
sources describe how Kim Jong Il wouldn't allow anyone to see
his father's body for some time and how the doctors who exam-
ined the Great Leader and performed the autopsy died soon after,
some in helicopter accidents and others of unknown causes.

Kim Jong Il made sure to maintain the draconian cult of leader
worship that his father had instituted, but he adopted a tactfully
less bombastic title than his dad's. He'd also begun rattling North
Korea's nuclear saber. He was going to turn Seoul into a sea of

fire. President Clinton had prepared for the worst. There was the chance of a military strike on suspected nuclear sites in the North, the possibility of a wider war. The U.S. embassy in Seoul later told us that they had, as ordered, drawn up an evacuation plan for Americans in South Korea. Of course, I wasn't going with them. My fate was tied to Tae Han Min Gook. If the North had attacked, I would have been left behind and one of the first lit up. I cursed my sense of timing. I tried not to think about it, copying the Koreans around me, who mostly ignored the menace and the tension and carried on with the hard business of their own lives.

Still, I could feel the pressure. We were at the doorstep of the most fortified border in the world, one of the very first and one of the last remaining cold war flashpoints. I was back in *M\*A\*S\*H* land, MacArthur world, pinned down in the harsh winter cold of a prison standing in the shadows of Stalinism, in the petrified remains of war. Not too far from Uijongbu were nearly two million troops facing off across the divide. I was often wrenched from my sleep in the middle of the night by the Korean soldiers manning the towers of the prison, who would randomly scream at the top of their lungs, *"Choong Sung!"*—a cry of loyalty and defense—out into the black, maybe hoping the North could hear them. The U.S. Army's Camp Stanley was right next door to the prison. The thunderclap of American artillery, dummy fire, and the staccato pounding of helicopter blades often shook my cell. There were giants at play all around. I was a tiny thing, an ant in its hole beneath the steep mountains of history.

IN UIJONGBU I met South Korean political prisoners for the first time. There was a group of four of them serving three-year terms for violating the National Security Law, the controversial legal legacy of the South's vigorous anticommunism. These guys had escaped what had been done to their predecessors as recently as the late 1980s.

General Chun Doo Hwan seized power in South Korea in a coup and shortly after, in 1980, sent soldiers into the southern city of Kwangju to crush a large protest against his military government. A massacre ensued when the troops opened fire on the crowds of students and other civilians, killing hundreds. A seminal event on the country's road to democracy, the Kwangju tragedy still holds an important place in the minds of Koreans. Some saw the U.S. Army in Korea and the U.S. government as complicit in the massacre, as having been aware of the volatile situation but having done nothing to calm it. During Chun's rule in the 1980s, Korean authorities fairly regularly used torture—against criminals, student dissidents, communist sympathizers, and other putative enemies of the state. One of the most notorious cases was Park Chong Chul, a Seoul National University student arrested for his involvement in a group opposed to the military government. In 1987 Park Chong Chul was tortured to death, like many others, while in police custody: officers from the Anti-Communist Bureau had severely beaten him before finally breaking his windpipe over the side of a bathtub. His death ignited a fierce national outcry.

They say that General Roh Tae Woo, handpicked by Chun as his successor in 1987, was the one who instituted the practice of denying parole to those convicted of the most serious crimes: gang violence, rape, murder, drug offenses. It's that legacy that saw the overwhelming majority of us serve every day of our sentences. But then, in 1993, came the country's first democratically elected civilian leader, Kim Young Sam. So after the rule of dynasties, Japanese colonial domination, and more than thirty years of military dictatorships, South Korea was at the cusp of a new era—fortunate timing for me. Things had changed considerably for the better since the 1980s. Outspoken watchdog groups had been formed. The country was a vaunted democracy now, and the new civilian government was more careful. Journalists were freer to write what they thought, even criticize the government. Citizens could speak out. Inmates could read newspapers now. Political prisoners could no longer be tortured with impunity.

So, Hun Rok and his crew of conscience, though branded enemies of the state, walked around Uijongbu like kings of the place. Smart, cultured, and well mannered, they had an aura of invincibility, of quietly righteous honor. And they seemed to bear their time with grace. I was drawn to them immediately. Just as it was with the Jehovah's Witnesses, these prisoners of conscience made me reflect on how empty and selfish my crime had been, how I hadn't stood for anything, really, other than my own satisfaction. (There were Witnesses in Uijongbu, too, only now they were getting three years for their refusal to perform military service. One gentle young guy began slipping handwritten Bible lessons into my cell. I couldn't bring myself to tell him I wasn't interested, not even in immortality on earth.)

Hun Rok and the other political prisoners walked around unescorted by guards. They studied calligraphy and English in the education office. They heard I liked basketball and one day took me, without a guard, behind a cell block. To my surprise they produced a real basketball and we played an exhilarating game in the dirt, trying to throw the ball onto a square drawn on the wall. Afraid that Hun Rok and his comrades would poison me with their socialist ideas, the guards tried to prevent us from spending time together. (There was no poisoning, although, ironically, I did learn the Korean word for "mine" from them, overhearing them trying to figure out who owned a particular shirt.) "To us, socialism is humanism," Hun Rok told me one day as we went to the hot prison bath. They didn't advocate a system like North Korea's; that wasn't a pure or decent state, he said. It was clear that he and his buddies felt a profound love for the country, and their pride seemed purer to me, less arrogant, than the nationalism expressed by the average Korean. I remember how excited they were to show me a picture of Chonji, the beautiful volcanic lake at the top of Paekdoo Mountain, which straddles the North Korean–Chinese border. In the mythology of North Korea, Paekdoo Mountain is where Kim Il Sung valiantly defeated the Japanese, where Kim Jong Il was born. But even for many South Koreans it is considered the spiritual center of the nation, the birthplace of the people, a place where tigers once roamed free.

Korean student activists like Hun Rok and his friends were often very critical of the United States and its involvement in Korea, but with me they were gracious and interested. I think they sympathized with my isolation, my being the only foreigner in Uijongbu. I think they could see me struggling. And although I couldn't speak enough Korean or they enough English, although our time together was very limited, I was glad that they were there.

IN SEOUL I'D mostly been called "American," but in Uijongbu I became an even less specific thing: "the foreigner." My first name is hard to pronounce for Koreans and never sounds good. But Thomas was easy, blunt, basic, and segmented: "To-Ma-Suh." This was provocatively close to "tomato," however, which is what many Korean inmates began to call me. I accepted it as an alter ego and willingly became the vegetable. But florid red Tomato was out of place. I grew accustomed to being laughed at, to being made fun of and insulted. Sometimes my limited Korean told me I was right, but often I was tense and defensive without reason. Simple requests and greetings could still be difficult; one side leaning, the other straining, both off balance and annoyed with the other because of it. This was not good, because greeting both prisoners and guards was an extremely important custom. I was a severe anomaly in a culture that inculcates conformity and sameness, doubly so in a prison that demanded them. I was a stuttering, retarded iconoclast, a lost American infant—predisposed to being a bad inmate, bad by those standards, unruly in the Confucian culture. Unaccustomed to it, I performed the respectful bow to superiors awkwardly or too late or sometimes, egregiously, not at all. The respectful form for speaking to superiors and elders still eluded me, too, so I unwittingly offended, unintentionally showed disrespect when I was only trying to say hello. There were many ways to say, for example, "Have a nice meal." All of them mean basically the exact same thing, but each carries a different connotation of respect, a clear statement on the speaker's relationship, superiority or inferiority, to the other. So if, with kind intentions, you said "Have a nice meal" to someone older and didn't include the right verb form, he might turn around and tell you to go eat shit.

The country's Confucian hierarchies of age and position were made cruder and more intense in prison; it was the most extreme form, social Darwinism among criminal Mongols. The language allows tremendous boasting and bluster, as if it had been designed in part by warlords or Mafia dons. Older inmates could address younger ones crudely and with condescension, putting them in their runt places with a little *ni* at the end of questions, summoning or commanding them with *Ya!* The younger ones were expected to respond submissively, making damn sure to use *yo* and *im ni da* and other respectful formalities. Dominating those younger, fawning in front of those older, leaping dexterously between the two: I was amazed by how Koreans seamlessly shifted between those roles. A man might yell at his younger cell mate, "Ya, Young Sun, you little fuck, get me my socks!"—then, without skipping a beat, turn around and bow to his *hyung,* his older brother "I'm sorry, dear older brother, what would you like to do, what can I get for you?" Korean required many faces, and like an actor you had to play them all well. Later, in Taejon, I would grow to enjoy the game and entered these language wars willingly. But in Uijongbu I quietly hoped not to be noticed or spoken to, cringed if I was, because something was definitely going to go wrong. "Tomasuh, *ya!*" they'd bark, and I'd feel my entire body tense up. It still sometimes felt hideous for me to have to address the guards by lowering myself, especially when they were mistaken, abusive, or deluded. But I had no choice but to keep eating that spicy Korean humble pie.

Writing with my left hand was a lurid affair. Guards and prisoners told me it was unnatural and unattractive. Several inmates from upstairs watched as I washed my clothes in cold water on the stone floor of the washroom. Not only was I washing my socks and undershirts incorrectly, apparently, but I'd offended everyone by doing so. They became indignant, and two came forward to teach me how it was done. With your near hand, pin the soapy item down on the ground, they instructed me, and with the other scrub it back and forth. That was the way, how all the inmates did it. But I, stubborn bastard, didn't want to be squeezed and trimmed to fit with all the rest. I threw my shirt down and told them to leave me alone. They shook their heads and left. A few days later a couple of guys found me brushing my teeth. They shook their heads again. One of them stepped forward and, like a gentle father trying to guide his simpleton son, showed me "the way" to move my hand and clear water from the brush.

Everything was decided for me: when to wake, when and what to eat, when to salute, when to speak, when to come outside my cell, when to lie down and sleep. I was autonomous in my writing, though, a secret world where I raged against them all. Bent over my notebook in my cell I could drive them from my sanctuary. (One Sunday there was music pumped into our hall; I sat there stunned as, along with a number of Korean songs, Nirvana's "All Apologies" incongruously played, echoing in our fort below Surak Mountain: "What else could I write; I don't have the right . . ." Kurt Cobain's lyrics washed over me. Juiced up, I clenched my fists and celebrated.) In my words I stretched and ran unwatched, played stupid games, spit venom, flew naked over the prison, and laughed as I remembered myself, what I was like, what I might want to become. I reasoned with myself, tried to explain the way things were, and through this stayed sane. The effects could be instantaneous. Often as soon as I put my pen down I felt energized, and I would jump up, shake the cold out of my body, and pace from wall to wall.

# 21

THE U.S. EMBASSY sent consular officers to see me in Uijongbu. They were supposed to visit once a quarter or at least three times a year after one's conviction, to see that we weren't being tortured, that we were receiving enough food, medical attention if we needed it. The embassy's standard disclaimer was that we had the right to be treated just as Korean prisoners were but no better. We should not expect preferential treatment or anything beyond what Korean law allowed. Later, the embassy gave me a pamphlet entitled "Legal Problems Encountered by American Citizens in the Republic of Korea." It stated that we "should not expect to be spared beatings if Korean prisoners would be beaten for the same behavior." We will not intervene, the embassy stressed. We cannot get you out.

This made perfect practical sense: why would the United States want to spend any kind of political or diplomatic energy on a criminal? The relationship with South Korea was a delicate, beneficial thing. Bilateral trade was booming. The North remained an unpredictable pariah. There was a stack of huge considerations for the State Department; they weren't about to complicate matters for the sake of American convicts. We couldn't see all this in the beginning, however, and we instinctively looked to the embassy for help. It was a natural, desperate reaction.

The first consular officer who came to see me in Uijongbu was a prickly man who looked displeased when I asked him questions or complained about my circumstances. I lamented having been sent to a prison where there wasn't a single other foreigner. He insisted that Uijongbu was a nice medium-security facility, with mostly low-level offenders. I asked him if the embassy could talk to the authorities about putting me to work. I was desperate for something to do to pass the time and get me out of the cell. He wrote my concerns down with a dyspeptic look on his face. Frustrated, I wrote Meredith, the chief of the embassy's American Citizen Services department, who'd visited me in Shin's office: "I don't know the extent of the embassy's work with American prisoners in this country, but I'd like to know precisely. I don't even know if you receive my letters. I never hear a response. I've been visited, but it felt like an insulting formality. I was treated like nothing more than a disturbance. What can I do to put you on my side? How can I make you consider my situation? Not to see me as just a convict, a dirty drug case?"

I shouldn't have sent it.

Soon after, I was compelled to write her again.


Dear Meredith:

I received your letter dated Jan. 20th; it answered some of my questions. I'd been waiting for the next visit to bring up the subject of my mail. My family was somehow under the impression that all mail had to be sent through the embassy. That didn't seem right to me, and now your letter proves it.

About two weeks ago I was shown an article in a Korean newspaper that talked about a plan to relocate all foreign prisoners. [Hun Rok had clipped it out and translated it for me.] The ministry of justice was calling for the creation of a "foreigners' prison." Then I heard rumors that I was soon to be moved to Taejon, where a section was going to be made into a facility for foreign inmates. Perhaps you can provide me with more information. If it's true, then I'll wait until I'm moved and permanently settled before telling everyone to write to me directly. Know that I never told people to send everything to the embassy, thus burdening you. Also understand that I'm in a passive position. I have extremely limited control over what my supporters send and where they send it. And your emphatic request that I "contact my correspondents and ask them to write to me directly" is not easy for me to accomplish. These short aerograms are my only line outside this place, and each one is inspected and delayed, so bear with me. Each silly letter I get keeps me afloat; remember that in your busy day. And don't worry about "the amount of tedious work" Uijongbu officials will have clearing my reading materials. If they have a problem, they can come to me. If I seem combative, it's because I have to be.

A week earlier my mom's friend Edie had sent me a funny little manual by Lewis Carroll called *Eight or Nine Wise Words About Letter Writing*. (It had been passed down to her from her grandmother.) One of Carroll's recommendations was that if you think you've written something incendiary, put it aside until the next day, when you can read it with clearer eyes and decide if you really want to mail it. It had come to me at just the right moment. I followed Carroll's wise words, put that less-than-friendly second letter to Meredith aside, and looked at it again the next morning. When I did, I saw that it would definitely make things worse, so I rewrote it, softening all its edges. My relations with the embassy improved from that point on.

They helped get me a job. I was made a so-jee, one of the first fully employed non-native prison so-jees in the history of the country. A so-jee is literally a cleaner. I was a serf, a food server, and damn proud of it. We gathered outside the cell blocks in the dark before dawn. There were always stars, and the deep dark ridge of the mountains stretching like a dinosaur's back against the sky, beginning to the right of our cell block, vanishing behind it, then breaking forth again on the other side. The other so-jees and I lined up in two rows, some of us carrying our bags of personal items for the day: books, letters, pens, gloves. I also carried my chopsticks and spoon, as I ate breakfast and lunch in the classification room, dinner back in my cell. All the small concerns and habits of a regular commuter, the humble repetitive acts on which you could build a life. I embraced them with joy now; they were miracles. Standing there in the soft and playful dark, soon to vanish, with the sense of preparation for a journey ahead, our so-jee crew at attention, I remembered the electrified mornings as a kid when Pop would wake us in the last hours of the dark, my brother and sisters and I dressing warmly, speaking in hushed voices through the house, enchanted by shadows and indistinct shapes. We carried our packs and supplies out to the Jeep in the dark. A drunk joy as muscles awkwardly awoke, eyes struggled for certainty, bodies bounced harmlessly together. We took our places under blankets in the Jeep, shivering from cold and excitement. Six hours to our forests and streams in Vermont. Dawn would break on the way.

My journey now was just a stroll down the hall about two hundred yards, then a duck of the head into the classification office. But something in the air held the same promise. Maybe it was the mountains around the prison or the few pines along the outside of the corridor or the sparrows we could hear. All of those in the moment, and memory carrying me from behind.

THE CLASSIFICATION OFFICE was a square room with an electric heater in the middle and desks around it. It was a choice assignment: I could keep warm. Unlike a true so-jee, whose job would be to clean, shine the shoes of the three officials who worked there, maintain the heater, handle the garbage, and do whatever else the officials needed or could think up, I had only to make coffee and do some filing. (The oldest man in the office, however, did once ask me to shine his shoes. I hesitated and he lost his nerve.) Lack of language was on my side, as was the fact that I was an American, which seemed to make the men reluctant to order me to do the most menial tasks. Maybe they thought that because I was from a rich country they couldn't ask me to do them. Whatever their reasons, they gave me preferential treatment. A Korean would have had a much rougher time, and I often felt a little spite from the other so-jees. I was something of an imposter, my appointment a sinecure.

The officials, men in their late thirties or forties, wore slacks and suit jackets, not the military uniforms of the guards. The one I dealt with the most looked like a contented, sleepy-eyed turtle. He seemed like a decent man who would do his job without a second thought, without considering the deeper issues at work, though it was obvious that he saw the prisoners as beneath him. As I was a different animal from all the others he'd seen, he looked at me with a half-smile on his face, his head tilted slightly back, trying to fathom exactly what I was all about.

Making him coffee didn't go well. It was just instant packets, with powdered cream and sugar. A kettle of water was always left to boil on top of the heater, its steam endlessly matching our minutes. The first time I made coffee for one of the men he complained about the amount of water I'd added. "American style?" he asked me dismissively, putting the cup down. "Uijongbu Prison style," I said. In their minds American coffee was an abomination: always too big, too much water, they told me. It was inelegant and over the top, not unlike America itself. They started fixing their own coffee, but they allowed me to make some for myself whenever I wanted, a tremendous privilege that helped the days pass more easily.

The classification officials interviewed every newly arrived convict, and through these proceedings, along with the filing I did, I saw how the Korean system worked. Once the inmate was seated quietly in front of him, the official would ask for every piece of the inmate's and his immediate family's background and history: the names and whereabouts of every man's parents, brothers, sisters; their occupations, education, addresses, phone numbers. They asked each inmate for his entire work history. Did he drink alcohol, and if so, how often? Did he have sex? How many times in his life? They actually asked this. I was floored, and a bit frightened. How can a grown man give an accurate number for that? What in fuck's name do they think that reveals? If the inmate was reticent or refused to answer, the official would rise in his seat and scream at him.

The first few times I witnessed these interviews, trying to keep my head down in my own business at the next desk, I was appalled—and grateful as hell that I wasn't going through something similar. Something about it felt like rape. The inmates could only give it all away, let the state arrogate all this to itself. An inmate's life was not his own, and his imprisonment bled onto his entire family. I felt for the ones who answered quietly with their heads bowed that their parents or siblings were dead or that they'd had no education past middle school or that all the jobs they'd held were dirty or undesirable—cooks, janitors, coal miners, drivers, laborers. Each one had a story, and it was more than what information came out in the office—that just traced the surface, the superficial markers. I would never learn the whole story, what they'd done and why, or who their victims were, what they might say.

As we warmed our hands together over a coal stove on one occasion, guards in Uijongbu explained to me that convicts would always be untrustworthy people and that a criminal record stayed with a Korean forever. They told me that ex-convicts had a red X or some such distinguishing mark put onto their national identification cards. This had me thinking that as difficult as my isolation was, it was a lucky thing, too. There was no red X on me in my country. My stigma and shame were far away; they could be hidden. Nor would I have to answer to Korean society forever, to face its judgments after I'd done my time. I'd be able to leave this behind me, I thought, on the other side of the world. The U.S. State Department would always have a record of my incarceration, but it was protected by privacy laws and would not, unless I authorized it, ever be disclosed to another party.

Inmates were grouped into four classes. Each of us started at fourth class with a certain number of points, based on the severity of our crimes and sentences. An inmate had to reduce that number, earning points against it by serving his time, extra points for behaving well or working. As we gradually reduced our starting numbers, we reached the third, second, and first classes, each one bringing wider privileges, such as more visits per month, the ability to send more letters, or the treat of watching movies periodically. Each inmate's file recorded his class and point totals, along with all the information gained in the interview, a brief description of his crime, his IQ test score, and graphs measuring emotional stability, responsibility, and sociability. I was often tasked with stamping the files and putting them in numerical order. Some days I went through hundreds. I began a practice of wishing each man well as his file passed through my hands. Those lines rising and falling, stability fluctuating, sociability edging below the half mark—they seemed like dry and feeble ways to try to explain a man. And the system never went much deeper than those fault lines flat against paper: too many of us, not enough time, not enough manpower, not enough will. The authorities got their answers and got out of there, leaving each man to stew away his time, to make of himself what he would.

# 22

THE WEEKS RUMBLE BY. It seems each time I look up it's night again, and I'm sitting on my mattress on the floor, back against the wall, reading or writing letters. Viewed as a whole, this journey is years, but I can see that it's really just a collection of moments: uncountable moments here, some joyful, others an awesome struggle, the same as everywhere. We really live only for a moment, but we can't see that when we stack together so many behind us, pile them up in front. Catching myself staring ahead at time, I remind myself that I have only this present second. I can't live next Wednesday, though I instantly want to pull it to me, or next year, or my final day here. They'll all be moments when they're ready. Today I drank blood soup, ate squid, juggled for a while, taught English for forty-five minutes to one of the officials in the classification office, glanced at the one bright star above the wall visible from my cell in the morning, sat briefly with another so-jee around the little stove in our hall, stood staring up at Surak Mountain, swept the dust out of my cell, thought of Morocco and the Philippines, was told to shave a dozen times, looked up the word "remonstrance" in my dictionary. Moments, strings of moments.

I was still struggling with many of them. A guard came by the classification office with letters for me. I got angry when he rudely tossed them down on the desk in front of me—I guessed that he wanted to show me his disrespect because he was put out by having to come to the office just to deliver my mail. When I picked up two of the envelopes, he tore them out of my hands, saying they hadn't been inspected yet and I wasn't to touch them. I grabbed the remaining ones and threw them on the ground, trying to imitate his callousness. He took a step toward me. Turtle Man shouted for us to calm down.

A week later I broke down. My cell was equipped with an electric buzzer by the door that produced a bird-chirping noise when pressed. With no guard on the ground floor, it was the only way that the guard or so-jee upstairs could hear me. Without water one night, I pressed the button again and again and listened as the damned birds chirped away alone in the hall. *Tweet tweet tweet tweet.* No one came. *Tweet tweet tweet tweet.* An hour passed like that. I must have pressed the button a hundred times. I could hear the guard's voice upstairs; it seemed he was trying to ignore me until I gave up. But I was determined to be heard. I wasn't going to be abandoned up there on the 38th parallel. Panicked and angry, I blew. I screamed and tore off the wall the wooden stick for hanging clothes and began hammering it against the door like a battering ram. I worked up a vengeful racket. After a few minutes of this madness, the guard and the so-jee appeared at my window.

"What's wrong? Are you fucking crazy!" the tamdang yelled.

"You can't pretend I'm not here!" I screamed back in English. He couldn't understand me. I couldn't endure the isolation much longer.

It was my luck that the rumors of the justice ministry's plan were true. In the next few weeks, all foreign inmates in the country would be transported to a special cell block in Taejon Prison. It was an enormous relief. I felt as if I were being called back from the ends of the earth. There was wild talk of beds, televisions, better food. And just like that, my winter in Uijongbu was over.

# THE GREAT FIELD

*February 1995–November 1997*

# 23

I WASN'T THE only convict in the family; there had been a great early precedent. That might sound like a strange consolation, but as I sat in a new cell in Taejon Prison, it was one. My maternal great-great-grandfather, Augustine Ellicut Costello, who was born in Ireland but had become a naturalized U.S. citizen, was convicted of treason-felony by the British Crown in 1867 for trying to smuggle into Ireland more than five thousand guns in the hold of a ship. He was accused of being a Fenian, a member of a rebel group also known as the Irish Republican Brotherhood, and of trying to aid a local uprising. I learned of his story through a photocopy of a letter Costello had written with a quill pen, in 1868, from his cell in Dublin's Mountjoy Prison to his sister in Philadelphia. My father mailed it to me shortly after I'd arrived in Taejon. Pops knew Costello's story would resonate with me: his international misadventure; his youthful recklessness; his time in prison far from home. He was sentenced to twelve years of penal servitude. He was nineteen. I can't imagine how it hit him. In the book *Speeches from the Dock: Or, Protests of Irish Patriotism*, published in 1899, Costello is quoted as having said to the prosecutor and judge in court: "It is hard for a man in the bloom of youth, when the world looks fair and prosperous to him—when all he loves is in that world—it is hard that a man should be torn from it, and incarcerated in a living tomb." It was as if I had unknowingly followed in this forebear's footsteps and was living a modern version of his story.

In his letter from prison, which I labored over with fascination, straining under the shitty fluorescent light of my cell to make out his tight, inky cursive from more than a hundred years before, he told his sister, "If I am not happy, neither am I miserable; I stand neutral as it were, between both. I only hope that I will through life preserve the same equanimity of mind." If that was true, how had he achieved it? He had managed the magic trick, mastered the puzzle of prison. Whether his self-evaluation was accurate or not, I admired and loved him for it. And I have the same blood in me, I thought, staring defiantly at Taejon's cement around me. His situation, he wrote, was "a melancholy one it is true; but it rests with ourselves to mitigate or increase the evils and the trials of this life. A patient endurance under sufferings is the true indication of a noble mind. . . . Even in the midst of our difficulties we have much to be thankful for. . . ."

By the time I put his letter down on the scarred wood floor of my cell, having read the two dense pages several times, this great-great-grandfather was more like a brother to me. He was talking to me across time, showing me the path through the maze, how the prison could be bested. I only had to follow him.

His became a landmark case. Though sons of Ireland, Costello and his fellow Fenians had pledged their allegiance to America (they'd also fought for the Union in the Civil War), and in exchange she had extended to these adopted sons the liberties and rights possessed by her native-born citizens, the benefits of her laws, and the protection of her flag. So, Costello argued, he could not be considered a subject of the British Crown and therefore could not possibly be guilty of treason against it. The U.S. Congress began to press for his release. President Andrew Johnson, keen on maintaining the support of Irish voters in America, put Secretary of State William Seward to the task of pressuring Great Britain to let Costello go. In response to his case, in 1868 Congress passed a bill entitled "An Act Concerning the Rights of American Citizens in Foreign States."

The following year England let Costello go. He'd served just under two years of his twelve-year term. He had the U.S. government to thank. He returned to America in April 1869. In New York he wrote and published a comprehensive history of the city's police department and followed it up with a thousand-page history of the fire department, *Our Firemen: The History of the New York Fire Departments from 1609 to 1887,* which was reissued in 2002 by an imprint of St. Martin's Press, in an abridged edition, under the title *Birth of the Bravest.* In a review of the book, the *New York Times* (May 30, 1887) found that "Mr. Costello's large and handsome volume does full justice to New York firemen. . . . [He] is very thorough in his information, and has left out nothing which is of interest." The history of the fire department is "part and parcel of the history of the great city." Costello died in 1909.

AT MY AUNT Patty's funeral in 2005, Costello's name came up. He was Patty's great-grandfather, and she had always been enthusiastic about him and the stories from his life. She kept a copy of his book on the New York Fire Department and that same letter from prison which she had sent to my dad before he sent it to me. Patty had been the one who had kept the memory of Costello alive within the family. As we got to talking about this, my mom's other sister, Sheila, mentioned that Costello was buried in a big cemetery in the Bronx—she couldn't remember which one—and that the family had visited his tomb once when she, Patty, and Mom were very young. The next day I tried tracking Costello down, calling cemeteries throughout the Bronx. I found him listed in Old St. Raymond's, a storied and sprawling rest for the dead just off the Bruckner Expressway, and went to visit him on a sunny morning in early summer. From my apartment in Brooklyn, I took a train and a bus to get there. There was no one in sight when I arrived. I wandered through the formidable obelisks and mausoleums etched with old Irish names until I found Costello's grave, section 3, right there on your left as you come up the stone steps. My heart jumped when I saw it. I felt as though I'd come to the end of a long road.

I sat down in the grass under the Celtic cross of rough-hewn stone that rises high above his little plot. The breeze softened the sun, and I patted the ground above his bones. I wanted to ask him how he'd carried his prison experience with him through the rest of his life, into fatherhood and life as a writer. What did he tell his kids or grandkids about it? Did he *ever* talk about it? What were the things that would trigger his memories of that time? In what ways did it shape him into who he was? I could only guess, mostly by thinking of my own answers to these same questions. Although Costello was a writer, he apparently left behind no personal account of his prison experience besides the letter. I've often wished he had. Maybe he did. Maybe someday I'll find it.

# 24

IN THE EVENINGS you could hear frogs burping in chorus in the rice fields outside the walls. A small cluster of old farmhouses with roofs made of clay tiles sat just outside our corner of Taejon, the Great Field, one of the largest prisons in South Korea and, according to proud guards, one of the largest prisons in all of Asia in terms of physical size. It held more than thirty-five hundred men, among them many of the country's most violent and hardened offenders, more than five hundred serving life.

All the rumors and reports had been wrong. There were no beds in Taejon, no toilets or televisions, no special facilities. It was the same life of sleeping on the floor and dumping in a pit. Water was still scarce and dirty; there was still no heat in winter or air in summer. We were all together, though, all fifty of us, a wild array of foreign convicts, pulled together from around the country and put into small single-man cells on the second and third floors of block 6: Pakistani cohorts of Mohammed and Jamil's; polite Iranians who'd raped; childlike Filipinos who'd bashed in brains; smiling Nigerians who'd run heroin; a Nepali who'd done what only his Hindu gods knew; Korean Americans who'd run drugs through Hawaii, kidnapped Korean girls, swindled land. It was like a criminal United Nations. We could've used the sensibility of a few Europeans; too bad none ever came.

It was an enormous relief to be with the other foreigners. They brought diversity, the same outsider perspective. And through them I vicariously traveled, continuing where I'd left off before getting myself in trouble. I learned about the histories and geographies of their home countries: the Biafran War; the Northern

Fulani Muslims, whom Joseph, an Ibo from Nigeria, liked to imitate by viciously yelling *"Bukashi! Bukashi!"*—Kill! Kill!, as he
translated it (he wanted to be like Fela Anikulapo Kuti, who had
"sand in his pockets," Joseph said, which somehow meant he was
invincible; not even death could touch him); the *saban-i-urdu,*
the language of the camps that the Persianized Pakistanis spoke;
the "five rivers" of the Punjab; the heavenly Hunza Valley. I was
in the Philippines again, too, through Manny and Arnel, and up
in the cold expanses of Manchu Guo.

The others seemed as glad to see me as I was them, the excitement born of exposure to something other than the vast Korean
homogeneity. But there was also a practical side to the others' interest in me, though I didn't see it right away. They wanted to
make friends with an American because they assumed he would,
in general, have more means than the others and more power in
the prison. Early on Joseph once cheerfully said to me, "If I was
an American like you I would have the Koreans on a leash from
my hand, like dogs on a leash."

During my first weeks in Taejon I would kneel at the window
in my door when the workers were let out in the morning in order
to check out the other inhabitants, to see whom I'd be dealing
with. Some of the guys had taken to stopping briefly at my window to introduce themselves. A humble and friendly Chinese
Korean in cell 44 slipped me the English textbook he'd been
studying from; he wanted my opinion on it. Assan, from the ill-
fated Pakistani manpower gang, slipped me the previous day's
newspaper. The Nigerians David and Freddy, who'd come by every morning without fail—chuckling and smiling as though their
lives were forever perched at the edge of a good joke—stopped to
say hello. Our block's *chooeem,* a higher officer who'd worked for
at least fifteen years in the prison system, began shouting at them
to keep moving. He'd come to herd the workers down the hall. I
couldn't see him, as the Nigerians were blocking my view, but

suddenly they were gone and in their place smack in front of my window was the chooeem. He slammed the metal window cover in my face, nearly catching my fingers against the bars.

We'd only been exchanging good mornings, I thought. What is wrong with these motherfuckers? I pounded the door with my fists, then flipped open my food hole and screamed into the hall, "Open my fucking window, *chooeem nim*!" It felt strange to be cursing and using the honorific *nim* at the same time. I kept pounding on the door. About a half hour later the chooeem, a young tamdang, our section chief, and a young soldier carrying handcuffs came to my cell and took me out. They led me and the Korean-American Mr. Chun, an avuncular man of fifty-three, downstairs to the chooeem's control station. I wondered what punishment was coming. The chooeem spoke and Mr. Chun translated. There were regulations prohibiting inmates from lingering at one another's cells, Mr. Chun explained.

"But we were just saying good morning."

"You should respect these officers," Mr. Chun answered me. "This is Korea, not the West. You have to understand."

"But they don't understand us at all. He didn't have to slam the thing in my face." I was surprised that a fellow prisoner was taking the guards' side. Mr. Chun should have just told me again that such were Taejon's rules, end of story. If a discussion strayed at all from that point, the details of incidents got lost. If you didn't tie them firmly down, they would invariably fly off like this, like charged balloons, inflating up to the same conflicted heights: East versus West, foreigner versus Korean. We foreigners could explain ourselves by crying difference—it was a bit of a cheap way out—and the Koreans would often allow the argument, because no one ever doubted the existence of differences, although neither side ever defined them clearly or determined exactly what they might excuse.

The rumor was that Mr. Chun had a fortune stashed away

somewhere, maybe back in the States, where he had citizenship. He'd illegally sold off government-owned land in South Korea for personal profit. Rather than turning the money in, he was taking his ten years. The temerity of that, the size of the dice he'd rolled, won him respect from other inmates and even some guards. I sometimes saw him as naked and weak, however, receiving from us non-Confucians few benefits of respect and deference for his age, for his status as a grandfather and a wealthy man. Although he was by no means mistreated by us foreigners, I could understand how he might have felt degraded among us just the same.

"You should apologize to chooeem nim for yelling," Mr. Chun said reproachfully. The chooeem sat calmly at his desk. The soldier played with the handcuffs in his lap. "I didn't have to react like I did," I told Mr. Chun, who turned and, ostensibly translating, made what sounded like a much longer statement in Korean to the chooeem. I was forgiven and escorted back to my cell. This was one of the first of many instances in Taejon in which the differences in language and culture would be at once a refuge and a burden, making me a favored criminal guest one moment and a disregarded outsider the next.

MY CELL WAS roughly four and a half feet wide—narrow enough that I could almost shimmy up with my back against one side and my feet pressed against the other—and nine feet long, coverable by four short paces. It was only about a foot taller than me, so with my feet flat on the ground I could extend my arms only halfway and have both palms flat against the ceiling. Lying down, I covered the entire wood floor, with my head hanging right at the edge of the wood, beyond which was a porcelain trough set in cement. A pipe with a tap at the end stuck up through the cement in one corner. Like everyone, I washed clothes there, right beside the trough—the sleeves and legs of things would often flop into it. Only cold water came from the pipe, and only during brief stretches of the morning and night. You could hear the pipes engage and hear the flow of water as other guys down the line opened them up. Often we had to wait for water, with urine or heaping kimchi dumps stagnating in the trough. That made even the most imperturbable among us angry. In ways like this, Korea's keeps were definitely still back in the third world, while the society at large had blazed its way into the first. This disparity was not lost on me or some of the others, and it sometimes enraged us. We'd complain to the guards that we had no water; then things would start to break down, with ever more rabid shouts for *"moool!"* echoing in the passage, the tense atmosphere full to bursting.

Two buckets sat next to the trough, so to bathe or relieve myself I had to move one bucket out of there. The second bucket was a privilege, given to us one summer because Korea's monsoons were late and there was a drought. The water rarely came from our pipes then. When it did we had to seize the moment and get as much water as possible into those two buckets before the taps were closed again. Problem was, the water smelled metallic and looked dirty. A viscous, rusty film formed at the bottom of the buckets. My skin went bad; the boils spread. The only soap available dried the skin badly. Every summer I got rashes in my groin. Diarrhea was common; intermittently over the final year of my term, I suffered weeklong bouts of parasitic pains. I was pretty sure my hair was falling out.

The water in the buckets was for washing clothes, bathing, clearing the trough, and rinsing your bowls and chopsticks. To wash myself I did what we all did: crouch on the cement over the trough and scoop water from the bucket with a blue plastic ladle. It took a while to adapt to the freezing-cold water. I remember daring myself to wash in December and January, trying to make a game of it. As the water hit and splashed, smoke went up in the freezing air at the back window, iced over right at my head as I crouched. I'd stand up, smoke sweeping off my limbs, howl, and clench my fists. I could make myself endure it. *I can do this,* I told myself again and again, in the same way that I sometimes attacked the time. The Korean inmates always swore by the cold water, saying that it was good for your circulation and nerves. That may be true, but every fall and winter colds and flu traveled through our entire population, and all of us dealt with the beginning stages of frostbite on our ears, noses, and toes. In the winter the walls turned the cells into little refrigerators. In summer they were sweltering, airless boxes. I think I preferred the cold overall. In the heat you felt like you couldn't breathe, that you'd soon run out of air. You had to get real still and sweat out the hours—sitting on the floor, the sweat from your back staining the wall; letting your brain baste as perfectly beautiful, sunny days cruelly passed you by just outside your window. You'd think about all the things it would be possible to do on such a day, if you were free, all the things the people you knew were out there doing, all the things you'd once done, all the little things that had never seemed as consequential or miraculous to you as they did now: doors left open; leaving a place when you wanted; walking down the street to the corner deli; hot water; Guinness; being around women; calling a friend on the phone. The simplest actions, self-made decisions far and wide, even the smallest ones gold. You wondered how you ever saw them for less than they were. And then you'd have to try hard not to think those thoughts at all.

We lived very simply; there was no other way. I didn't mind having few possessions, and could see the value in being removed from the noise and consumption of the outside world. Those conditions agreed with my character. But they had been forced on me now; I hadn't chosen them. Ecologically speaking, we were light and easy on the earth; we created very little garbage, used incredibly few resources: no fuel for heat, just enough electricity to power the fluorescent lights in the cells—and we would have gladly done without those much of the time. We took up very little space. We might have been reprobates, but we were also living like progressive ascetics. I can't say that I'll ever again be able to live a life so simple.

The fluorescent lighting tubes sat behind a clear plastic casing slanted forward from above the door. They didn't provide enough light to read or write by in sharp clarity; yet it was just enough to disturb your eyes as you slept. I put a paper flap above the light and at night, when the guards weren't strolling around anymore, folded it down over the tubes just before going to sleep, creating more shadow. Most of the others made similar devices—cardboard coverings and the like—though the guards periodically made us remove them. I missed the dark and the night. It wasn't enough just to look out into it through the back window. I wanted to be out in it, enveloped by it like a warm bath. One night, the lights throughout all of block 6 suddenly went out. There was a moment of stunned fascination and then whoops and cries of delight broke out from all quarters. The entire prison had gone sumptuous black. Dark in the hall, the defeat of the eternal little lights in our cells: it was like an act of God. The authorities struggled to bring the power back on. The lights blinked back for a moment (expressions of disappointment), then went black again (whistling and screams of childish glee). The guards shouted for quiet, but without light they were helpless. It was the closest thing to a party Taejon had seen. I went to my back window and looked out at the small village, and beyond it to the shelf of mountains in the distance. They were velvety smooth and lit from behind by the last lambent glow of twilight—most beautiful seen in the dark. I savored the moment, knowing it would probably never happen again.

I got tired of the gnarled metal screen between the back window and the bars on the outside of it. It blocked what little natural light was available and made seeing out much more difficult.

I took matters into my own hands and blasted the screen out, using one of the large water buckets. I would smash it, then quickly put the bucket back in its place and sit down, pretending to be reading in case the guard came over. The operation must have taken me the better part of several hours; the screen didn't want to give. But it was old and rusted and finally did. This small act was surprisingly exhilarating, and not unlike untying our own ropes. I had done something myself to positively alter my tiny world. I was master of my closet, still an autonomous, creating beast, in spite of all the attempts to control me. I was the light bringer and screen smasher. When I told a few of the other foreigners what I'd done, they followed suit. Soon the unnecessary screens were taking a beating across block 6.

I THOUGHT I could hold on to myself through all the little decisions I made in the cell, whether to read or write, sleep or daydream. I tried to remind myself that these minor acts, little habits repeated daily for years, would shape my character. It seemed like I had all the time in the world, but sometimes I saw through that illusion. It wasn't as abundant as it seemed. I had to be disciplined. I often thought of performing experiments on myself, fasting, depriving myself of sleep. I went weeks sometimes without bathing. I thought about trying to go days without moving a muscle, without opening my eyes. I'd try not touching myself for as long as I could go. I was going to attempt a comparative study of the world's major religions. I was going to count every breath for entire days. I was going to eliminate desire. I thought about trying to make myself into a special freak of nature, a fakir capable of feats of endurance. Instead, more often than not, I learned too well how to kill time. I often read and wrote, but just as often I paced, trying to get the rice to go down, or allowed my mind to spin out into the void from meal to meal, sleep to sleep, from one minor self-pleasuring to the next, an animal existence measurable only by the rough regularity of its basest needs.

≡≡

WE SOMETIMES SPENT three or four days in a row locked in our cells, with not a second outside them, stewing, everything slowed to a crawl, Koreans hanging off the hour and minute hands of the clock I couldn't see. The silence ticked like time—a vacuum of silence swirling in the stone hall. My little gray closet was a punishment capsule drifting out in space. Thinking was a kind of hallucination. We lived in our own heads—nice places to visit, but not to live. Guys imploded, craniums busting inward. Sleep was always around, tempting you from the side: *Escape in me—come on, escape in me.* The cell siren song.

Some days it felt like all the gray stone was on top of me, and the weight just beat me down. There was no color and no good in the world. I just couldn't see it. It was close to being buried alive, except I was still breathing. And I still had so far to go that it wasn't worth thinking about. I was tired as hell of being surrounded by so much dirt and murder and weird men, tired of my dried-up skin, the gray, the barley rice, the fucking cold, the fucking heat, the scum in the water bucket. The relentless horns would wake me and I'd open my eyes to the gray and white cement of the cell standing over me. My stomach would be boiling and ready to burst, the sky one thick cloud of gray without a break. Just get through the day, I'd tell myself. The sky color can't last. The water will come back on. My stomach will settle down. Just get through the day.

# 25

IN APRIL, AFTER having been in Taejon about two months, I snapped. It was a haircut, of all things, that set me off.

On my way over to the guard I kicked one of the haircutting crew's blue stools and watched the stool and my left shoe crash into the corner. "Medium! I told him medium!" I screamed. Lurch, our floor tamdang, stood next to a massive Korean prisoner who'd just cut off all my hair. The big man was *gangpey*, a member of a powerful group on the outside. Along with the guards, these gang members held sway in Taejon, as they did in many of Korea's prisons. They were meaty, hierarchical bastards, and their codes of loyalty and respect made them the most united force outside of the authorities; they got the choicest work assignments, and brooked no opposition. Somewhere in me I knew I was lucky not to have already been beaten senseless; but everything—Taejon's walls and all her wretched souls, the whole damned country—fell like a burning tower with spite before my rage. The world could go to hell.

The haircutting crew, a half-dozen Korean inmates in white coats, seemed as surprised as Lurch. A crazed American was something new for them. The big man stood stolidly, staring at me. I turned to some of the other cutters to see whether they sympathized with me, but they stood silently by their stools amid the hair strewn on the gray stone floor. Inmates usually had their heads shaved, that was the letter of prison law, but the guards often made an exception for the foreigners. The gangpey, however, had made a nice little game of my head. I'd seen too many large clumps fall to the ground, heard him laughing above me.

When I'd reached up to feel my head, there was no doubt about what he'd done.

"Finished," I'd told him, ready to burst.

I'd gotten up and walked back to my cell. I looked at myself in the small mirror pasted to the stone. My head was a hatchet job, and when I saw myself I wanted to cry. This wasn't the kid I knew; there was no room for this in my mind, but there I was, looking very much like the foul convict I was struggling so hard not to be. My skin was oily and marked with boils; I had red-pepper diarrhea, was thin, in shock, on a hair trigger. The daily challenges were finding their mark, pricking me, and I was flying off in wounded fury like a mad horse in response to all of them. But I could rage against the butcher job on my head if not against the entirety of my situation, though I tried that, too. I slid back into my blue prison shoes and walked back down to the end of the hall. I would knock through the stone walls to let myself out; these bastards will find out who I am. Something in me, feisty Irish, a perverse American pluck, wouldn't let me just take it smoothly. I threw myself forward blindly, heeding little. I'd wrongly assumed I'd always be protected. I'd discounted tragedy, comeuppance. I was a kid who still hadn't learned to take "no" and "fuck you" for answers. But, of course, we often get what we don't want: deities rip the carpets out from under us, limbs drop off, control slips away; we find ourselves overshadowed by forces much larger than us. Now more or less bald, I was angry because of the humiliation of having once again been powerless, just as I'd been in Seoul and Uijongbu, something less than a man. And at twenty-four I still was—once invincible in my own head, now broken and not accepting it.

It would have been so much easier had I gone quietly; I would have suffered so much less visceral stress and psychic mangling. I used to think about that lying on the floor of my cell—how all the nuances of personality spelled out the unique ways a man suffered, just how exactly and to what degree. I couldn't understand how the other inmates weren't enraged like me, how they didn't rail at the treatment, at being demonized and packed away into oblivion. That the Koreans didn't rebel much I understood. I'd been observing their Confucian codes and the ways in which these were intensified in prison. Those codes were strong on obedience, acquiescence, hierarchies that the Koreans couldn't escape. They were bound together by strong ropes of pride and shame. But I was out of my head, lost in my own westernized, selfish, individual madness. I was still disturbed by the fact that, to me, my crime, however inexcusable and deserving of punishment, had nothing to do with the guards or the other strangers who'd judged me. I felt as though at every turn, when there was one to make, I was being told that I was small and shitty. I never took that well.

"Medium length, damn it—I know he heard me!" I kept on yelling as best I could in Korean. The gang barbers did nothing. Who the hell does this arrogant foreign *kay seki*—son of a bitch—think he is? I'm sure they thought. I knew then that I should go before things got worse for me. I took steps back toward my cell. Lurch jumped in front of me.

"What is the problem?" he asked, awkwardly sounding out each syllable in English. Not a bad man, Lurch; but hooked and gaunt at six foot four, he looked like a hideous bird. He often tried to practice his English with us.

That Lurch saw no problem only enraged me more. "Fuck you, fuck you!" I spat the words in his face.

I watched him grow angry; his lips went white and trembled. And it seemed so pathetic to me, as my anger must have to him. We were all so damned small, so locked into our own petty existences. We fended for ourselves like crabs, scavenging like Korean mutts for dirty water and rice, for hope and respect and little scraps of self-worth. And yet there was nothing else to do; those were our battles. Your day was having someone watch you shit in a trough in a cell the size of a closet; being awakened by someone cursing you and kicking your metal door; being forcibly shut out of the world's goodness because you didn't deserve any, when somewhere in you, in a submerged and now barely reachable place, you still believed you did.

"Fuck you?" Lurch repeated questioningly, examining the words. "Prisoners' heads are shaved; it is prison law!" he screamed at me. He pronounced "law" the same way Prosecutor Shin had, so that it sounded like "low." The hideous sound of it was following me, and so was Lurch as I made my way back to cell 45.

"Get the hell out of my face!" I yelled. I refused to have him escort me, but he kept at my heels until I finally turned and lunged at him with my arm raised. I wanted to hit him. He recoiled, and inside I loved it. He circled around me, went to my cell, and stood there with the door open, waiting to shut me in. The sound of the thick doors always pounded home our impotence; the bang meant you didn't matter, you were no more than a broom, a disgrace to forget. The guards often slammed the doors roughly; their indifference—a blasé toss of the arm—or the perverse enjoyment you could see in their faces, was enough to make me hate them. I often felt like lunging back at the door, telling them they could fuck themselves; I wanted to scream ridiculous things: *I'm worth more! I don't deserve this! I didn't hurt anybody! You don't even know me, for the love of God, you fucking idiots, how can you make this decision on my life without knowing me?*

"I'm going alone!" I shouted at Lurch. He conceded and stepped away from the cell. I felt I'd won. I went in and shut the door myself, pulling it closed by the bars in the window. Then I screamed into the hall as loud as I could, "You don't own my head!"

Pacing uneasily in the cell, I could hear my heart hammering away in my chest—alive, pulsing with blood, how marvelous, but how sad and rabid! This wasn't the guy I wanted to be. I was struggling against something unbeatable. With all my fiber I hated the primitive place I was trapped in. Somehow life had cheated me. I was a failure, a loss, a disappearance. American, though. They didn't send me to solitary for what I'd just done to Lurch. I got away with behavior the Korean inmates and other foreigners would have paid for simply because I was an "original"—what the Koreans sometimes called Americans. As bad as I thought I had it, I was in many ways the fortunate son of forces much larger than me.

THE NEXT MORNING I went over to Big Green's cell when they let us out for exercise.

"How'd you sleep, man?"

The thirty-five-year-old American from Milwaukee looked like hell. He was pasty and his eyes were red. His cell smelled acrid. His Bible was out. Green had pieces of metal inserted into his left leg to prop up the bones. He struggled to his feet.

"I thought about Mark and David all night, couldn't sleep," he said.

Big Green had suffocated his two Korean-American sons. For a while he was the only other American with me in Taejon, and one of the few I would meet during my sentence. I nicknamed him after the Jolly Green Giant, because despite having been sui-cidal and manic-depressive his entire life, having killed his own children, there was still a strain of joy in him, of goodness, and he used to lumber around the hall and between the blocks during exercise, all six feet four inches, 240 pounds of him, dressed in a green sweatshirt and sweatpants. Despite his size and the horrific nature of his crime, I didn't fear Green. He was broken and de-fenseless, ripped apart by a sordid life. And you could see, if you looked, that the very real pain he bore for his deed, having killed a part of himself that he no doubt loved, was ravaging his soul. I pitied him. Though we were judged by the guards and other prisoners for what we'd done, there was also a curious, distorting detachment from our crimes. Taejon was a new life. Our crimes had happened in another, one lived before in a different world, under drastically different circumstances. Without my being consciously aware of the rationale, my brain sometimes had it that the killers weren't killers there, just as I was no longer a drug smuggler. We were all just convicts, shells of our former selves.

Exercise time was really the only chance the foreign prisoners had to talk. As nonworking inmates we got an hour outside in the dirt between the blocks. We were given the choice of deciding not to work only because we were foreigners, because the authorities could see, just as we could, the kinds of difficulties that might arise if we were in the prison factories surrounded by Koreans: we didn't know the language or its delicate hierarchies of respect; communication was badly strained. So twenty-three hours a day locked in our single-man cells, and an hour outside between the walls.

"You're out of control," Green told me in his slow, emphatic tone as we walked side by side around the small space. We could see the faces of bored Koreans watching us through the bars of their ground-floor cells. "You're making yourself look like a fool."

"What the hell should I have done? You saw what was happening."

"If you fight for the little stuff, how're we gonna fight for something bigger?" he shot back, looking down so as to concentrate on his steps. "You're wasting our chance to get in good with the guards. You're just gonna piss them off."

I could see Green was right. But it was easier to be sane out there between Taejon's blocks, under the wide sky, in the open space of the world.

# 26

I had dropped one form and not taken on the other ... with a resulting feeling of intense loneliness in life and a contempt, not for other men, but for all they do. Such detachment came at times to a man exhausted by prolonged physical effort and isolation. His body plodded on mechanically, while his reasonable mind left him, and from without looked down critically on him, wondering what the futile lumber did and why. Sometimes these selves would converse in the void; and then madness was very near.

—T. E. Lawrence, *Seven Pillars of Wisdom*

I KNEW MY personal struggle well but was barely acquainted with the suffering of the others. On our floor were forty-five-odd men serving a combined three hundred years, and they all tried to present a brave face. I could only wonder what they went through when they were alone in their cells. Most of the Korean prisoners lived in group cells, so they never had the chance to be alone, not for years, not for the rest of their natural lives. That seemed to me a crueler punishment than solitary. But we all seemed to have gotten our culturally appropriate deserts: group-oriented Koreans sleeping side by side in fifteen-man cells; more individualistic foreigners locked away in single units.

I didn't see the others cry or break down. I couldn't see them in their rooms, hunched over, blank, lost. I saw scarce signs of their struggle, though I knew they must have been deep in it. Guys with ten- and fifteen-year terms would speak about it as though it were nothing. That was true of Joo Shik, the ethnic Korean from China who got life for killing a Korean on a fishing boat off the coast of Kenya. Joo Shik said three of his fellow ship workers started a fight with him on deck. He'd grabbed a knife to defend himself. Kenyan authorities held him in a Nairobi jail before the international laws were worked out and Korean authorities came and got him. They'd insisted that they should be the ones to punish him. Joo Shik just announced, as though it were a trivial detail, an incidental conversation piece, that he gets out in 2015. Cell 44, next to mine, fifteen years; cell 2, across from me, ten; and yet they carried on without incident, almost without sound. I knew that they ate and read and looked out their windows, that they slept within feet of me. But I knew nothing of their personal agony, nothing of their task to battle through to an acceptance of their lives. I wanted to know it. I wanted to see the struggle, not numbed static. They had so much more to deal with than I did, and yet they left me to wonder if I was the only one who cried at night, who cursed and threw things at the walls, who hid under his blankets trying to escape poisonous feelings of lowliness and despair.

I remember being shocked at myself one night when, for the first time in my life, I tried to go to sleep at around six o'clock in the evening. I couldn't stand my conscious mind anymore. It was hammering me relentlessly with condemnation, tearing apart the fragile little tower of self I had built in twenty-something years. For the first time in my life I was rejecting life. Not even when I was paralyzed by disease as a kid and lay dying in the hospital did I ever reject reality so desperately. Many days I tried to make myself tired, to force myself to escape into sleep. When I woke in the mornings, my eyes slowly opening to the faded white cement of the cell ceiling, my ears to the echoes in our hall, I shut them again and tried to keep them closed. I prayed more sleep would come to me. I wondered if the others were sinking like me, twitching in the silence as they unraveled. Or were they stronger than me? Did they feel and hide it, or had they been anesthetized? I couldn't get a sense from them—as I had with Billy—of what was important in our fate, what mattered. I wanted to scream for them to speak to me, to rage with me. But for the moment we were close only in physical terms, and they didn't expose their insides because we weren't brothers, just strangers held tightly together.

≡≡

WE READ IN the *Korea Herald* that our uniforms were marked for change. "The ministry has decided to change the color and designs of the prisoners' robes epochally," the paper reported, "because the current ones do not match with the atmosphere of the times and they psychologically oppress inmates." The article quoted a justice ministry official as saying, "We have stuck with the current clothes since the national liberation [from the Japanese colonial rule in 1945] according to a theory that deep blue has an effect of restricting provocative psychology of prisoners. However, we decided to change them because deep blue clothes create too gloomy an atmosphere in prison." The new uniforms were to be bright brown or orange.

So that was it: I was just reeling from a case of oppressive fashion. It was a revelation to see that the authorities truly did put thought—to say nothing of the merit or reason in it—into their plan for us. Maybe things weren't as accidental or random as they sometimes seemed; maybe our suspicions about their denials and experiments were right. I can say pretty confidently—though who can know for sure?—that brown or orange uniforms weren't going to make things any more festive.

IN JUNE OF that year an officer from the education department came to see Tracey and me. A Pakistani, Tracey was just a few years older than me. He was part of the same manpower gang as Mohammed and Jamil, the Pakistanis I'd been with in the Seoul Detention Center, and had been convicted along with them. Some of the Koreans told Tracey he looked like a movie star, perhaps one of those Bollywood heroes who sing and dance. Tracey could have entertained like that. He was somehow more man than most of us—strong, intelligent, and high-spirited—and yet more woman, too, starting with the androgynous English name he chose to go by. He was whimsical and effeminate, and yet he was the shrewdest, most subtly and exquisitely manipulative inmate I met. Nobody messed with Tracey. He was too clever, and he had many friends. The Pakistanis always numbered more than six, one of the largest national contingents among us, and they were a unified group. Tracey was the best Korean speaker out of all of us and seemed to have a knack for language in general. (Overall, the Pakistanis were the best linguists; they all had grown up exposed to three or four regional dialects.) He threw himself into new things with abandon and made himself adept at them quickly: chess; the different jobs in the prison factory in which we eventually went to work; his sentence. To me he seemed fearless.

Tracey and I were dealing with two letters: one that I'd written and mailed to the Korean justice ministry; another that he'd sent to the Pakistani embassy in Seoul. In mine I'd asked why the possibility of parole shouldn't be considered in the case of foreign inmates.

> In providing the possibility of early release you are not excusing the prisoner's crime; you are not telling society that your justice is soft and weak. What it does is provide strong and real encouragement for the prisoner to work on himself. Why should an inmate do everything the jailers order, work hard, behave well, even repent or attempt a reform of character when all this is disregarded by the justice ministry?

One should for one's own sanity and progress, of course. But that was *my* answer; I wanted to hear theirs. I thought that if the justice ministry heard this directly from an inmate it might make an impression. At the very least it felt empowering to write. Of course, the letter wouldn't make any difference. It might not even get read. I had no illusions about that. But it seemed natural and right to want to share an opinion on my life, and that of the others with me, with those who owned us.

We followed an officer from the education office to the empty room at the end of our hall. He began by telling us that my letter could not be sent. Tracey's letter, rife with complaints about our conditions, would not be sent, either. Tracey argued in Korean, asserting that there was nothing outrageous in what we'd written. I broke in awkwardly. "I wrote only true things, a simple request for parole."

"I know you didn't lie," the guard answered me. "What you said in the letter is not the problem." It was something about his country's custom or the prison law or appropriate steps. He was, of course, only a messenger, a herald of denial sent by his superiors to deliver the "no" and absorb the brunt of our reaction. I could have made his job easier, could have recognized the futility of the situation and just let it go. But I was angry, because I knew they could take away what they wanted, and letters were my oxygen line, stretching up to the outside world through an ocean of surrounding depths. And what was wrong with calmly and respectfully asking if we could be considered for early release? Where was the harm in that?

Tracey made sure to tell the soft-spoken mail guard that we knew it wasn't his decision and that we weren't angry with him personally. "Hey, listen, the shit and invective you're about to be showered with aren't personal, okay? I mean, we like you."

Guard: "That's all right, really. I understand. And hey, this afternoon your letters are gonna be torn up and thrown away. But it's nothing personal."

Just the law; no need to take it personally. In my head it was a bodiless, intangible force that owned me, served by all these bodies simply doing their jobs. I couldn't appeal to the former, couldn't even see it. But the latter, the guards—they gave me something solid at which to throw my rage.

"*Fuck the law!*" I screamed before I knew what I was doing. I punched the desk. "You've gotta send this letter!" Before the mail guard or Tracey could respond, I walked out and went into my cell.

An hour later the section chief came for me. We took up the same argument in the same room at the end of the hall. A large man, he told me very calmly that legally the prison could refuse to mail the letter, and destroy it. Now being a real pain in their collective ass, I asked to see that specific law; I wanted to read it. The chief was a step ahead of me. He'd brought a blue prison-law book. Adorned with the rose of Sharon on the front, it seemed to radiate. There it was, our bane, the catalog of all the minutiae of our closet world. Through its hundreds of pages it gradually, but expertly, cut us down and hemmed us in.

He found the page and placed his finger down on a particular passage, then flipped the book around and pushed it over in front of me. "*So shin pay gay*"—which basically meant "We can tear up your letter if we feel like it." When I asked to see the law in English, the chief got annoyed and left.

LATER THAT DAY Tracey sent me a note through the so-jee.

I am sorry if I did different from what you thought. As I told you to advise the ass is a waste of time. It's really useless to talk with them, on the other hand kaejang said he will send your letter out. They can if they want, but never do the things which they don't want to do, and we're in here, help less, so we have to use our minds and politics. I have an idea, give me the copy of your letter. I'll write to my uncle in 'urdu' then he will write in English and send to the justice ministry. My uncle is very kind hearted person. We need to be nice in front of them. Think about it, there is only two person who they think are very bad, if we all behave like that (like you) then OK. Because every one is same. But this time many prisoners are kind with guards and agree with guards that Tomas and Tracey are wrong. That encourages guards. Please try to understand what I mean, what I want to tell you. I don't know how to tell you the situation, you know every think, don't be alone.

He was wrong about me knowing "every think." It was closer to "no think." Reason wasn't yet an appealing course, unless I was using it in my journal to debate them, to prove by argument and polemic how primitive and useless this kind of punishment was. I wanted the guards to understand. I think I was literally trying to change their minds, to convince them that things in this prison of theirs should be different, that there was no sense to Taejon, to that same sorry-ass system of retribution and punishment that man feebly falls back on all over the world. (Man, 人, in a box, □ = 囚. That's the Chinese character, which is sometimes used in Korea as well, for prisoner. It's amazing that they haven't come up with a new idea—and that goes for most of the world—in thousands of years, or a new character to represent it.) Inside I was raging. They weren't fit to hold me, these moralizers and idiots, I thought. They had no fucking clue what to do with me other than shut me away. I wasn't interested in considering how our circumstances could have been far worse or how I'd already been quite lucky not to have been beaten or put away in solitary. If I had been, my outlook might have changed. Then again, I might have only gotten worse. I didn't give a damn about anyone, and, in retrospect, I was hideously appalled by myself most of all. There was no Jolly Marauder then, only an angry and wounded cipher. I threw my cheap Korean textbook out the window during a lesson at the end of our hall (a study hour that lasted about a month and yet was trumpeted by the authorities as a major concession to the foreigners). The kind foreigners' tamdang who taught us sat there and did nothing. He didn't know how to react. Why am I learning Korean? my head screamed. How can everyone act like everything is all right and we're just having our neat little language lesson while our lives are made every second to rot away in front of us?

Only later did I realize that I was caught up with raging against the system and acting out against our conditions because that was easier than facing myself. I couldn't look at myself honestly yet. I had screwed myself beyond reason and it was unforgivable.

Tracey—a good friend, I realized—tried to reach me again.

Hey, kid! There is only one thing I wonder. Tell me if you don't mind, why you be so different from others? I mean you don't care if someone detest you, that right you have your own way to live your life. I know you don't need any of us. You can live your own life by your self, and you don't have any greed to us. But dear, do you know what is humanity or affability? Life is not just that come in the world, eat, sleep, sex, live own life and go (death). No, I think, be a good person, and live also for others, at least give a smile to others hearts, try don't to hurt them even by any of your action. I am sorry, I am not a person who should speak like this. Because there is so many things in this note to you but even I do not act like what I am saying. I will try to live for others.
P.S.—Don't care who is saying. Care it or see what he is saying.

He must have had his dictionary out. It was remarkable, not yet knowing Tracey well, and yet seeing that beyond being jailed for five years for his apparent involvement in several brutal murders, here was a compassionate friend reaching out to try to pull me back from a dangerous place. He was part killer, perhaps, and part able counselor, the lovely, shrewd Khan.

# 27

MOM, POP, AND my brother, Chris, brought up the idea of visiting me. My reaction to this surprised me. Despite missing them all and needing to keep the link to them, to my former self, alive, I would have been ashamed to have them see me in that place, in my prison uniform. I was ashamed of where I was and what I'd already cost them, but there was something more: the realization that this experience was mine to face alone. And there was a perverse pride in that, in the thought that no one I knew before would ever be able to mediate my experience in Korea, to dilute or alter it in any way with their own version. It was my own foray into a world beyond anything anyone I knew had known before, and I was taking the trip alone, and that was satisfying. Halfway through my twenties, I was living a life of my own now. However silly, brutish, or undesirable the particulars might have been, I was cutting my own path.

Of course, I also knew visits were seven minutes long. I knew that flights cost about a grand. I knew that I would feel worse after seeing my parents through the hard plastic wall of the visiting rooms. I knew it wouldn't do them any good to see me or Taejon with their own eyes, because neither would have been a pretty sight. I told them not to come. I would see them when it was over. I couldn't have been any surer of the decision.

When I slipped from the discipline I'd been trying to maintain in my letters home—keeping them as light and positive as possible, revealing little of the actual mental struggle I was experiencing—and told Mom that I had been acting out of late, arguing with guards and exploding with anger, Mom was worried that I was ruining my chances for parole. It was hard to have to tell her then that my crime had placed me in the category of killers, gang as-sassins, rapists, and enemies of the state, and that there would be no parole.

Mom had helped nurture in me the will to seek out the un-known, and she hurt worse than anyone when I landed myself in trouble in Korea. Much of the guilt I bore was due to that, that I had caused her so much pain. When I was first arrested, the U.S. embassy in Seoul told my family that the minimum penalty for my crime was seven years. Mom nearly fainted. Then there was the nervous breakdown she had in a King Kullen grocery store while wheeling a cartful of food through the aisles. She was pick-ing out cans of corn and refried beans when the weight of her son's folly sat right down on the great woman's head and she wept and raged and threw herself on top of her discount items. They didn't know if they'd see me alive again. The uncertainty about what was to become of me was part of the worst of it. And then the powerlessness. There was no way for us to communicate ex-cept through letters. No matter how often I told them that I was all right, they were left to their own visions of prison: rapes, mur-ders, and torture. To this day my brother thinks I'm lying about never having been involved in any prison sex; he likes to joke to me about young Korean boys or how I must have been a treat for the Korean sodomites. It's his fraternal love at work.

On the night I was born a large, loving black nurse stood over Mom, desperately urging her to push with all her might to get the baby out before the late night passed into the next day, Friday the thirteenth.

"You don't want no Friday-the-thirteenth baby, honey, push!"

Mom did it, pushed and sacrificed and got it done for me as al-ways: on Thursday, November 12, at 11:41 P.M. I emerged, spared by nineteen minutes from being born under a bad sign. But, as Pops sometimes likes to spin the story—and nothing could help me once my brother and sisters heard his version—my head was large and it tore magnificent Mom open, bursting an artery in her leg. (In fact, the complications she suffered were the result of a poorly done episiotomy.)

For three and a half years, without fail, she wrote me at least once a week. She was a lifeline to me with her letters and cards—once one of Tintin hanging off an emerald-green train that looked a lot like the Chinese one I'd taken through Mongolia and Siberia. She gave stacks of prestamped envelopes with my address on them to the others to make it easy for them to write me. She sent me a steady stream of books, asked if I needed socks, if my health was all right, my spirits intact. She made sure her love reached me even at the bottom of the ocean. Had I been exiled on the moon I'm certain she would have found a way to cheer me. It shamed me, and when, after a time locked down, I began to understand that my actions had a profound effect on the rest of the family, I wept with the realization. From my cell I canonized the woman.

RUTH, AN OLD family friend, wrote me about how Mom would call her on break at St. Francis Hospital when she was sick with worry for me and needed to be talked down. Ruth reminded Mom, and me, that if I'd been in Singapore or some other places I might have been hanged. Another good friend of my mother's—like Ruth, a wise woman in her eighties—told Mom that she had done her work and now had to trust me. She told Mom to be like the mothers of bears and birds: "The way they send their kids off, when well prepared and ready to take on their world, is motherhood at its best." I came to know this amazing lady as Aunt Mil, though she was actually the aunt of my mom's closest friend, Edie. Aunt Mil was close to ninety. When she heard about my situation, she began writing me once a week, just as Mom and my sisters did. The overwhelming majority of the letters I received were from the women in my life, and this was true, I found, for many of the other inmates. The women, these angels, were constant and unwavering in their support. They were full of compassion and concern, measurably more so than the men, it seemed. The men in my life, my dad and my brother included, were far less present. They wrote far less frequently. But I didn't hold that against them. They seemed to be up against a biological disadvantage.

Aunt Mil had lived her life in the service of her husband, an accomplished pianist who had played with many of the best classical musicians of his day, and their three sons, a writer, an African adventurer, and a musician. She filled me with visions of all their lives, especially that of Conrad, the son who had lived in East Africa for more than thirty years and ran a river-rafting tour company. I loved hearing about his trips through Ethiopia and Tanzania. Aunt Mil was going blind but could see black and white, shadows, enough to write in big looping cursive that often strayed endearingly at oblique angles along the page. She was reading voraciously while her eyes could still manage it. "As long as I can read and write I am in the business of living," she once wrote me. I adopted that as my slogan. We were birds of a feather in that. Like Mom, Aunt Mil regularly sent me books, including some of the spiritual ones she was reading, others that I requested: *The Tibetan Book of Living and Dying*, *The Satanic Verses* (though she had qualms about sending this one, knowing its history and the fact that I lived with Muslims who might be offended by it), Lawrence of Arabia's great adventure, Nelson Mandela's memoir, a book on Madagascar called *Ark on the Move*, which was full of amazing pictures, of lemurs and baobab trees, and provided a great window outside the jail.

Like me, Aunt Mil lived in relative isolation, in a retirement community in Kansas City where she had few kindred friends. But this circumstance had led her to begin examining her life as never before, and she valued that above all else. In her letters she never looked down at her life, never complained, not about her blindness or the forty years that she'd spent standing dutifully by her husband's side, to some degree at the expense of her own exploration, or the untimely death of her son Conrad. She humbled me when she told me that her oncoming blindness was a trifle and that, to her mind, what I was going through was much more difficult.

I thought she was wrong about that, but I was amazed by her spirit. She was taking blindness with grace, without complaint, and she was assuming that I was reacting to my challenge with the same poise. If only you could see how small I've been here, I wrote her, feeling embarrassed and young and sloppy. But Aunt Mil wouldn't hear it; she had her eyes on the prize, on the better self. She told me that I was strong, positive, and wise in the way I was taking my time, making it easier on my family. How could I not try to be that man, then? I felt I owed her that. Your mother still has high hopes for you, she wrote me. If you can accept your situation with grace and work to be kind and wise, you will still make her proud, even from a prison on the other side of the world.

I READ EVERYONE'S news greedily, noted their changes of address, tried picturing their trips. I told my twin sisters everything I knew about Seville before they went there to study. I encouraged them in everything they did. I talked to them about their breakups and crises. I commented on every trivial piece of personal news that came to me. My letters were evidence of a kind of starvation. Mom and my sisters told me how they fasted for me, toasted and remembered me during holidays and birthdays. I wasn't missing anything, they always said, to make me feel better.

As the months went by and turned into years, Rocket began to write me. Enough time had gone by that she knew she was no longer in any legal danger. I can't imagine the pain and utter powerlessness she felt during the first year, when her family and lawyers forbade her to contact me. She was so sad in the beginning, she said, that she had crazy thoughts of skating off the Brooklyn Bridge. When she finally did begin to write me, it was tough, because there was a certain delicacy and restraint to our correspondence. My feeling the urgency and pain of wanting to see her and be with her, the sensation that I was losing all this time as her life went on without me, was something that she seemed to be consciously trying to avoid. She wrote me, but there was an emotional distance, a caution in her words that matched the physical separation. As Billy had encouraged me to do, I had tried to eliminate urgent, romantic thoughts of Rocket, and I did let her go in large part. I told her in letters that I was sorry and that I knew she had to live her life. I didn't need to tell her, of course; she was doing that—and yet always, often unconsciously, I kept up some thought of her and me together, of her being still in love with me, waiting for me, even chastely, a silent hope that I stored away and preserved in a quiet part of my mind. I never heard about her lovers: the hot guy at Downstate Medical Center, where Rocket had enrolled to study physical therapy when she'd pulled herself together and settled on a career; the older Brooklyn man who became her Rollerblading partner, then her lover. He had wanted to marry her. I heard these stories when I was out, and they hurt me even then, though I knew Rocket had done nothing wrong. It was inevitable.

I think Rocket also held on to the thought of us all the while, even as she moved forward. She sent me a postcard of a Georgia O'Keeffe painting, which I stuck to my cell wall: *Black Hollyhock, Blue Larkspur*. In the deep center of the jet-black petals of the hollyhock is what looks like a star of light, a glowing white core with a little golden yolk in its center. It's consumed by the black petals around it, and yet it seems to be insulated there, incubating. Rocket said that the central yolk was me surrounded by the black of the prison but undimmed. She said that she was living the blue of the larkspur, a different flower in a different place, but still somehow touching the hollyhock. I tried not to put any pressure on her in my letters, but other times I would tell her that I loved her and needed her still. To describe a woman leaving a man, the Korean inmates used the phrase "She put her rubber slippers on backward"—meaning the woman was walking away from the house, not toward it as in happier times. This was something on all our minds, locked away as we were in our house of sad men. Rocket appeared in my dreams and I'd lie there hugging her in my empty cell. I saw us in Chefchaouen, up in the Rif Mountains of Morocco, where I was fever-stricken and weak and could barely climb the blue-and-white mountain steps, and Rocket held me up. She once sent me a large envelope full of autumn leaves from New York. Improbably, the guards let me have it (especially surprising as my crime was something of a "leaf" offense). That night in my cell I cleared the wood floor, spread the leaves out, and lay down in them, threw them over me. Their colors, flaming reds and oranges, burned the cell. It seemed unreal that nature was capable of such a thing. She sent me the identification number that had been pinned to her shirt as she ran the New York City Marathon. Green asked me if I could smell Rocket's sweat on it. She ran the race two years in a row. Greater than my personal regret that I wasn't free and out there with her was the sincere joy I felt that she was living so fully, that she hadn't gone down with me in Seoul.

She sent me a picture of herself on a mountaintop with her top off, her big breasts blazing. I couldn't believe the letter office let it through. I told Rocket that it was possible that at least a dozen government workers might have seen that picture. Sometimes I told Rocket, risking a response from the guards, that I was going to escape to come see her, break the bars, pick the locks, scale the walls, fly the mountains, swim the seas.

EVERY YEAR ON Buddha's birthday, the eighth day of the fourth month of the lunar calendar, Taejon authorities had a few sweet tomatoes or apples placed in the food hole of each man's cell. This always reminded me of a trip Rocket and I had taken during the three months we spent together in Korea.

With nine days off from our teaching duties during the Lunar New Year holiday, Rocket and I had gone down to Kyongju, the ancient capital of the Buddhist Shilla Kingdom, perched in the southeast of Korea, near the sea. The Shilla kings had reigned long, and we walked the little hills that were their tombs as an old custodian swept the short grass with a bamboo broom. Die and become a hill, I thought—how marvelous! I wanted to be buried like that. We climbed Namsan outside the city, about twelve hundred feet at the top. It was sunset, and rather than miss the colors in the sky we decided to stay and watch them fade into the hills. It grew dark and cold. Rocket and I walked the summit and found a clearing. On a rock looking out over the valley and the three clusters of lights that were towns in the distance, we found an apple and a bottle of rice wine, the top unscrewed and placed at its base, that someone had recently left there as Buddhist offerings, humble gifts to the Compassionate One. We demurred, then decided that in our state of need, the Buddha would want us to partake of his tribute. So Rocket and I said a blessing for Kyongju, blessed Buddha and all the Buddha beings, then made a fire and roasted the apple and drank from the rice wine. We battled through the entire night, trying to sleep there at the summit, with small patches of snow and ice around us, huddled together between rocks with my coat over us. The temperature dropped and the wind picked up. We slept what felt like only a few minutes at a time. We woke often, stumbled shivering in the dark, searching blindly for twigs and branches to relight the fire. The moon and stars were naked and gorgeous above us. We wondered how long till dawn.

Delirious, we were awakened just before dawn by chanting and the gentle knocking of wood. We stood on the rocks and peered down into a niche of the mountain to see a temple set against a cliff under the pines about two hundred feet below us. We talked and held each other, then stood on the rocks with anticipation as the sky began to soften and turn shades of pink. We waited for the top of the red ball to peek over the hills, and when it did, we seemed to be standing in the center of a straight line connecting the points where the sun had vanished over the hills the previous night and where it was now rising in the east. We raised our arms and cheered, warmed our bodies in the sun. We had Namsan to ourselves. It was an intimate, magical mountain as it woke all around us. In sleep-deprived languor we took the path along the curving ridge, stopping in clearings to stare out at the brown, fallow rice fields in the valleys on both sides. In a blissful daze we descended, encountering birds and strange squirrels, chipmunks and earthen burial sites. I thought of the temples and pagodas that must have dotted those hills more than a thousand years before, and imagined monks sitting silent among the trees. A tranquil spirit infused everything. The air and light seemed to shimmer with a special charge. After spotting a few stones with Buddhist images carved in them, we began to see faces and forms all over—lines in rocks that here looked like a brow and eyes, there the suggestion of a placid smile or the curve of a gentle head. Buddha and bodhisattvas were everywhere, it seemed. We wondered if we were hallucinating. At the base of the mountain, in a grove of pines with wavy trunks next to the rounded hill-tombs of the kings, Rocket and I lay down in the sun and slept.

BACK IN NEW York, Rocket went to Rockaway Beach in Brooklyn and made a small fire on a rock jetty. She skinned a red apple, roasted it in the fire, just as we had on Namsan, and cut a deal with Buddha. "I give back the apple sacrifice and they give you back," she wrote me. "Who knows who's listening?"

# 28

MR. AND MRS. Lee stood before us, a slightly mad but kind Korean pastor and his big-boned blond American wife. They came to Taejon regularly to save our prodigal souls. Mr. Lee had also talked in the past about advocating for our early release, and that to us was an even more tempting salvation. So Tracey, a liberal Muslim; Green, a suicidal Catholic; and I, a devout believer in getting out of the cell regardless of the reason, often accepted their visits. We'd meet down by the education office in a large room where we'd sit in comfortable chairs and listen to this sweet couple talk to us about penitence and guidance and transformation through Christ. They'd bring pastries and cakes. Sometimes they persuaded the guards to bring us coffee.

Mr. Lee had just come back from a retreat. "Ten days on Prayer Mountain north of Seoul; fasting, no food for ten days, only water, reading the Bible," he told us. "When you are released, I can sponsor you and take you to Prayer Mountain with me. We can go to a public bath." We shifted uncomfortably in our seats.

"Let's say a prayer together," Mrs. Lee said, looking like she might cry. Her hands were locked in a furious grip and she began to rock her big hips. Green told me that night that he loved women her size. She began Psalm 23: "The Lord is my shepherd, I shall not want. . . . Though I walk through the valley of the shadow of death, I will fear no evil. . . ." A powerful incantation indeed, full of beauty and high drama. I'd heard it many times, but only Green knew the words well enough to declaim it with Mrs. Lee. Green had come to Taejon from Seoul National Mental Hospital, where the courts sent him after finding him half-crazy and sentencing him to seven years for killing his two sons. Just seven years for two deaths. They must not have known what to do with him.

He wanted to be moved to a different prison. He was suffering from depression and thoughts of suicide, the same things that had plagued him since childhood. Left here in Taejon, he was surely going to kill himself.

"I was at peace at the mental hospital, you know. Everything was taken care of for me," he told Mr. and Mrs. Lee, hoping they might talk to Taejon officials about a transfer. "I need to go to a place where they can deal with me. Somewhere I would be with my kind."

Mrs. Lee was nodding. She said she knew of a good place. "It's a lovely facility and honestly, I've never seen, well"—she maneuvered her head, shoulders, and hips like someone trying to pass gas discreetly—"crazy people there."

Everyone looked at Green.

"My wife has my pictures. I want to get them back," he said, already on to the next need. "I don't know what you can do about that—pray for me?" For a religious man this sarcasm was a particularly low blow. Must have been the thought of his wife that set him off.

GREEN TOLD ME that when he was about two his parents were sent to prison for their role in the death of their other son, who was a few years older than Green. He could only remember being told that his brother had fallen down a flight of stairs, and that somehow his parents were found responsible for the accident. He was sent to live with a foster family. His foster mother sexually abused him. He remembers lighting upon the idea of killing himself for the first time when he was eight years old. How the hell does an eight-year-old consider killing himself? I wondered. How horrific must a life be to drive a kid to that? By twelve Green was drinking often, letting older men go down on him in their cars in exchange for beer. Drug use and depression followed. He joined the air force and was stationed in the Philippines, where he lost himself in alcohol and prostitutes, fondly referred to, he recalled, as "three-holers." He was moved to South Korea, where he repaired electrical wiring on U.S. military aircraft at Yongsan. He met and married a Korean room-salon hostess, an uneducated woman who sometimes slept with customers. In Taejon, it dawned on Green that during their eight years of marriage he and his wife had never truly spoken to each other, had no decent or productive communication. It seemed incredible, to go that long with someone so close and yet never reach her at a deep level. But something about Green's story had the hard ring of truth, and I thought about all the countless lives, the families and friends, passing the same way, sad, lonely lives lived out within arm's reach of one another.

Green and his wife had two sons. His drinking was affecting his job. He either stepped or fell off a Seoul rooftop, shattering his left leg in several places. His wife, he said, only tormented him. She bragged to Green about the businessmen who took her on trips. Green raged but couldn't stop her. He hated her. He quit the air force and relied on his military pension after serving fourteen years. He wanted to kill himself but couldn't bring himself to do it cleanly. He especially wanted to kill his wife. He thought they were unfit to raise their sons. He worried about how their relationship was scarring the boys. What kind of father could he be, drunk and suicidal? He imagined his sons growing up surrounded by instability and abuse; their childhood could easily become like his, he thought. He didn't want that for them; he wanted to spare them the horror. There was no way out of it. Only blackness and death. Death, the constant thought.

Numb from depression and weeks of drugs and alcohol, Green put tranquilizers in his sons' food one night while his wife was out. The older one was seven, the younger four. When they passed out, he put plastic bags over their heads and then wrapped his hands around their necks and squeezed until they stopped breathing. His wife found the bodies in the hall closet, piled one on top of the other.

IT WAS EASY to reject such a monster, to hate this big, sloppy, cowardly man: fat beer gut, limping gait, massive head covered with receding red hair. It so happened that on one U.S. embassy visit to us in Taejon the consul was a pregnant woman. Green spoke about wanting to do something to help Amerasian children, as he knew firsthand how his sons had suffered ridicule and prejudice. He said he loved his kids. The consul, one hand over her belly, repeated in a contemptuous, incredulous tone, "You loved your kids?" She quickly straightened herself, realizing, I think, that personal judgments, as easy to have and difficult to suppress as they were, remained outside the scope of her job.

He'd committed the unimaginable. How could a father murder his own children? I'd never had to ask myself such a thing before, but I was now living with the question, taking stock of the very animal that could do it. Most of the inmates and guards avoided Green. They never gave him a chance. Call it tolerance or pity, chalk it up to the fact that for long stretches he was the only other American with me, but I did. There was more to him than just the child killer. Rejecting him was too easy. Something told me to hold off.

In his own account of the crime, which he was required to write as part of a psychological evaluation, Green called his sons "it": "I put the bag over its head. It stopped moving." (The authorities had given Green a copy of the account for his own records. After I'd won his confidence, he let me read it.) I don't think that this was a conscious ploy on his part, a way of mitigating, even for a semantic moment, his guilt or responsibility. I saw it as a chilling sign of the fact that he simply couldn't bear to write his sons' names in relation to what he'd done to them. His brain, perhaps suffering from dissociation, wouldn't let him draw the human connection, handle the thought that he'd done this to human beings, to two individuals, his own flesh and blood. I think he was sickened and appalled by it more than anyone else. This is not the case with all murderers, of course, but it was true for Green. His crime was, and perhaps rightfully so, eating away at his soul. It was, for all intents and purposes, his final act. I'm sure that hell was in his head then, in those quiet days in our cells, as his mind and memory tortured, shamed, and condemned him beyond all reason.

WHEN GREEN FIRST told me about his wife, I said, "She's bad news."

"I know it. Look where I am!" he responded.

I wasn't inclined to let that go and dug in. "Come on, man, you know that's not right. You've got to take responsibility for what you did."

"I won't do it," he barked back like a defiant child. "That's the one thing I won't do!"

But through our conversations and his own soul searching, he began to do it, to look at his deed and his life in the full harsh light.

## 29

IN THE DIRT between blocks 4 and 6 we arranged a daily *jeem bong* game, a kind of poor man's baseball. One of us had a small, hollow rubber ball with an elusive flight and bounce to it. The pitcher, standing about twenty feet away, lobbed the ball underhand toward the batter, who swung his hips, let his arm fly, and slammed the ball with a clenched fist. Smashed well, the ball would collapse into a whirling disk and scream toward the back wall of our lot—a home run if it got there. Some guys concentrated on the shape of their fists when hitting, but that wasn't the secret to jeem bong, not as I saw it. It was all about arm speed, pure acceleration. Catching the ball was tough. Your hands had to be quick and soft, converge on it with precision, otherwise no catch; the ball would bounce away, the runner would be on.

One day, as a group of us were in the middle of a game, I suddenly started to go sour. I was in my roving position behind the pitcher when I began to feel dissatisfied by the game, the dependency of our little group of cretins, the familiarity of our wasted cage world. I stared down uncomfortably at my thin legs. I told the others I was done and walked away. They got angry and yelled at me; there were still fifteen minutes left. A few days later came a form of payback: a heavy rain of green-white shit from a line of pigeons on the roof above me. I was at bat, standing at the ready, focusing on the pitcher and the ball to come and not the backed-up birds above me, cooing and hanging their tail sides over the edge, when suddenly there was the violent rush of what sounded like pancake batter falling from a height. It dropped right on my head and over my back and shoulders. I staggered away. Mr. Chun, Tracey, Green, and the others were cheering and laughing in fits. I threw off my shirt to see what was on me. Laughing, Mr. Chun told me, "In three years here I haven't seen this happen. It's a sign of good luck in Korea. Soon you'll have money!"

From then on I watched the pigeons through my window. I watched them kiss and mate on the roof throughout the spring and summer. I thought they must have a specific mating season, but they humped right through the fall and winter, too, whenever the spirit moved them. When the air was buoyant and charged, they'd fly together in a whirling mass, wheeling in large playful circles above the blocks. I thought I saw the pigeons show emotion when they dropped from the top of the cell blocks, caught currents, eased their wings into broad angles at their sides, and glided. They had to work hard, beating their wings strenuously, to get back up on the roofs, but then they'd have their cliff-dive again. I wondered if in those moments they imagined themselves to be hawks or eagles, something grander, something beyond the life of a pigeon.

Below my window in our exercise space was a little shrublike tree. There was no other plant in the area, and the shrub seemed to be stubbornly holding to its solitary life there. It was about three feet high and had branches like the antlers on a big male deer, very few leaves. When we played jeem bong the little tree was sometimes in the way of the action, but we left it alone. The guards began to cut it down, though, bit by bit, over a period of several weeks. I kept tabs on it, observing each change and abbreviation, watching it with admiration. There it was enduring its slow death without a scream or protest. There was something noble in the way it went so quietly. Each progressive cut seemed to do nothing to diminish it. Its dignity was the same as when it was full, and it stood there with grace just the same. At the end it was just a small root barely sticking out of the ground, and yet I could still see the full tree in it somehow.

AT THE END of my first summer in Taejon, workers on our floor began stopping by to look in on me and ask if I played basketball. The promise of a new athlete, especially a tall American, could cause a stir. They tried to persuade me to join their factories, bribing me with soup and cookies and promises of special treatment. Come to the garment or woodworking or printing factory, they said; you can live all right there. You'll be taken care of.

The gangsters in the factories arranged basketball contests, played on Saturdays usually, half-days of work when two factories at a time had to share the exercise grounds. They'd bet cases of yogurt drinks, bags of apples, boxes of ramyun on the games. Victory led to bragging rights and prestige. The games, therefore, though sloppy and wild on the loose dirt of the one court, were far from a joke, and they led up to the annual fall sports competition, a prisonwide month of contests between all the factories. I'd basically been playing jeem bong for six months and was charged up for the chance to play some real ball. And the time was right, because if I was to keep my sanity I knew I had to get out of the isolation of the cell and start work in a factory. There I'd have space and light and much more human interaction, though that was always a double-edged sword, especially when it meant navigating a room of Korean convicts with whom I still had trouble communicating. On my side were my pent-up rage and the gathered potential energy of six months during which I'd spent nearly twenty-three hours a day alone in my cell. I was ready to explode into action. The downtime, though, had also left me out of shape, thin, and a little deranged.

My love affair with basketball began when I was about ten. I got a new ball for my birthday and bounced it all around the house. Soon I was playing every day at the Main Street School courts near our house in Port Washington. I played in the dark and in the rain, on top of snow. I practiced by myself or with friends and got in games whenever I had the chance. It was always street ball: pickup games anywhere and everywhere I went on Long Island and in New York City. In my admission essay to Notre Dame, I wrote about how basketball was a method of self-regulation and healing for me. I played ball in Seville, Spain—good run in La Triana—and worked for two days teaching Spanish children how to play. I ran with some young Filipino hotshots at a streetside basket in a poor section of Manila, sewage puddled at the curb. We even played up in Sagada. I got into a full-blown game at a court inside the first wall of the Forbidden City in Beijing—traveling alone and cruising around the Chinese capital on a bike, I'd been stunned and elated to find the sacrilege of a full court inside the magnificent palace. It was me and the ghosts of the Ming and Qing. With a crowd of spectators around us, I'd created several great shots for myself right near the basket, only to blow them. I redeemed myself with a couple of resounding blocks. Mao seemed to smile down at me on my way out. I also played in Seoul. Once, a fellow teacher, a Korean American, and I took our classes of kids to a court near our school. We tried to give them a good show, dribbling fancy between our legs, trying to dunk the ball through the rusty rims. The game was just starting to take off in popularity in Korea. The kids knew of Michael Jordan and the NBA. A fairly new professional Korean league existed. Some of the teams had foreign import players on their rosters, guys no one back home had ever heard of.

The Korean-American Gary on our floor was the most persuasive recruiter. He and his older buddies had run millions of dollars of methamphetamines through Hawaii and Korea and Hong Kong. He'd somehow gotten just three years. Gary spoke English like a native and worked in Peehyuk, the shoemaking factory. In quick conversations over the course of a week that September, Gary told me briefly about Panjang Nim, Peehyuk's captain. He was fair and highly respected, Gary said. I would be looked after. I finally told him yes, and that's all I had to do. The rest was taken care of for me. So I became a convict cobbler, and Peehyuk my employer for the next two years. This was appropriate, in a sense, as our sentences in Korean were *jin yuk,* or terms of forced labor.

Out into the halls, then, on my first day, a Saturday, when all new workers started. I was blasted by the space and light of the wide exercise grounds at the far end of the jail, framed by the low two- and three-story white concrete buildings that housed the more than a dozen factories. I was looking around wide-eyed as we marched forward in single file. We passed a peacock and rabbits in cages in front of the sewing factory. Later, I'd come up with a pretty good imitation of the peacock's warped baby-cry call. We had no work that day in Peehyuk, but a game had been arranged. We were to play Paysun, the car-wiring factory above us. They were a good team, Gary said, due mostly to the presence of the Nigerians Joseph and Zeke, established big men who played physical and dirty if they had to. As guys began getting ready for exercise, I was called over to meet the other members of our squad: the fun-loving, wild gang member who called himself Charlie (when he learned what I was in for, he slapped me on the shoulder and exclaimed that he was a "doctor of happy smoke"); the fairly tall and athletic-looking Min Chul; our team leader, Peehyuk's oldest gangster after Panjang Nim, who became known to Tracey, Green, and me simply as Gang Guy; and Chang Ho, a good-looking and popular kid who was doing life for killing his stepmother when he was nineteen. I nicknamed him Gorilla Man (there was no rational explanation for the name; I just thought of it one day and gave it to him; I think he was fond of it). Although he and I became very friendly—studying English and Korean and eating ramyuns together, talking about and playing basketball, singing songs—I never felt close enough to ask him about the murder. Others told me that Chang Ho's birth mother had died tragically in a car crash and that, maybe angry at life, he had strangled to death his father's new wife. That all seemed like a shame, pain leading to pain.

Charlie gave me a pair of shorts. Chang Ho brought me a pair of sneakers that fit. (The prison sold us only one kind.) The morning raced toward eleven and exercise. Suddenly we were out in the dirt. Hordes of blue-clad prisoners from Peehyuk and Paysun were gathered around the perimeter of the court, out in the middle of the dusty grounds. My heart raced in anticipation. I took a couple of practice shots. I noticed that the rims were lower than regulation height. It would be hard to cut, or to defend opponents when they did, as there wasn't much footing on the sand and loosely packed dirt. The Nigerians looked enormous and like exotic ringers out there, warming up with the Korean gangsters from Paysun. Joseph and I knew each other from our cell block, but now he was all business, preparing himself for the impending combat. Still, I thought I saw in him and Zeke the same thing I was feeling: a natural interest and even admiration for the other foreigner in such an odd spot. But pride was at stake, personal pride, factory pride, one's place in the factory pecking order. If you acquitted yourself well as an athlete, life could be better for you. Some factory captains gave their athletes special treatment, I learned, gave them sneakers and special food, a good table to sit at, excused them from actual work. Later, other factories tried to lure me into defecting. I might have been able to arrange some nice privileges through a transfer, but I became a full-blooded Peehyuk man. In time, I felt loyal to Panjang Nim, even though he insisted on not giving us players any preferential treatment. That was something I liked about him. He had a principle and stuck to it, making you want to rise to do the same.

When the game began, I saw that Chang Ho had a good natural stroke and coordination; he looked like a star in the making. Though Charlie was rough and didn't quite get the movements of the game, he played with such hustle and physical abandon that I was glad he was on our side. Several times he crashed through the defense, knocking Paysun players down on his way to the goal. Min Chul might have been a murderer, but it was clear that in competition he lacked the killer instinct. Gang Guy, appropriately enough, would never have made the team if selection had been based on skill. Despite his excellent size—about six foot two and more than 220 pounds—he was slow and deliberate. A minute into the game I felt my body completely take over from my mind for the first time in what felt like years. It was a palpable release. I was lost in every single second of the game, not following months and years now or wondering who the hell I'd become. Only the ball mattered now: putting it through the rim, stopping Paysun from doing so. It was the same glorious simplicity of basketball, and sports in general, that I had always loved. I received a pass on the baseline with my back to the basket, Joseph guarding me. This was familiar and a piece of home. I faked right, toward the center of the court, then quickly broke baseline. Dirt flew. Joseph was a full step behind. One Paysun gangpey in front of the hoop. I picked up my dribble and jumped to the rim, dunking the ball with both hands.

It was as though a depth charge had been set off. The prisoners all around the court and exercise grounds erupted in a wave of cheering and screaming. Taejon would never be the same again. Gang Guy and Charlie slapped me five and hollered, "Tomasuh, guuut shot ya!" Several minutes of frantic play later, Charlie stole the ball and I broke down court ahead of everyone. I grabbed his bounce pass, dribbled toward the basket, and went up, turning my body in preparation for a two-handed reverse dunk. I remember thinking that everyone was going to enjoy seeing me pull it off. In the excitement and thrill of the moment I might have gotten too far ahead of myself. Suddenly I was radically off course and soaring out of bounds. One of Paysun's players, a muscular young gangster, had slammed into my back. I must have looked funny, hurtling helplessly through the air in little shorts that didn't fit too well and showed far too much of my pale, skinny legs. I landed hard on my back and my head slammed against the ground. The inmates exploded again, shouting above one another.

Dazed, I got back up on my feet.

"What the fuck is that?" I yelled, pointing at the guy who'd floored me, holding the back of my head. "You can't fucking do that!"

He stood there stone-faced, his body bristling. He'd done what he felt he had to do, and I'm sure his squad was pleased with him. He'd defended Paysun's pride. Gang men from both factories got between us. The Nigerians took no sides and stood away. In all my time of playing I'd never had anyone take me out of the air so viciously. I was surprised that I wasn't seriously hurt. I was looking around for some kind of justice and wasn't finding it. None of the Koreans in Taejon knew the traditional rules of basketball. They really didn't know how to play yet, how to create shots off the dribble, how to defend without clutching and grabbing. Their style was mostly spastic and rough, and I'd just had my wings clipped by it.

"This isn't basketball!" I yelled several times in Korean at my assailant, pleading for a purer version of the game, as though prison might be the place for it. It was all I could manage, and once again I was sure that it made me sound like an asshole. Several Koreans laughed when I repeated it. The gangster who was refereeing the game conferred with the factory captains. When the dust had settled, I was awarded the absurd number of four foul shots for my pain. Feeling slightly vindicated, though perplexed by the number of free throws, I went to the line and, not intending to but getting lucky, banked home all four shots off the backboard.

"*Oondong guuuuuuuut!*" Panjang Nim yelled across the wide space. Exercise was over. Peehyuk had won. No longer was Peehyuk a poor-to-middling team; we'd become an instant contender, and as we reentered the factory inmates young and old approached me, smiling with their thumbs up, paying me compliments. Despite a sore head and back, I felt better than I had in years.

≡≡

FROM THE EXERCISE grounds you could see the bent backs of grandfather hills over the walls. Chang Ho and I often practiced together. He copied me, learned a mean behind-the-back dribble, honed his jump shot. I soon became aware that a lot of inmates across the length of the grounds were watching me from the windows of their factories as I practiced. I soon found out that they were studying how I played, carefully observing each and every move. They themselves would sometimes tell me in the halls, "Tomasuh, I'm watching you and learning how to play. Watch out!" I'd watch during other factories' exercise how guys were trying out moves they'd seen me execute: dribbling between their legs, taking jump shots on the run, trying to protect the ball with their bodies. I saw the better and more athletic Koreans begin to slowly polish their games. All they'd needed was to see it done live. Most had never had that chance, nor even seen an NBA game on television. Many people ask me if, at six foot two, I was a giant out there. It's amazing how widespread the stereotype of the short Asian man is. While I was probably taller than the majority of the Koreans in Taejon, I was certainly not the only tall guy. There were a fair number of guys easily as tall as me or taller, and many who were more powerfully built.

In the ensuing months our team took on the garment factory, the toughest group of athletes in Taejon and the usual winner of the prisonwide fall tournament's overall crown. They had the young gang lifer Kwon Ahn, a chiseled and superior athlete, the sports god of the jail. But we could beat them. We could handle the woodworking factory, whose best player was Joo Shik, the

Korean-Chinese lifer from our block. The printing factory was another top-notch squad, with a Filipino who had played a lot before and Na Moon, a gangly Korean who stood about six foot three and learned the game fast enough to become a headache on both sides of the court. The sewing factory seemed to have no fit men.

Opponents were always gunning for me. Seeing that I had a temper and would sometimes lose focus if I became angry, opposing teams would play us using that as their strategy. This worked for a while, until I realized they were playing me like a puppet. Gang Guy pulled me aside one day and told me, "Don't get angry when they keep fouling you. Just stay controlled." I made a conscious effort from then on to prepare myself mentally before games: they're going to climb all over you, I'd tell myself; they're going to keep holding you and hitting you to try to piss you off. Preparing myself this way meant there were no surprises and I kept my cool. Our opponents didn't always.

In one game against the exasperatingly long and quick Na Moon and his printing-factory team, we went down to the wire with the game up for grabs. Close to the end, with the score still tied, I smashed knees with Na Moon as he tried to drive around me. I came up lame, unable for the moment to walk on that leg due to the shock to the knee bone. As I limped off the court, the action was halted and the chatter of the spectators died down. But one of the printing factory's players began jumping up and down at the center of the court, yelling, "He's injured, he's hurt, he's hurt. We won! We won!" It didn't really bother me; in fact, I thought the guy's naked display of how much he wanted to win was funny. But Gang Guy and Charlie were furious and they started to tell the guy off. Gangsters stepped in from both sides and began pushing and shoving each other before Panjang Nim broke it up with one of his fearsome shouts: "Stop fighting, you fuckers!" I appreciated the way my teammates had stuck up for me. The guy who'd celebrated my injury had hit a nerve with my

Peehyuk gang, because a week after the incident they were still cursing him. Other printing-factory workers seemed ashamed of what had happened and came up to me to offer their apologies for the behavior of one of their own. It was vintage Confucian class, even among convicts.

I saw my star rise. On the way back to the cells at the end of each day, inmates from other factories, guys I'd never seen before, started calling to me as we passed each other in single file on opposite sides of the hall. "Tomasuh, nonggoo good! Nonggoo numba one!" I'd get nods, thumbs-up, and approving smiles before they disappeared down the line. Soon they were calling me *nonggoo hwangjay,* basketball emperor. Guards began to call out to me as I passed them and to clownishly pantomime the dribbling of a ball. Called to the education office to give an English lesson a year later, I was surprised when an older, dignified political prisoner I'd never seen before gestured to me and told everyone in the room, including several high-ranking officers, "The entire prison has learned basketball from him." They all nodded their heads at me as though I were really something special, the Taejon kid, basketball emperor of all Hades.

# 30

WALKING SINGLE FILE through the hall, I feel myself stick close to the wall like a well-trained animal. As always, I'm jolted back to life at the very point at which the hall ends and I step out, following the man in front of me, into the open space of the factory grounds. The peacock gives a cry, *Wooaaaoooohhhh!* As we reach the front of Peehyuk, two young guys from our factory are just arriving from the kitchen with large silver vats and blue buckets full of barley rice, kimchi, and seaweed soup. The greetings begin. This is more than just a formality, I know now. This is Respect Central. This is where I can make my life in here a whole lot easier, just by bowing generously, giving respectful hellos and good mornings. *"Annyong hashimnika,"* I say to all the Peehyuk workers I know as they arrive. *"Chal chaso?"*—Did you sleep well? my older brothers ask. *"Yeh, chal chasumnida,"* I answer them respectfully. "A fresh pleasant morning to you," I say to a funny character that Chang Ho has nicknamed Stone Wall because of his bricklike build. He doesn't expect me to know this greeting. "Yaaa, Tomasuh, good one." *"Shabaherr,"* I say to Tracey. He greets me in Korean as we shake hands. We sit down at our table in the front corner by Peehyuk's open office and the guard's desk, which is raised up on a kind of dais so that he can see everything going on at all times. It's early to start the day like this, but out comes our *yoot nori* board, a square piece of cardboard with round dots drawn around its perimeter and crisscrossing through its center. It's an old Korean game, played on special holidays. The traditional version of it entails throwing foot-long wood sticks in the air to determine the number of spaces one can move one's pieces. We make do with a smaller board, little black and white buttons for pieces, and instead of long sticks, four little wood chips. Green, having been up all night staring at his walls, has plopped down in his chair with a sigh.

"I got to tell you guys about the epic dump I took this morning."

"I don't want to hear it, you demented bastard." I cut him off before he can get going, but this has already been enough to cheer him up, and he laughs himself red in the face. The whole motley crew of eighty is still filing in, making for their sections throughout the factory. Through our windows I can see blue lines of men, like ants, entering the other factories around us.

"*Chum-guuummmmm,*" Panjang Nim calls out over the noise, announcing the first inspection and head count, one of at least six during the day. We straighten our jackets and line up in neat rows in front of the double doors. I can see out into the exercise grounds and see the kaejang approaching from the central outpost, across the dirt at a brisk, authoritative pace, his stiff blue hat, the pins of rank along his collar, the folder in his hand, all getting slowly larger as he nears. Our factory tamdang looks us over. One of the guys flicks the ear of a younger Korean in front of him. Kaejang steps into the factory and tamdang bellows in his best stern voice, "Be quiet!" Then he turns to the kaejang, they salute each other quickly, and tamdang reports, "Seventy-three men, *kaejang nim!*" Kaejang nods. Chang Ho yells out "One!" from his spot at the front of the first row. Min Chul follows with "Two!" and so on down the line with the escalating speed of a lit fuse until fat Bek Soo, in the eighth spot, daydreaming of God knows what at the critical moment, gets caught off guard and calls out "Nine!" The rest of us fight not to laugh out loud. Tamdang again yells for quiet. After our numbers are straightened out and the kaejang has gone, Panjang Nim calls out, "Ya, Bek Soo ya, you clown, get yourself together!"

I'd yelled out the wrong number during a morning count before, but like Tracey I would sometimes test myself and step up into one of the front-row positions when chumgum was called, just to get it right, to prove to the Koreans that I could do it.

Before we disperse to our different sections in the factory, Panjang Nim has something to say to us. Perhaps the most respected man in the prison, he is fifty and built like a brick wall, with a massive chest. In his former life he was the leader of a gang that controlled the Tongdae-Moon market area of Seoul. He'd lived the wrong way, he told us, by his fists and his power. His life sentence was the result of his having stabbed a man to death over an unpaid debt.

"Be good to each other, you fuckers!" Panjang Nim bellows at us as we stand in rows in front of him. He's referring to a fight the day before in Peehyuk in which one inmate hit another over the head with a chair. "Fight if you want to. Go ahead. But when you're in solitary you'll see how good you have it here in the factory," he thunders. "You can still make your lives harder in here. Each of you has to lead himself, watch himself, by your own mind control yourselves."

We never called him by his name; he was always Panjang Nim, Captain, to us, or, to the younger gangsters, Hyung Nim, a respectful form of address that means something like Esteemed Older Brother. When I met him, he was in his thirteenth year in Taejon. After our head counts in the factory, he would often stand in front of us and go red in the face trying to teach us how to live, to see things differently, to work hard, to embrace our prison lives. He was really the only person in the entire prison who tried to reach us in our minds, the only one who had the undeniable strength of character to make us want to listen. I always listened closely to try to catch his words, feeling that there was wisdom in him. He often spoke of the great battle we wage in the flesh, of how one could stand in that fray of eating and suffering, both caused and received, and still carry oneself with dignity.

"You cannot live halfway!" he would warn us sternly. "Do you think life is easy outside? Don't fool yourselves. It's the same as it is in here. You have to work hard to survive; you must be disciplined and constant. Half-assed will not get it done."

I had heard that Panjang Nim had left the gang world behind him, yet all the gangsters respected him implicitly. He was not only our captain, but also the chief of all the factory bosses, almost all of whom were gangsters. The gang members in Peehyuk still came to his table before each meal and bowed to him, one after the other, wishing him a good meal with the highest respect. He'd sometimes mumble an acknowledgment, often without looking up. He wasn't caught up with the idea of his power and often seemed bored with the manifestations of it. He led by example, through hard work, fair play, and a hard-nosed acceptance of life in Taejon. He gave us room in Peehyuk—to read and walk around, to play games when we had no work, to put eggs in plastic bags and lower them into the hot-water heater. He didn't dominate or terrorize us, but no one dared cross him. His deep, rough voice alone was formidable enough to shake you if he turned it on you in anger. I saw him as an old Mongol warrior, a guy who would have fought with Genghis. Peehyuk was his relatively peaceable fiefdom.

The guards respected Panjang Nim because, though he gave us that bit of grace within the factory, he also brooked no bullshit. More important, the guards knew that Panjang Nim was highly respected across the various regional and city gangs with members in Taejon. He helped to keep the peace between them, to hold them together. The various gangs, in turn, helped to hold the prison together, enforcing their code of respect and obedience, ensuring that no non-gang inmates ever rebelled against the status quo.

Though not a gang member, Chang Ho attended to Panjang Nim the way the young gangsters did their elders: washing his clothes, bringing him his towel when he stepped out of the shower room, arranging his belongings in his personal box kept under one of the tables, taking care of his food, washing his dishes. In exchange, Chang Ho was untouchable and got to enjoy some of Panjang Nim's status and privileges. But their relationship was more than that: Panjang Nim was like a father to Chang Ho, and the latter an adopted son to the former. The mutual respect and understanding between the two was special to behold. It was feudal master and retainer, old teacher and his promising pupil. I knew Chang Ho truly admired Panjang Nim, and so I felt free to tell him how I liked the way Panjang Nim spoke to us and tried to make us think. I could laugh with Chang Ho as we imitated Panjang Nim's inspection commands, his brutal, hilarious vulgarity when he was angry. And I know Panjang Nim looked at Chang Ho with pride because of the way Chang Ho carried himself: avoiding trouble, bringing good energy to the factory, not wallowing in sadness or self-pity. He admired Chang Ho for his basketball skills, his ability in English—even though Gorilla Man never studied diligently—and his quick wit. Although Chang Ho felt lucky to be under Panjang Nim's wing, he wasn't obsequious to him. Panjang Nim didn't need or want that. Chang Ho would say sarcastic things to him, though carefully and always within limits. They would make fun of each other lightly or argue at times, over a game of chess or a missed order from the commissary or the state of Panjang Nim's clothes. When Panjang Nim stepped out of the shower room naked, water dripping down his body into his rubber slippers, he would sometimes shock us by saying something like, "Chang Ho, you little fucker, where's my towel?" He'd look over at us with a mischievous smile and wink as we began to laugh. He never talked to Chang Ho that way seriously. He didn't wield his power vulgarly or ostentatiously. He was parodying a kind of man that was common in the prison, the kind that he so easily could have been, but wasn't.

GREEN, TRACEY, AND I eat breakfast together at our table, bowl of barley rice for each man scooped out of the steaming silver vat, one bowl of communal kimchi for each table scooped from a blue bucket. In no time there's another call to attention and a head count. We wander back to our table and our yoot nori board.

"None of that calibrated-wrist shit today, Green," I say. "You won all those games yesterday only because you're cheating."

"Would you quit your whining, sweet cheeks?"

"You've gotta throw the pieces, man. You can't just turn your wrist and lay them down. It's bullshit." Panjang Nim walks by and gives us a look. We stop talking and wait to see if he'll order us not to play, but he only shakes his head. To him yoot nori is a silly game. Chess, that's a real man's game.

"Ya, Western fuckers, what are you up to?" It's Jang Soo at our table, looking to get in on the yoot. It was only a matter of time.

Jang Soo came to Peehyuk because Panjang Nim was one of the only authority figures in Taejon, guards included, that Jang Soo respected enough to obey. He'd been responsible for one of the very few cases of violence against guards that I heard of: demanding better treatment, Jang Soo had once taken a knife to a kaejang's throat and held him hostage in one of the prison offices. He had no release day and would most likely die in Taejon. He'd set fire to a house and killed several people. His own face, arms, chest, and neck consisted of severely burned skin that had healed into white and pink patches that looked like stretched rubber, or spackle that's been smeared and pushed in different directions. His eyebrows and eyelashes were gone. His lips were burned off. His hands were gnarled and badly scarred, but he could still use his fingers. He was allowed to wear a baseball cap in order to cover his scarred, raw-egg head. He was also allowed the special privilege of keeping birds in little cages in his cell. When he brought his sparrows and colorful cockatiels to Peehyuk, we'd scoop flies off the tables, throw them down hard to stun or kill them, then watch as Jang Soo's birds hopped over and ate them.

Being a murderer and burned up like he was, Jang Soo seemed to have let all pretenses go, and that made him maybe the most idiosyncratic, the most colorful, and the goofiest Korean I ever met. He was always cursing, slurring insults under his breath at people, cracking himself up, chuckling dementedly. He was small and thin, so you didn't worry about him, but you also knew you couldn't trust him. He loved playing yoot with Tracey, Green, and me, and I suspect that he might have felt more at home among us foreigners than with his fellow Koreans. Those were some of the most enjoyable moments I spent in Taejon: shouting with the suspense and fun of those games, telling Jang Soo to stop calling us sons of bitches when we were in the lead, catching him when he cheated. Some days we played yoot for hours on end. I can still see Jang Soo raising his burned and gnarled hand in the air in an imitation of the stick toss, challenging us to another game, or his lidless red-and-white eyes going wide whenever someone came from behind to beat him. "Ooohh fuck!" he would say with resignation, and scuttle away scratching his hairless head.

WE'RE JUST GETTING into our second game when Kee Jung, our doorman and lookout, yells out, *"Chagop!"* A truck loaded with materials has come through a gate on the far side of the grounds and is heading right for our front door. "Work is coming!" Panjang Nim shouts, and orders us all to our sections. The double doors are thrown open. I grab my tattered work gloves and head for the front. I'm not officially assigned to this duty, but I can't resist it: jumping into the back of the truck with Kee Jung and Tracey and a few other inmates, unloading the heavy bags of heels and soles, meeting the work head-on. I embraced the chance to throw my hands into something, to busy the body so that the mind could take a break. No one had to tell me to snap to it, to help out where extra hands were needed. I felt as though I had a storehouse full of energy and needed only something to pour it into.

Peehyuk's work was putting together boots and shoes used by Korean soldiers and riot police. We joked about how we might make them undetectably defective—skimp on glue so that the soles of a policeman's shoes might come off as he chased a suspect down the street. But productivity and quality were keys to keeping the contract with the outside company alive and our factory afloat. We had a vested interest in seeing it go well, then, as life in the factory, while challenging for us in all its Korean demands, was better than life in the cells. I was grateful to be in Peehyuk's wider space, the walls pushed farther back from my sides, to be able to eat with others, to see all around the wide grounds, to come and go each day from cell to factory, commuting as one would in the free world.

The heavy bags are carted in and divided up at each section. Il Hwan, who along with Chang Ho formed Panjang Nim's core crew, unlocks the tool cabinet and passes out hammers and mallets. I look at the men around me, these criminals, now with weapons in their hands. I watch how they hold them. But there is no violence with the tools. The work is the thing, and moving as one body—old inmates chipping in where they can, in ways their broken bodies will allow, Panjang Nim directing the action, we blue dwarves pummeling away our sins—we take up the task. The individual lives of our eighty-odd men are suddenly tied together, united by our shoemaking. Some of the men have done physical work like this all their lives, some never. Some hammer with skill; others struggle to get it right. At our section Tracey, several Koreans, and I are nailing black rubber heel pieces onto harder brown plastic ones. We hammer nails into eight holes in a half moon around each heel. Another man at each section wields a bit and mallet and, as fast as he can, smashes the nails down deeper in rapid-fire sequence. The final step is to tap the nail points down where they have come through the hard plastic part of the heels and throw them into the completed pile. They'll be bagged up, wheeled or dragged back out to the front, and loaded onto the truck when it returns at the end of the day to collect our labor—for which we are paid six hundred won, about eighty cents, a day. Off the truck will go to bring our work to the outside world, the dust of the exercise grounds chasing its wheels. We'll trudge back to our cells no worse for the wear.

With a hammer in my hands, I couldn't help thinking of Mom, carpenter that she was. I'd grown up seeing her and Pop hammering things, shelves, stairs, wood floors, desks. There were always hammers and nails of all sizes in the garage and basement. So as I worked away at our table in Peehyuk, paying my debt, I wondered if Mom would be hammering faster than me. I thought she could probably beat even the fastest of us with the mallet and bit. She'd put us to shame with sure and steady swings. These thoughts drive me on. We're going fast now, ripping like a revolution through our bags, our crew, like the others, heads down and determined. We take turns with the mallet and bit; those require a special touch and lightning speed, *bang bang bang bang bang bang* across the tops of the nails. Tracey and I race each other, competing to see who is faster. Hours pass. We still have several bags remaining, but I'm not discouraged. I don't give a damn about the eighty cents a day, about working away in this factory buried in a South Korean prison. The alternative is rotting in the cell. I put my head back down into the black-and-brown heels, the nails in loose piles atop the heavy, pitted plastic boards we worked on—to protect the tables, on which we also ate—the nails wearing down the skin of my index fingers and thumbs, leaving them tender, my hand getting tight from gripping the hammer too long, reminding me of the cold in Uijongbu, my frozen hand unable to write.

My ears are filled with the irregular beats of dozens of hammer blows, rising and falling, the metallic cacophony filling our factory. It'll be done when it's done, I tell myself. Keep your head down and in it. This is the ironwork of time. I'm above the mythical anvil, the hot furnace of life raging beside me. *Bang bang bang bang bang,* eight more in a half-moon to join the heels, throw it to the mallet man, on to the next. *Bang bang bang bang,* throw it to the mallet man, on to the next. *Bang bang bang bang,* days nailed together, forming weeks—*il, wol, hwa, soo, mok, kum, toe*—weeks glued and nailed forming months, months stitched and bonded into years, hammering home the lesson of time, of works and days that no man escapes.

We got high on glue, inadvertently. A conveyor belt sat across the back of Peehyuk. While some men brushed glue onto the black rubber and leather soles, others stood at the opposite end of the machine. As the disembodied feet slowly made their way through the machine's covered section, lights inside heated the glue, sending its vapors throughout the factory. It got to the head and sent you for a loop—not a welcome kind really, though at first it was a novelty, Peehyuk's little chemical secret. Once the heated soles were through, we carefully matched black rubber pieces to corresponding leather ones and pressed them carefully together. They were then pressed in a vise, stacked into piles of ten, and tied round with plastic ribbon.

WE BREAK FOR lunch, clear off the tables, and eat together, chopsticks digging into our bowls of kimchi and soup. When we're done, and everything is cleaned up, each crew's bowls washed in the shower room—usually by the youngest inmate at each section— the boards come back out and land with thuds on the tables. Our work continues. As I pull my gloves back on, I look over at the guard reading a newspaper on his perch. Il Hwan, whom we've nicknamed Slim, is painting at a free table. He's a thin, nervous, intelligent man who can barely see without his glasses and is always sniffling. Like Chang Ho, he is one of Panjang Nim's right-hand men, and while they don't work with the shoes, they have other responsibilities.

Slim was serving life for murder. Jailed when he was around twenty, he'd lived almost half of his life in prison. His parents and most of the rest of his family had died while he was in Taejon, but Slim had found a new life in his mind and was determined to educate himself. He earned high-school and college equivalency degrees in Taejon, the last part of that intellectual quest while I was there. I helped him with some of his reading in English literature: Yeats, T. S. Eliot, Shakespeare. It was inspiring to read those writers again, so far from the Western world that gave birth to them, to see Slim's enthusiasm and talk to him about *The Lake Isle of Innisfree, The Waste Land, Macbeth,* the great themes of nature, time, death, and treachery in those pages, mirrored all around us in Peehyuk's crucible. But aside from my interest and encouragement, poor Slim was an odd man out in all that. Neither of us knew of any other Korean prisoner who was studying such things or who had any interest in them. Slim didn't mix much with the others and mostly busied himself quietly in his studies and painting. He once told me that he wanted to write a book about prison life under the ex-presidents Chun and Roh, when things were much tougher. He said I could help him translate it into English. The two ex-presidents had just been convicted of corruption committed during their terms and had been brought to the Seoul Detention Center. We wondered what block they were in.

Slim was about five foot ten and could jump, leading to his achievement of a cruelly brief bit of athletic glory when the rims of the basketball court were lowered and he found himself one of the few Koreans who could dunk. He never played basketball and couldn't even dribble the ball, but once he discovered that he could pull off the dunk, he did it over and over, jump-stopping awkwardly, his glasses nearly falling off his face, leaping, and just getting the ball over the rim to throw it down—over and over, with a look of absolute bliss on his face. A few days later the rims were raised. Slim took one look up at them and knew his time had passed. He went quietly back to being the bookish scholar.

He painted in the classical Chinese style, mostly mountains and water, or images of the "four gentlemen": orchid, chrysanthemum, plum blossom, and bamboo, traditional East Asian symbols of integrity and refinement. Prison officials began putting in requests for paintings, and Panjang Nim put Slim to work making them. Slim grew weary of it but couldn't possibly refuse. He even framed them and wrapped them in brown paper before Panjang Nim took them out of the factory to give to the guards. No doubt this was good for Panjang Nim, good for Slim, and maybe, in intangible ways, good for Peehyuk as a whole.

This reminded me of Joon, a young doctor fulfilling his military service, whom I'd met in Uijongbu Prison. From an elite family, Joon was about my age and had studied medicine at one of Korea's top universities. All the medical texts were in English, so he could speak it fairly well. In the afternoons he often came by the classification room to practice his conversation skills with me. His wife was pregnant, with twins, Joon once told me happily, though he seemed to temper his joy when he informed me that they were girls. Sons were more highly prized in society, regardless of what he personally thought. I always felt sympathy for Koreans when I saw the reality of the restraints, the sharp prejudices and value systems their relatively rigid culture forced them to live under. I didn't envy them that. I admired the way they endured it, though, made sacrifices, honored tradition, bore up under what was expected of them—I thought I should become more like that. In these ways Koreans seemed more mature and less selfish than Americans. Men had to go to the army. People married these their parents selected. Tradition usually won out over personal whim. So much of the bittersweet sadness in the Korean character and art seemed to arise out of that dynamic, a resigned acknowledgment that their dreams were, in a world of duty and unchangeable laws, impossible; that personal yearning caused the soul to bleed. And yet, naturally, a person could not stop dreaming, straying in desire and whim from what life required, and would eventually claim.

The prison's second-in-command had asked Joon for a paper on the process of fermentation that Joon had written while at university. The officer's son was now in school and needed to plagiarize something.

"I didn't want to give it," Joon had told me, "but I could not refuse. You can't change these old men. Just like my father. They are set."

On one occasion, one of Slim's paintings, along with a few other prison-made works, was included in an exhibit at an outside gallery. Someone bought Il Hwan's piece for about four hundred dollars. It was the first time in his life that he'd ever sold his work. I was excited for him, but Slim seemed to shrug it off. He was glad, but he wondered if it had been bought mostly out of pity.

Slim was in charge of Peehyuk's tool cabinet and held the key to it. He was beside himself one day when five razor blades, kept in the cabinet for us to shave with on designated days, went missing. By the end of the workday, they still hadn't been found. The factory doors were locked; no one was allowed to leave. Panjang Nim lined us up and said that whoever had the blades should come forward now or else things would get bad for all of us. All the workers from other factories had filed past on their way back to the cells. We scrambled around trying to find the lost blades. Guys even searched down in the drains in the shower room. It looked like we might spend the entire night in Peehyuk, and despite the tension, there was a thrill in having our normal routine so disrupted. And there was the intrigue: Who could have done it? Was a violent plan under way? Was someone going to get cut?

Was someone plotting suicide? Slim, shaking and sweating, finally thought to look in his other uniform jacket that was hanging in the locker room. There in a pocket were the blades. Everyone threw his arms up and sighed. Poor Slim could barely bring himself to look at any of us. Panjang Nim gave him a light smack on the head and cursed him with a smile.

WE BREAK FOR exercise. Here again Peehyuk is privileged because of Panjang Nim. We get fifty minutes of exercise a day, guaranteed. That's more than most of the other factories receive. Today is one of the rare days I decide not to play basketball. I feel like doing the leisurely stroll that many of the old or infirm or just out-of-shape Koreans prefer. I want to take it easy, step back, look at the sky over the walls, and observe what goes on. But no sooner am I out on my own in the dirt of the space than a young inmate, new to our factory, approaches me.

"Oh! What's this?" he says in *pan mal,* or informal speech, with a kind of condescending, mock surprise. "Are you American?" he asks, again in pan mal. It is disrespectful to use pan mal with a stranger, but he's betting that I won't know any better or call him out on it. But I've played this language game a thousand times now. It is the unavoidable language war, the most common form of aggression in Korean prisons. The Korean inmates were very quick to correct us and to make sure that we foreigners were speaking to them properly, but they also tried to take advantage of our ignorance of their language's nuances. While I understand that this new guy is probably genuinely interested in making some kind of contact with me, he's doing it rudely. He's made this less of an introduction and more of a power play, because by speaking to me in pan mal he's assuming a kind of superiority over me straightaway. It would be foolish, maybe even dangerous, to let this happen. If I refuse to respond, not wanting to be petty, I lose. I may be spoken to rudely and inappropriately by this guy from now on. Other inmates who overhear our exchange might assume they can speak to me the same way. They'll try to peg me into the role of the subordinate, to bully and order me around. They'll seize this cultural advantage dictated by Taejon's extreme version of the Confucian hierarchy of age. It is, therefore, a serious matter of face and place.

"How old are you?" he asks me. He's right at my side now, and still speaking in pan mal. I can see that he's around my age. Predictably, it was most often the young ones who came at us like this.

I take him down from the little perch he's made for himself. "Why are you talking to me in pan mal?" I ask him, in pan mal, delicious revenge. It stops him cold.

Like the other foreigners in Taejon, I went through this kind of Darwinian linguistic face-off so many times that I grew tired of it—constantly having to engage in what, to us, seemed like ego games and confining, marginalizing power struggles to determine who fit where in the ancient system. But we were trapped in this Korean milieu. We were smothered and drowned in it.

The Korean inmates all seemed to have learned the phrase "When in Rome, do as the Romans do." Their version of it, in Korean, translated as "When you've gone to Rome, follow Rome's law." They seemed very pleased to be nailing us with this locution straight out of the foundations of the Western world. We had little choice but to take it even further than that, to *become* Romans, as it were, and they loved us when we did. And the Korean inmates pretty much insisted that we did. "Follow our country's laws," they told us, making sure that we were showing the prison, and Korean society in general, the respect it deserved. In that way they were Koreans first and foremost, and convicts second. When we were different or didn't adapt, we met their strong walls. So we were forced to embrace the Korean way, to bend and be pliant, to efface for a time parts of our old selves. It was an incredibly difficult task, being like children again in that pressure cooker, learning from the rudiments up.

It was not rare to hear inmates in their fifties arguing passionately about who would be *tongseng*, the younger brother, and who would be *hyung*, the older brother, even if the difference in age was just a matter of months. (Koreans consider a baby one year old when it's born. One hundred days after the birth the family officially celebrates the child's first birthday. And that makes sense, if you begin counting time while the kid is forming in the womb. That womb time counts, that's aging, that's living, too, the Korean system seems to say, even though the child hasn't yet touched the earth.) In prison it made a big difference, as did any shred of advantage or power. Not all Confucian men are created equal. As trying as these battles were, however, there was an immense pleasure when we finally understood enough, and could speak enough, to demand justice in their language by invoking the very Korean code with which they sought to gain the advantage.

"How old are you?" I ask the new guy sharply in pan mal to drive home the point. If you gave your age first, the Korean prisoner would often put his age at a year or two older than yours—a dizzying coincidence.

"I'm twenty-five," he answers. I can't be sure this is true, but what's more important is that he said it with the respectful *yo* at the end. This is progress, a great linguistic leap forward. It means he's been chastened into speaking to me properly.

"Really? I'm twenty-six in Korean age. I was born in 1970. So I'm actually your hyung," I tell him. I'm the winner in this particular skirmish. "Don't speak to me in pan mal, you understand?" But the guy isn't so enthusiastic about talking anymore. Most of the fun has gone out of it for him. There were always those younger and those older; no one was without that balance. But it was clear that being the younger, the one who had to take shit and be spoken to in pan mal, was usually not as much fun. It is the nature of all inequality, I suppose, with everyone vying for the top that not everyone can have, a tilted race for a limited prize.

The new guy mumbles something and walks away.

I got better and better at this, and each time I held my own I felt my confidence grow, my sense of myself, especially the Korean version, strengthen.

AS WE'RE USHERED back into the factory when our time outside is up, a guard arrives from the education office with a stack of letters. They have to go to our factory guard first, but sometimes we can get to the stack before he does, before they are placed on his desk, and flip through the envelopes quickly to see who received what or if any has come for us. I always felt a jolt of excitement when I saw my mom's unmistakable geometric print or the distinct writing of my sisters, Aunt Mil, or Rocket. Their letters were bolts of lightning, flying out of a distant sky, entering our closed world through the thinnest of cracks, striking me with electric force. Along with visits, which we foreigners rarely received, letters were king, and receiving one gave an inmate a kind of favored glow, at least for a day. Letters said that a man was remembered outside, that he still had connections to the free world, that his life was more than just Taejon. You watched a man receive a letter and you were reminded of all the things he was or might still be besides a convict: father, husband, friend, businessman, lover, relative. It was so easy to lose sight of all that because of the way the system allowed us to be, in general, only convicts and inmates, shutting off other sides of us, limiting what was available for us to become.

Before turning the letters over to Man Yong or Chang Ho, the guard looks through them at his leisure, for his entertainment, in part, as they've already been inspected. Even after years of this, I still sometimes felt that little shock of violation upon looking up at the guard in his raised perch and seeing him casually opening up and looking through letters addressed to me, taking his sweet time, acting like they belonged to him. There were miraculous days on which I received as many as seven or eight. I'd smell the pages and the envelopes, hoping somehow to get a whiff of freedom's fragrance. Usually I'd open them right away and read them at our table, with Man Yong asking me for the stamps for his collection. But sometimes I would wait until I was alone in my cell to read them. Today I get one, from my sister Gillian. Chang Ho comes over to ask me what she wrote. I read several sentences to him.

"Do your sisters always call you Cullen?" he asks me.

I tell him it's the customary way. Panjang Nim happens to be walking past and he overhears us.

"Your sisters call you what?!" he says incredulously. "The disrespectful . . ."

Chang Ho and I laugh. They should call me Older Brother, he thinks, as it's done in Korea. I decide against trying to explain to him that if my sisters called me Older Brother I might feel more distant from them, and that what may seem casual or disrespectful is actually, to us, intimate and preferable.

WE FINISH WITH our heels and soles for the day. The conveyor is turned off. The bags of finished shoe parts are carted outside and piled into the back of the truck when it returns. The tools are returned to Slim, counted just as we are, and locked away again in the cabinet. I know that Slim had been hoping to be released as part of the annual August fifteenth amnesty, which just passed. Rumors had been swirling around Taejon about who might get lucky. Maybe someone had gotten Il Hwan's hopes up. But he's still among us.

"I cannot believe our government anymore," he tells me sadly when I ask him about it. He doesn't know if he'll ever be let out. A week before, he told me about a dream he had in which he was released and found himself wandering a nameless city, only to slowly realize with growing horror that the street he was on, along with all the other ones he ran to, were still somehow part of the prison.

As we're cleaning up and getting our uniforms straight, preparing to head back to the cells, we watch as the Demon Catcher weaves his spell around us. He's impeccably polite and there is a persuasive quality to his voice. None of this, however, fools anyone into thinking that he isn't out of his mind. He sees little demons everywhere—he tells you so if you ask him—around his own body mostly, encircling his head and feet, tugging at his arms, but also around other inmates, around chairs, in the locker and shower rooms, everywhere. He snatches them out of the air like a man being attacked by a swarm of bees, turning suddenly on his heels, waving his arms, clutching at the air, reeling his tormentors in, one stern hand over the other. He gathers them up in invisible bundles and throws them aside. He does this nonstop for hours, striding about Peehyuk like a mad paladin, waging his eternal apocalyptic battle. It's frightening how many demons there must be. This place is apparently crawling with them.

PANJANG NIM CALLS us to our final head count as horns sound over Taejon. He stands in front of our rows to address us.

"I tell you not to throw out juice boxes and ramyun cartons in the shower-room garbage can and today people do it again. I can't accept that. You are not fucking children! If one section doesn't have work, another does, go over and lend a hand. We are in here together! I can't do it alone. We have to clean this place together."

"*Yeh!*" we answer him in unison with the Korean affirmative.

"Oh, and we have a man going home tomorrow. Let's give him a hand and hope he lives well outside." We clap and the lucky man thanks us. Then we face the guard and salute: "*Keng seng!*"

we shout (hand up sharply to the forehead on *keng*, snapped back down on *seng*), from the Chinese characters for "new life." We would leave our old, corrupted lives behind us; we'd repent and relearn and be made new here, in the fire of oblivion. For me the words are unreal, a game, a challenge, and at times, the strongest phrase I'll ever utter.

We're out the double doors now. The light is fading behind the hills over the walls. I can see the top of block 6 waiting for us in the distance. Panjang Nim is standing in his brown first-class uniform out in front of Peehyuk. All the factory captains are in front of their buildings as the long lines of blue march past. As we go by him, each of us bows his head and shoulders. "*Sugohashusumnida*, Panjang Nim!" we say, telling him he did a good job. We're saying it to each other, too, with varying degrees of formality. At its best, it's an acknowledgment of each man's journey, each man's fight.

Before we leave the open grounds and enter the hallway, we stop to form lines in front of guards standing next to square pieces of wood with numbers painted on them. I line up behind the block that corresponds with the last digit in my number, 6125. When I get to the front, I slip off my shoes and step onto the wood block. I spread my arms at my sides, and the guard pats me down. They seem to always check our socks, but surprisingly they sometimes neglect the pocket of the jacket, one of the most obvious spots. We're able to bring back glue and nails and coffee packets. Today I have nothing to hide, as I stare straight ahead but not into the guard's face. I don't mind the patdown so much, but I feel my anger return if I see dislike or judgment or arrogance in the guards' faces. We're down the hall, thousands of us. Back on our floor in block 6, I see the other foreigners arriving. I wonder what it was like for Joseph in Paysun, or Joo Shik in woodworking, or Reza in the sewing factory. Good job, we tell each other. Newspapers and books are quickly shuttled from cell to cell. Shoes are stepped out of and left in the hall. More horns over Taejon as we step into our little private boxes, and then the last bang of the day as the so-jee or guard shuts us in. My last bit of fun before I'm truly alone involves the final head count. As soon as we're all in, the tamdang calls out inspection and then, when the chooeem arrives, he turns toward our cells and yells, *"Chariot!"*—Attention!—each guard with his own distinct voice, a variation on the theme (I appreciated it when they got creative). The guards salute one another; then the chooeem, his clipboard in hand, starts off at a brisk pace down the line of cells with tamdang following right behind him. If any of us is screwing around or not sitting properly, legs crossed under us on the floor directly in front of the door, the chooeem will stop short suddenly and yell at the inmate to snap to it. That reflects badly on the tamdang, and the chooeem might reprimand him, and then the tamdang will be pissed at us and may call us all animal fuckers.

My little game, which somehow made me feel empowered and helped me through the five thousand times I did it, was to be able to time the chooeem's pass. I could after just a few runs with a new chooeem more or less learn his speed and be able to gauge how much time I had from the start of his inspection, his first step, to the moment he crossed my cell. I could take a peek out the window, if I was feeling bold, leisurely put my uniform jacket back on and button it, maybe take a drink of water, and then with a bit of satisfaction, calmly sit down and look up attentively at the window in the door just a fraction of a second before the chooeem passed, staring in at me, the flash of a stern, disembodied Korean face followed immediately after by the tamdang's. I felt like a master of the routine, and a part of this grand Korean penance, this soul-and-shadow play. Another point against my total, another step closer to home.

## 31

"YOU, I MEAN, you've got a family waiting for you. You've got Rocket. What have I got? Nothin'." Green and I were talking at our table in the factory.

"There's a lot you can still do. What about taking pictures? You could do something in photography." He'd put a lot of energy into taking pictures when he was stationed in the Philippines, and he'd taken a lot of shots in Korea.

"Come on, once people know what I did, they'll never give me a chance. They'll fucking run away. My family, whatever's left of it, they've disowned me. My one aunt still writes me, but the rest of them . . . in my family if you're in trouble they just throw you to the wolves. No, man, what you did was nothing. People think it's cool. You don't understand."

"When you get out, you'll be, what, forty-something. You can start over," I told him.

"What would I do on the outside?"

"I don't know, but you should give yourself a chance, man."

"I don't mind being here," Green said. "It reminds me of basic training. The reveilles, all the rules. It's the same deal. I'm used to it."

I REMEMBER HOW surprised I was when I first heard myself telling other inmates that they could start again. But if you think about it, I'd say, you'll be fifty or however many years old, and you'll be out. You might have half your life left, or twenty, thirty years. Whatever it is, this isn't the end. I think I might have started saying this just to give guys hope, but later I could feel myself starting to actually believe it. Before prison I never thought in terms as long as years. I was even scared by the thought of a one-year teaching contract. And now I was telling guys that after fifteen, twenty years in prison they'd still be standing. I could see them—myself, too—at the other end of this. Life was huge and I could see more of its breadth now, its start and middle, on toward its end, a trajectory guided by all the units of time we live, just like our sentences. They had the same shape. They asked you to keep going forward; to take what you had, whatever skills, all the accruing weights and wounds, and keep carrying it all forward; and as I began to do so, I felt like I was beginning to see over the wall and the mountains, out into the wide open sea of what we'd be next.

I CAN'T SAY why I kept seeing the good in Green, child killer that he was, and felt the need to draw his attention to it. He reminded me of a little boy himself, a man-child waging one of the worst wars. So much had been stacked against him, and it seemed to me that he had never had much of a chance. I know that some succeed and rise high from there, but many never have enough of a line to pull them through. Green believed in the death penalty; he told me that he thought he should have gotten it. I don't think he considered himself damned, though. He clung to his Christian faith and looked for answers in it. Damned or not, he wanted to die. He was hoping to kill himself and seemed assured that he eventually would, somehow. For him this was just a fact of life, his life anyway. But he was haunted by the idea that the Church would judge his suicide as his final sin. That bothered him. He saw it more as mercy.

He often said I was lucky to have my family, lucky that I'd had the education I'd had. He was right about that. Both had given me words and a perspective with which to understand and assimilate prison. Philosophy, literature, language. All the things my parents had taught us growing up about using our minds, about taking lessons from experience. They got rid of our TV for several years, tried to teach us how to quiet our minds. They had given me so many tools. If life for me had ended in my mid-twenties in Korea, I still would have had all that. I was never more grateful. Green, like many of the other inmates, hadn't had that. He didn't even really know what manic depression was or how it helped to explain his weak memory, his problems with sleep, his death wish. He'd heard of it before but didn't know exactly what it meant or that he was living the life. I read about hormones in the brain that act as natural antidepressants and are released through exercise. I told him about this and encouraged him to study up on the disease. But Green wasn't very mobile and he was lazy and he ate too much. His sleep patterns were screwed up. He'd lie awake late, almost the size of his cell, sweating, staring at the walls or reading the Bible. Taejon's infirmary didn't have antidepressants. They would give Green little blue sleeping pills, but those only fucked him up. I got so fed up watching him edge closer to trying to kill himself in some foul way that I decided to press the embassy on the issue at our next meeting. I did, and it might have saved Green's life, for a little while.

The guards were remarkably nicer to us when they knew the embassy was coming to visit. It was the power in South Korea of our home country again, who we were, whiteys from the States. And still more than that, it was the Confucian ethic of keeping up good appearances. Speak well of Korea and Koreans, guards sometimes told me. When you leave Korea, say good things, they requested. I would smile and say I would. (On one such occasion, a high-ranking officer in his fifties told me that eight out of ten Americans are good and two are bad. I wasn't sure how he had me placed.) They cared about what the United States and the world at large thought about them and their country as a whole. The embassy visited us about three times a year, and when they came it was incredible to watch the guards become gentler and more careful with us, a little extra cushion that was expressed in subtle ways, such as how they looked at you in the hall or how they spoke when they gave you an order, their tone of voice, their physical presence. Green and I and the several Korean Americans who were U.S. citizens floated on air those days. The whole event was mostly just an appearance, a kind of gesture, but that was precisely the kind of thing our Korean hosts responded to and tended to respect. To them, the visits showed somebody had our backs.

I spoke up during the next visit and told the consul that Green was sick and needed help that Taejon simply couldn't give him. He was going nuts, and it could be a problem for everyone. He was severely manic-depressive. Green didn't object to what I was saying, just sat there solemnly without saying a word. During the following visit, I pressed the embassy again. Taejon was no place for anyone suffering from any kind of serious illness. It wasn't uncommon for us to hear that a man had died in the infirmary or in his cell—diabetes, heart attacks, the *chasang nims* who went peacefully of old age. At the infirmary you stood in a long line until it was your turn to sit in front of an overworked doctor in a white coat at a little wood desk. He had a couple of prisoner assistants and a nurse or two, rare females. They were not attractive. (One of these ladies once gave me an injection in my butt cheek, through my pants. I took it kind of personally that she stood as far away from me as possible, as though I was contagious or nasty or dangerous—and yet the episode still managed to give me a strange little thrill.) The doctor listened to your most recent sad story, scribbled stuff down, and quickly prescribed some pills. Then your minute was up.

The embassy spoke to Taejon officials and arranged for Green to receive a supply of antidepressants. These helped him occasionally, but more often they gave him headaches or weren't strong enough or made him sleep too much or somehow didn't agree with his system and left him feeling the same or worse. Because it was hard for him to move around a lot or exercise to get his blood flowing, he always had problems with frostbite in the winter. It would get to his ears, his hands, and, especially, his huge feet. (The Koreans were susceptible in the winter to getting red sores that looked almost like burns on their lips and noses.) He started becoming obsessed with fresh vegetables, and he complained enough, scaring several guards with his vehement, insistent requests for raw cucumbers and carrots and onions, that they gave in and started bringing him what he wanted. The Koreans didn't seem to know what to make of Green and regarded him with what looked like a strange mixture of tolerance and disgust. Yet all the while he was doing a lot of headwork, in fits and starts, fighting through all the debilitating shit that held him back. I was proud of him for that. He told me that he knew his wife wasn't to blame. He understood better how his family had screwed him up. He'd done some reading into manic depression. He called himself an alcoholic. He told me that he saw clearly now how screwed up he was around the time he killed his boys.

He'd try to study Korean, even Chinese characters, taking them up every few months. He knew a small collection of phrases in Korean but could never seem to advance beyond that. "My memory's shot, dude," he'd say. "Too much beer. But you, you surprise me, man. The memory you got. You and your big words. If you didn't write 'em down I'd be lost." Someone back home had gotten me a subscription to the *New Yorker*. After reading through them and looking up and writing in the pages the definitions of words I didn't know, I'd pass the magazines on to Green. He was no dummy. Even though he'd lived in Korea for more than ten years and had a Korean wife and yet couldn't speak much Korean at all, he was the best Chinese chess player among the foreigners. He spent much of our downtime in the factory squaring off against Panjang Nim and various old-timers. Green said it was harder than Western chess, more difficult to learn. But he gave himself to it fully and gave those old-timers—just like the ones I used to like to watch in Seoul's Pagoda Park—some good competition. They appreciated Green for that, for his interest and ability. I liked watching him, big-headed pale Polish giant, his face tense with concentration, surrounded by old Korean men in various frozen states, silent, all eyes on the battle below.

Green cut his wrists late one night. He didn't have a razor, only a crude piece of glass, so he couldn't cut enough. Maybe he didn't want to go all the way through with it; maybe he lacked the courage—though I'm not sure if it's courage that's required. It was sad and a little sickening for me to see the raw, red gashes on his wrists. Panjang Nim welcomed him back to Peehyuk a week later. Green was still in a daze. Everyone knew they were dealing with a wounded animal. Some of the Koreans approached him, stuck their fingers in his face, shook their heads, and, with a mixture of sincere care and harsh censure in their voices, told him, "Don't do that. Just stop it." It was at times like that that I loved the Koreans for their stark and unambiguous morality. Green's situation, however, was not so simple. I knew he needed to go to a different facility. The next time the embassy came, with Green sitting before the two consuls with bandages still on his wrists, looking down at the floor, we made a good case for why we needed help in getting him transferred as soon as possible. The embassy came through. They must have appealed to Taejon officials or the justice ministry. Green was soon taken out of Taejon and transferred down to Chinju, meaning pearl, a city near the southern coast. I'd asked my mom if it was all right—she was wary but trusted me when I vouched for Green—then gave Green her address so that he and I could communicate through her. I was sad to see him go.

## 32

THE FIRST WESTERNER known to have been held captive in Korea was a Dutch sailor by the name of Hendrik Hamel. (While Hamel is considered the first, he did report in his journal that there was another Dutch captive there when he arrived.) In 1653 he and a few dozen other survivors washed up onshore after their ship, the *Sparrowhawk,* ran aground off what was then known as Quelpaert Island and is today Cheju Do, the vacation island off the Korean Peninsula's southern coast. Hamel kept a journal of the thirteen years he and the others spent in captivity before escaping to Japan. It is the first European-language book written about Korea. In it Hamel says they were not allowed to leave the country because the Chosun dynasty court wanted to keep Korea secret from the rest of the world.

In *Corea: The Hermit Nation,* published in 1882, William Elliot Griffis offers a translation of Hamel's journal and uses available sources in a number of languages, including Korean, along with his own experiences in the Far East, to examine punishment and penal customs in the late Chosun dynasty.

The inventory of the court and the prison comprises iron chains, bamboos for beating the back, a paddle-shaped implement for inflicting blows upon the buttocks, switches for whipping the calves till the flesh is raveled, ropes for sawing the flesh and bodily organs, manacles, stocks, and boards to strike against the knees and shin-bones. Other punishments are suspension by the arms, tying the hands in front of the knees, between which and the elbows is inserted a stick, while the human ball is rolled about. An ancient but now obsolete mode of torture was to tie the four limbs of a man to the horns of as many oxen, and then to madden the beasts by fire, so that they tore the victim to fragments . . . For some crimes the knees and shin-bones are battered. A woman is allowed to have on one garment, which is wetted to make it cling to the skin and increase the pain . . . When an offender in the military or literary class is sentenced to death, decapitation is the rather honorable method employed. The executioner uses either a sort of native iron hatchet-sword or cleaver, or one of the imported Japanese steel-edged blades, which have an excellent reputation in the peninsula.

In Griffis's somewhat imperialistic and condescending view, Chosun was a "semi-civilized nation." But he notes that things had improved greatly since Hamel's days in Korea. Back then, according to Hamel, a husband usually killed his wife if she had committed adultery. A wife who murdered her husband was buried to the neck in the ground at the side of a road so that passersby could strike her head with clubs and axes if they felt like it. Thieves might be trampled to death. One of the worst punishments consisted of pouring vinegar down the criminal's throat and then beating him until he burst. However, Griffis also reported that, since Hamel's time, among the "many improvements on the old barbarous system of aggravating the misery of the condemned," there was one surviving practice, a "disgraceful form of capital punishment, in which the cruelty takes on the air of savage refinement":

The criminal's face is smeared with chalk, his hands are tied behind him, a gong is tied on his back, and an arrow is thrust through either ear. The executioner makes the victim march round before the spectators, while he strikes the gong, crying out, "This fellow has committed [adultery, murder, treason, etc.]. Avoid his crime."

ABOVE PEEHYUK, PEGGED to the white façade in large blue Korean characters, was a line from Francis Bacon: *Be true to yourself.* The sticky problem was that many of the prisoners had been exactly that, I thought to myself as I walked under it every day, true to their devious, greedy natures. Above the woodworking factory, Goethe: *Life is love and that life is spirit.* I spent a lot of time trying to parse out the translation of that one. It still seems a little too cryptic. In the halls and above certain offices there were proverbs and exhortations, little maxims hanging from blue signs, smiley faces with *New Heart* written in place of teeth. *Love of neighbor, Respect for parents* was hanging above the entrance to our block 6. Every day coming back from the factories I saw it and thought of Mom and Pop, thought that I would treasure their lives more when I got the chance. It was a rudiment of Confucianism that I hoped would seep into my character. I certainly took some of it with me, and have been a better son since. *Deference is a virtue:* another Confucian correction. *As you would yourself, forgive others,* another sign read. There were many others, and I set myself to try to understand what the authorities were trying to teach us.

*When faced with the opportunity of an advantage, weigh its righteousness:* that's a damn good piece of advice really.

*Instead of shouted slogans, take action to achieve the goal.*

*The greedy, the gluttonous, through control and moderation, can overcome.*

*The mirror by itself does not become dirty.*

In front of the kitchen, where I once thought I saw a man standing up to his knees in a vat of kimchi the size of a swimming pool: *The sea receives all waters.* This was my favorite. It seemed open to various interpretations, and I worked it over in my head during the course of several weeks. I concluded that it meant that a wide and wise heart accepts all things, even dirty streams and rivers, which the larger body can absorb and assimilate without becoming dirty itself. It made me think of the Dalai Lama, whose divine title is sometimes translated as "Broad Ocean." That was how I wanted to be, broad enough that my years in Korea would open my eyes and prodigiously increase my volume of experience, of things felt and seen, without leaving me stained or bitter. Open and yet unspoiled, like a big sea. Reading *Soledad Brother: The Prison Letters of George Jackson,* a fascinating perspective on prison life and American society as a whole in the 1960s, I came across his inclusion in a letter to his father of a quotation of Mao Tse-tung's: "In shallow men the fish of small thoughts cause much commotion, in magnanimous oceanic minds the whales of inspiration cause hardly a ruffle." "Oceanic minds," that aquatic metaphor for wisdom, just as in Taejon's hall.

This was by no means the first time I'd seen something in a piece of prison literature that floored me and had me shaking my head. It's always amazing to me to see how across time and re-gardless of place the experience of imprisonment retains a consis-tent echo—whether it be George Jackson's letters, Solzhenitsyn's *One Day in the Life of Ivan Denisovich,* Mandela's account of his nearly three decades behind bars, Henri Charrière's *Papillon,* Brian Keenan's *An Evil Cradling,* Joseph Brodsky's reflections on his time in the Gulag. Marco Polo, imprisoned during a battle in Italy after he'd returned from the East, is said to have whispered the stories of his adventures to Rustichello through a chink in the walls of their cells. So many lines that remind me of things that I've thought or felt or written down in regard to the experience. Speaking in all humility, I say it's a true brotherhood. It's some of the best stuff I read.

LOVE EACH OTHER, *help each other, believe each other*: this senti-mental trio was all over the place, in the halls, in the mouths of captains and guards, writ large on the wall at the side of the stage in the auditorium. Sometimes I could truly feel them at work. We were all Korean brothers then—waiting in the factory for the first inspection in the early-morning cold, before the sun was up, all of us jogging in place as Panjang Nim led us in the chant *"Tongsang yaebang! Tongsang yaebang!"*—Frostbite defense! Or when the Sampoong department store in Seoul collapsed during a busy afternoon, and Taejon authorities played us a live radio broadcast of the ongoing search for survivors as it stretched into the night. We stayed up late listening in our cells. Five hundred people died. Every time the radio broadcaster excitedly reported that another survivor had been found in the wreckage, you could hear cheers and joyful shouting explode from every corner of Taejon, echoing across the blocks and through the dark empty halls—a night I'll never forget.

Some of the messages were insultingly trite, of course. I hated when the guards, fat, happy, and warm, would glibly tell us to mind our health. "Nothing more important than your health. Stay healthy," they constantly reminded us. Thanks a lot, fellas, I thought after hearing it for the thousandth time, I'll try to remember not to get ill and die in here. Oh, and by the way, thanks for stacking the deck in our favor. After the morning horns woke us each day, the speakers hidden behind the light panels in the cells broadcast the sound of birds and running water. Then a gentle Korean voice would announce what day it was and tell us to stay healthy. In the evenings, after a few maudlin Korean folk songs played, the voice read us epigrams by the likes of Lao-tzu and Emerson.

I think the vast majority of guys simply walked by these signs and listened to the messages day after day for years without paying them any mind, in many cases without ever ingesting them. The voices and slogans just blended into each other, were repeated so often that they faded far into the background. It was the same with our constant pledge to begin new lives. After shouting *"Keng seng"* for months and years, you often lost track of what exactly it was you were saying. The phrase ceased its life as a thought in your head and became just words in your mouth. And like that, the lessons would be lost, the promises forgotten. When I asked Slim and Chang Ho to help me translate the signs in the halls, they kind of laughed at me and seemed to be looking at them for the first time.

The main rehabilitative part of the prison was *chung shin kyo yuk,* the annual two-week "mental training" that every Korean inmate went through. We foreigners never did. The logical guess is that the authorities simply determined that we'd be unable to understand the group lessons and lectures. But I wondered if they also decided not to bother wasting their very limited time and energy on inmates who were marked for deportation as soon as they'd done their time. We weren't going back out into Korean society, after all. When I asked Chang Ho about the mental training, he described it as more of the same, exhortations to respect one's parents, obey authority, abide by the rules, stick to the conventional routes society had sanctioned. "It's nothing new," he told me, and left it at that.

DURING THE STIFLING summers, I meditated on the mosquitoes as they came to hang out with me in my cell and suck my blood. Nets for our windows always came late, leaving us for several months a year at the mercy of all manner of flying beasts, the mosquito the most persistent and disturbing among them. The fluorescent lights in the cells drew them in, or maybe they could smell our warm stench wafting out over the fields. If it's light they want, why don't they just fly off to chase the sun? I thought. That's some light for them. But no, it was light in darkness that they especially liked; they needed that mingling of opposites, the contrast, the fastidious little madmen.

The lone spider near my light looked engorged and exhausted. Maybe he was disgusted by the sight of so many mosquitoes hanging in his silk. A catch and a meal is one thing, but a living room full of bodies? The searchlight on the outer wall near my cell revealed a hideous reality. In its conical shaft of light carved out of black floated a sea of terrifying things, species I've never seen before, ones that may yet be undiscovered, flying out of Taejon's fields to hover at the walls. Some of them looked as large as hands, with huge wings and hideous buzzing. We were sitting ducks and you could only pray that they didn't randomly make your night hell.

As I smashed the mosquitoes into my walls and dreaded them in my ears at night, they buzzed their way into my thinking. I thought about why I slaughtered the mosquito but let the spider live, even rooted it on. Well, I kill the mosquito because it drinks blood out of my body; I kill it in self-defense. But the mosquito is only following its instinct and biology, its nature, I countered, playing devil's advocate, smearing another into my cheek. It was incredible to watch how smacking them did nothing. Didn't they see me right in front of them hammer three of their buddies into bloody smears on the wall? Don't they know that their odds aren't good against me, that scores of them are going to get crushed like little toy helicopters? This, of course, made no difference. It must be the most recidivistic, irredeemable fucking animal in all the world, I thought. Perhaps that's the truth of it, but not the end of the story. With nets I don't have to kill them. I can avoid the confrontation by anticipating and defending against them. I keep them away and save us both the blood loss.

Like the mosquitoes, we convicts were too many, and we just kept coming. How to reach men like Big Green or a kid like Chang Ho? Time and a serious bond; a huge and personal commitment of time and effort. Who can do that? I thought. Who has the energy for such a colossal task? There aren't enough guards. What teacher or psychiatrist wants to work in a prison? Who has the intelligence and grace and will to sit with such stigmatized and difficult men, each individually in his turn, and try to reach them in their hearts and heads? A system designed for thousands cannot do it. It is as if each man, each criminal, requires a treatment of his own, one tailored to his specific inclinations and traits, a system that appeals to him personally, that gets at him from the inside, using keys that may fit only him.

Too many of us and we simply get lost. It is the bittersweet tragedy of life: not enough love, care, or interest to go around. I saw this written across Korea, in the faces of her criminals, her unwanted and lowest. Look into any institution—schools, hospitals, prisons—and it's easy to be overwhelmed by the sheer tidal mass of need. I realized that I didn't envy the government its job, not the Korean justice ministry or any other, to be the caretaker and manager of society, charged with pressing back against the force of so much damage and neglect. I wouldn't want the job. I knew how hard it was for me to open up to some of the other inmates, how often I simply had no energy or stomach for it, how often I had chances to reach out to the others, to talk to them, to show them a bit of friendship and care, and how seldom I did it. So many missed chances, so much sadness and failure.

# 33

As I stood considering the walls of solid stone, two or three feet thick, the door of wood and iron, a foot thick, and the iron grating which strained the light, I could not help being struck with the foolishness of the institution which treated me as if I were mere flesh and blood and bones, to be locked up. I wondered that it should have concluded at length that this was the best use it could put me to, and had never thought to avail itself of my services in some way. They plainly did not know how to treat me, but behaved like persons who are underbred . . . As they could not reach me, they had resolved to punish my body . . . Thus the State never intentionally confronts a man's sense, intellectual or moral, but only his body . . . It is not armed with superior wit or honesty, but with superior physical strength.

—Thoreau, *"On the Duty of Civil Disobedience"*

GODFREY THE NIGERIAN, one of a crew of six that bought heroin in bulk in Thailand, swallowed little bags of it, and sold it throughout Asia and Africa, had been a friend of Billy's when the Kid was in Taejon, and so I gave him the benefit of the doubt. He seemed gentle and soft-spoken, but you could see the time wearing on him, and very subtly his smile shifted from friendly to crazed. He quit work in the garment factory. They shouldn't have let him, because as soon as he was back spending twenty-three hours a day in his cell, his mind began slipping faster.

He kept asking the rest of us, very politely, to lend him stamps, paper, and envelopes. He had no money left, he told us, and had used up all his supplies. Convinced that his sentence was four years, which he'd just passed, and not the six that was written on the little plastic identification strip outside his cell, he was furiously writing letters to the Nigerian embassy and the Korean justice ministry. It seemed as though, feeling his brain slipping, he'd desperately begun to look for a way out before the damage set in. But the Nigerian embassy looked into it and confirmed to Godfrey that his term was six years; there was never any doubt about it. Godfrey would hear none of it, though, and said that if they didn't let him go he was going to stay in his cell for the next two years to show "what they've done to me." It was terrible to helplessly watch him struggle against the poison in his own head, not least of all because the rest of us knew we were vulnerable to the same thing. We tried talking to him. Godfrey would smile shyly, almost like a little boy, look away, and say, "I'm doing all right. I'm okay." Guys told him to go back to work, to settle down and try to relax and do his time. He wasn't so far from the door now, if he could just hold on a bit more.

He no longer spoke to his West African accomplices, the four other Nigerians and the wily older Liberian—too many suspicions and grievances. They didn't trust one another. Paranoia set in. Godfrey slept too much. While asking me for stamps one day, he told me in a whisper that at least four times guards had passed by his cell late at night and thrown something in at him. I asked him what they threw, and he asked me if I believed in shamanism, powers of the spirit. He insisted that the guards were trying to drive his spirit out of his body while he slept. He swore they were poisoning his food and had arbitrarily added two years to his sentence.

I spoke to our hall tamdang and section chief, warning them that Godfrey was in need of help. The officers shook their heads as if they understood, but they made almost no effort to get him out of his cell or to reach out to him. Korean prisons had no formal counseling, nothing of that kind for the foreign prisoners. The task the justice ministry set for itself was simply to hold us, as effortlessly and cheaply as possible, to sit on our chests and pin us down until they'd said we'd had enough. In court and during sentencing the ministry seemed to have all the answers, to know exactly what was needed for our lives. But when some of us cried out for help in prison, the master was nowhere to be found. The ministry had no answers then. They couldn't understand Godfrey's accented English much, his native Ibo not at all. They didn't want the dirty job of dealing with his delusions.

Not long after, late one night when it was dead quiet, Godfrey suddenly cried out and began smashing his door, screaming, "Why do you want to poison me? They're killing me!" He screamed that he wanted to die there in his cell, to die in Korea. Awakened, the rest of us kneeled at our doors as though in prayer and looked out into the hall. Godfrey continued raving and smashing his door. A group of guards hustled into our hall and opened up his cell. They told him to calm down, but he was past consoling. When two guards tried to grab him by the arms, he shrieked as though he were being stabbed. They dragged him out of his cell into the corridor as he desperately tried to fight them off.

"Foreign prisoner! Foreign prisoner!" he yelled, desperately trying to invoke their mercy. "You want to inject me!" he screamed. They must have tried to tranquilize him. The guards kicked and pulled him and tried to cover his mouth with their hands. It was terrible to watch. When they had him sufficiently subdued, they carried him by his splayed arms and legs out of our hall, his head dangling lifelessly. He looked like a corpse. I heard they put him in a restraining jacket and handcuffs and placed him in solitary. Shaken and unable to fall back asleep, I lay awake on my floor wrestling with thoughts of justice and madness as Godfrey's screams still echoed in my head.

A week later he was escorted back to our hall. I wondered if he was embarrassed by his breakdown, but then I thought of my own and realized that embarrassment was beside the point. Maybe it had been cathartic for him. When I got the chance, I went to his cell to ask him how he was. "Fine," he said, looking up from his spot on the floor. Then he put his hand over his heart and said, "My case is special here. I'm suffering." I told him to try to take it easy. He thanked me, and then as I turned to go he asked if I could lend him more stamps.

I REMEMBERED VIKTOR Frankl and his *Man's Search for Meaning* again. When I read it, I was a sheltered high-school kid in safe middle-class Long Island. I never could have guessed then the meaning Frankl's book would come to have for me, that I'd be in a place where its wisdom and guidance would strike me so profoundly. One of Frankl's ideas in particular kept returning. Despite the relentlessness and unyielding nature of the conditions they faced in the concentration camps, he said, what became of each man in the end was up to him. If this was true there, in a place of horror, brutality, and cruelty worlds beyond anything we faced in Korea, then it was certainly true for us. The final choice always belonged to the prisoner. What became of our lives depended less on what the authorities did to us, the specific conditions under which we lived, than on how each of us took them. And there was freedom in that.

The Filipinos Manny and Arnel took their fifteen hard. They had the easygoing languor of their sunny homeland, but the sentence had filled them with an underlying sadness. Manny had given a pair of sneakers and about one thousand dollars to a fellow Filipino, another factory worker in Korea, to mail home to Manny's mother. As Arnel told me, the guy never sent the stuff. So Manny and Arnel paid him a visit, which ended with one of them, or both of them, smashing the man's head in with a concrete block. When Arnel, a father of two, told me the story in the factory, I got the feeling that he might not have directly participated in the violence. It seemed to me that he was sickened by it. Manny seemed the more likely to run amok. I tried to size the two of them up, looking for clues as to who might have done what. I peered at all the convicted murderers, hoping to learn something. I'd parse through their seeming normalcy, try to pick my way past their pleasantries and ordinary ways, looking for the side of them that snapped. In most cases I never found it. I tried to imagine Manny, Arnel, and the other murderers passing me on the street in the free world and asked myself if, without knowing they'd killed, I'd be able to guess it just from looking at them, as though they might bear some clear sign of it on their surface. But there was little or nothing to distinguish them except the stories of what they'd done. They didn't seem so different from me, and I could see myself in them. I could see myself in a rage—like the rage I'd felt there in Taejon—with that brick in my own hands, set to smash it into some opponent's head. Manny and Arnel were no more violent than I was—less so, even; I was convinced of it. But I had never killed. For the first time in my life, however, I thought myself capable of it.

With the Korean murderers, things were even grayer. No doubt there were great pathologies there, degenerates and killers, wickedly manipulative men, men with destructive anger. But then they must have also been adaptable, or expertly submissive, because I could see no clear sign of those negative attributes. If they were once recognizably evil, I thought, they've since surrendered. I was struggling to discern what part of that was the result of the Confucian culture, and what part of it was the fundamental nature of all men. How can a man seem to be kind, generous, and good and yet at the same time be a killer? I kept setting up such equations in my head, but finding no answers. It didn't make sense. Only with time did I see that men most often have both sides. The difficult truth was, as I found it, that the two poles are in no way mutually exclusive. A man may truly smile and smile and yet be a villain. What the other convicts with me revealed is that they were far broader in their characters and more complex than I might have guessed, certainly more so than the system acknowledged.

Daily and hourly I observed how murderers and thieves, rather than acting as I might have imagined they would, instead bowed and saluted and submitted dutifully to the rules. I often wondered if stable, law-abiding Korean citizens would have been able to recognize the Korean convicts with me as disturbed or wayward just from observing or listening to them. As a foreigner it was very confusing to see their consistent adherence to the commands given them, to see them behaving like children or sheep: whether lining up or kneeling or reciting factory rules or surrendering personal items or keeping quiet when told to or greeting and bowing to the guards respectfully or answering anyone in authority when called. When we were out of the guards' earshot, the Koreans sometimes cursed and made fun of the authorities, but those were just words.

The surface display of forms and appearances, carried out conscientiously, could be radically deceiving. It reminded me of how so many other foreigners and I in Seoul had believed that there really wasn't much crime in Korea. We'd look around and marvel at how safe it seemed, how predictable all the interactions were. I sometimes thought of this as the miniskirt dynamic. Young Korean girls in Seoul often dressed like sexual fantasies, with steep high heels and shockingly tiny miniskirts or super-tight jeans and flashy makeup. You could be forgiven for looking at them and guessing that they were naughty, freewheeling girls, but more often than not they weren't. Many of those girls abided by parental curfews and in many cases probably weren't very sexually experienced, if at all. The outer appearance was saying one thing, but the reality was quite another.

It was revealing for me to see that even in a homogenous culture with little or no ethnic, racial, or linguistic differences, where morality is stark and obedience to authority has deep roots, men still broke away and deviated, still committed all kinds of crimes. It seemed that no matter how insistently you define for a man what is good and what is against that good, his nature will do as it is inclined.

MANNY, A SHORT, stocky kid with a chubby face, was friendly and well liked. He was a good basketball player and had a great voice, honed in karaoke and at family gatherings in the Philippines. When I was in the cell next to him, I'd sometimes ask him out our back windows to sing for me. Into the sticky, then cold, then moonlit Korean nights he would belt out Whitney Houston's "I Will Always Love You" or Céline Dion's "Power of Love." He liked those big weepy ballads. These are female songs, I thought to myself, but in the hardened male world of Taejon, they moved me. The lovers and love in the lyrics represented everything we'd left behind, parts of us that had fallen out of use. They evoked bittersweet nostalgia. When Manny finished, we'd hear shouts of approval go up into the dusk from Koreans who'd been listening along, unbeknownst to us, in the cells below us.

Manny told me that when his father, a big shot in his town on Luzon, heard about his son's fate, he went nuts and charged into the street with a gun and began shooting it off wildly, injuring three people. Manny seemed to take this as a positive sign of his dad's love and concern. I thought of the Philippines and its culture of guns and machismo.

"If you speak Latin it protects you," Manny once told me. "Bullets won't even kill you. That's why the Philippine army uses Latin."

Not only was Latin not dead, apparently, but it was keeping people alive.

Ali the Pakistani, with his downturned mouth, under the weight of his twelve years, fell upon his Shiite faith, shouting oaths to Ali, his namesake, son-in-law of the Prophet—"'Li, 'Li,

'Li, Haidaaaar!"—screaming out that ancient Muslim invocation, sharply breaking the quiet of our lockdown days. Reza the Persian was unfailingly courteous with his *shabaherrs* and *shabhorshs*, but you could feel his sadness, too. He was innocent, he said. He hadn't raped his Korean girlfriend, he swore. They'd simply done what couples do, only he was a working-class Iranian doing menial jobs around Seoul, and she was a Korean girl whose family, the males mostly, as with many families everywhere, resented the foreign incursion. This opened serious historical wounds. Green often told me about how he and his wife were accosted on the streets, how Korean men seemed to purposely bump into them or would spit and say things like "traitor" and "whore" when they saw big whitey with a native girl. Reza described for me what he called his bad luck, how his girlfriend's brother had found out about their relationship and either turned the girl against Reza or raised the charge of rape himself. Reza's buddy Samad carried a great sadness, too. When Samad got word that his mother had died back in Tehran, the big gentle Persian wept and didn't come out of his cell for days. One by one over the course of a week, on our way back from the factories, the rest of us stopped by to express our condolences. Samad, jowly and sallow-faced, gracious and impeccably polite, stooped in the window of his shadowed cell and thanked us for our kindness, his hand over his heart. It meant something to him. A little humanity, even from such transient and wretched neighbors as us, was a welcome thing.

And while most struggled, men like Tracey and Joseph the Nigerian seemed to float right over the top of it all. Smiling, energetic, scheming, not a moment of weakness revealed, not a chink in the strong armor of their character: these were men who wore their punishments lightly. As others sank, they rose, and seemed to reach higher still as some, like Joseph's former associate Godfrey, went under around us. After work, locked back in our cells, I'd look across at Joseph, his smile filling his window, his huge head and shoulders dwarfing the space. Somehow the cell didn't seem to hold him. I'd shout, *"Reeany off ma!"*—his Ibo for "Have a good meal." He'd say it back, then give me the wolf cry, his name for his defiant, big-toothed howl. He'd let it rip as a celebration of life, as an expression of his joy. His seven years could have been fifteen or twenty, I think, and I would have found him just the same, larger than life, bigger than Taejon. Maybe he'd found that strength there. Maybe he'd always had it in him.

MOST GUYS DIDN'T seem to change. Their old ways just kept coming back. They angled toward one another, tried to get close, sat at one another's tables in the factories at "meetings" to discuss business with fellow traffickers, gangsters, and frauds. That stereotype of prison is dead on, of course, even in a Confucian one, where everyone had submitted to the penance arranged for us, in the collective Korean style. It went on even as we saluted and shouted about our new lives, day after day, with Panjang Nim, the guards, the Korean state, and our own consciences as witnesses. In their minds these men had suffered setbacks, lost years, lost money, lost property, lost respect, so there was added pressure to get it all back. Many naturally fell back on what they knew, only now with the determination to make it bigger and better. That the Korean system did little to present these men with healthier alternatives does not negate the fact that, again, in the end we made of ourselves what we would, regardless of the circumstances. However much the system was to blame for its shortsightedness, the final responsibility rested with each of us individually.

Being an American, I think the other foreigners looked at me and saw capital. They saw a big, robust market. They saw access and the ability to cross borders. Mr. Wang, a fat middle-aged ethnic Korean from Taiwan, was a man with money. He was also generous, always buying a lot of goods from the commissary and sharing them with his friends in the factory. His relatively short sentence was ending soon, and he was full of business plans. He wanted to set up an arcade-game and slot-machine parlor in Dalian, the bustling Chinese port city just across the Yellow Sea from Korea, and he wanted me to help him. He gave me his contact information in Taiwan, talked up the plans with me at my table, his hand on my knee. I really don't know what help or investment he thought I could offer him, but it was clear that he considered me a potential asset. "Write me or call me when you get out. I'll be waiting to hear from you," Mr. Wang said.

I knew Joseph had been thinking for a while about the possibility of gaining a contact in the States. He finally brought it up, asked me if I would consider it, told me the percentage he'd give me, explained how I could go about finding buyers for him and his crew of heroin runners. At the same time, a gang leader named Mr. Kim began taking me under his wing and walking with me during exercise. He was charming and personable, very much the gentleman gangster. He had money and clout in Taejon. He was getting out soon, but he wanted to establish something with me before he left. He told me I could help him in New York, organize people, set up an office, be a contact for him—who knows what such a position would have really entailed.

I knew all the while that I was never going to do any of these things, but I listened. I felt I understood these men even though they were unlike anyone I'd known before. And when would I ever meet the likes of them again? They were showing me the battle-scarred, battle-ready side of life, the Darwinian one, the animal fight for advantage and opportunity, conscience, morals, and the law be damned. As immoral and crude as it might be, that world, I realized, was huge and real and no less true than any other. Life in many ways was a dirty fight, but one you could still love. So even as they propositioned me with schemes, I saw not business opportunities but a chance for a rare education. I like to think I was after a bigger prize, the knowledge that this trip into the underbelly might make me wiser. I wasn't just a callow kid anymore. I knew so much more of what was out there, about the infinite ways in which people live and make money, about the paths they choose. And that was why I'd left New York in the first place. It wasn't just to teach English and learn about Korea. It was to learn more about human beings, whoever they are, Confucians, cretins, killers, pirates, the mentally ill. My journey didn't happen as I'd planned or as I thought it might, but in a roundabout and more forceful way, I still got what I was looking for. That's why I will never regret my time in Korea.

I kept thinking of what Man Yong, Peehyuk's secretary, had told me once when he heard me jumping from English to Spanish to Korean one day as we worked. *"Tomasuh, ya, akapda!"* he said, slapping me on the back. *Akapda* meant something like "almost, close but not quite, something that had just missed." That was how he saw me, my life. I was smart, he meant, I might have done something with myself, might have made myself into something better than a convict. Man Yong had intended it as a compliment, but his words stung deeply. I didn't want to be an almost, an also-ran. There was nothing worse. And after all the advantages I'd been given, it was a damn shame. But as bad as that felt, I had one incredible consolation, one straw to cling to. Unlike Man Yong, I'd be let out before too long and I'd have the chance to redeem myself out in the world. That meant everything. It wasn't too late for me. But there could be no akapda this time, no more criminal gambits, no almost-but-not-quite.

# 34

PANJANG NIM MAY have been a rare breed of gang leader, but in the factory we also dealt with other powerful gangsters, none of whom was as easy to deal with as Panjang Nim. These guys were toughs, and they strutted and fought, they barked orders and cursed at people, they punched their underlings in the face if they talked back or failed to show enough respect, they bullied the common Korean inmates, they flaunted their privileges and power. The gangsters were in control of the four little coal stoves that were set up in the factory in the winter. They boiled water for themselves in the all-important and scarce kettles whenever they wanted, so that they always had hot water for bathing and shaving. They always got nicely tailored uniforms from their associates who ran Yangjay, the clothing factory. They didn't have to do any actual work. In Peehyuk, for example, the gangsters never touched a single shoe. While we pounded away for years, they read or twiddled their thumbs. Their groups on the outside ran racketeering rings and big business. Money was always coming in to Taejon's gangsters from subordinates on the outside. They bribed guards. The way it looked to me, any established gangster with money in Taejon could have his own guard on the gang payroll, a personal conduit for *bumchigum,* contraband. This corruption was a welcome thing for us. It meant the occasional packet of coffee or a good magazine or even getting one's journals out. Gary, the Korean-American on our floor, who was not a gangster but had enough money to do the trick, had a young tamdang from our block well greased. I didn't know which guard it was, and it was probably better that way. Gary said he could give the guard my journals to mail home from outside the prison. And so twice over the course of years I taped together brown envelopes full of pages, wrote my mom's address on them, and gave them to Gary. The next I heard of them was weeks later when my mom wrote me, saying that she had received something curious from me in the mail. On one of those occasions, the bribed guard had even repackaged the mailing, using a better envelope than the one I'd had at my disposal, rewriting my mom's address for me. I kept imagining him at a post office on a day off, out of uniform, writing my mom's name and the name of the street in our Long Island town on the stronger envelope he'd picked out. Did he know who I was? Did he care? Had he ever been to New York? I was amazed that you could pay a guard and he would flip so far around as to be of such help. I had smuggled myself into prison, so to speak, and now a prison guard was helping me smuggle my story out.

GANG GUY, MY basketball teammate, would call us to his table and we'd sigh and shuffle over. We didn't want to go, but we had to. We knew we were in for a didactic, warped, and tendentious talk on some topic. He was fascinated by the Jews. He was reading a book that claimed the Jews owned all the media in the United States, that spoke of how smart they were, how unified, how they always helped their own. All of that appealed to him. He told me that he was fond of Hitler, Stalin, and Castro. He respected their power. With a laugh, though he was by no means joking, he told me that poor countries should be Korea's slaves, and he gestured over at Tracey and the Filipinos. He judged other nationalities by their wealth, their per capita GDP, the color of their skin. He would giggle to me, calling the black American Fred, who worked in Peehyuk for a few months, a *gamdoongee*, like saying blacky, or a *yontan*, a coal brick. Korea was the tenth-largest trading nation in the world, he reminded me, the eleventh-largest economy, the fifth in car production, whatnot in coffee consumption, a bragging seventh in this or that obscure category. In this and all their other forms, the gangsters were often the purest and most extreme examples of Korean hierarchical structures and nationalism, of the native culture of winners and losers, those riding and those ridden. It was a mean and bleak view of the world, I thought. But their code was also rooted in the ideal of the gentleman gangster, the well-dressed man of culture and refinement—even as he twisted your arm till it broke. My guess is that the Korean gangsters share a lot in common with the yakuza, the infamous Japanese gangs, and may even be modeled on them to an extent. The Korean gangpey did try to behave with a sense of honor, to serve as gracious hosts to us as foreign guests in Korea and in their prisons. They often took it upon themselves to make sure we weren't abused in the factories, to help us if we needed it.

ANOTHER OLDER GANGSTER, with a scarred face and wildly colorful dragon tattoos covering his entire back, strutted and preened his way around Peehyuk. He was a rotten seed and you could see it right away. Tracey and I once got into a conversation with him about betting; and new to the factory and to being around these gangsters, I said something about the way Koreans seemed to love betting. They bet on everything. Suddenly this man, whom Tracey had nicknamed Difficult Guy, began to seethe. He came up to me with his jaw clenched and let loose a torrent of vulgarity. I was a little American bastard, a motherfucker, a fucking asshole. I don't know how I escaped a fight, but I did. It was fortunate that at that time I didn't quite understand the things Difficult Guy was saying to me and so stood there hoping it would pass. Soon after, he was removed from Peehyuk and given a few extra months on his sentence for damaging a regular Korean inmate's face with his fist. We were glad to see him go and breathed a sigh of relief.

Another one took his place, though. This one was younger than

Difficult Guy, but still old enough to have many subordinates and to act like a petty tyrant. He was big, fat, and strong. I avoided him safely until one day, as exercise was ending and we had all run back to the front of the factory to get into rows to be counted off before going back in, when I found myself next to this gangster in the last row. Row by row we were dropping down into a crouch so the guard could see us more easily. Just before it was our row's turn, the fat gangster turned to me and roughly ordered me to crouch, and for some reason, on this day, I was just a touch less compliant, just a little bit resistant, perhaps disturbed by the manner in which he'd spoken to me. I went down into my squat too slowly for his liking. As soon as the count was over and we were free to stand and move back inside, I tried to get away from the fat man, because I had a feeling he was going to blow. Fortunately I had put a crowd of guys between him and me as we made our way through the double doors, but I heard him behind me starting to go nuts. "You fucking little animal! I'll fucking kill you!" I looked back and saw him pushing guys out of his way trying to get at me. No one besides the two of us was quite sure what had happened. It had been such a subtle moment out there in the sun and dirt. Like an ogre, he was clawing his way over men on his path toward me. "You American fucker, why don't you go back to your shitty country, you motherfucker!" No one in the factory had ever spoken to any of us foreigners this way. Others might have had similar thoughts or felt animosity for the foreign strangers, but no one had shattered the veneer of propriety like this. The other Koreans were stunned into silence by what he was saying, in part because they still viewed us as guests in their country, and a guest shouldn't be so reviled. My Irish was up listening to the fat bastard say these things to me, threatening me with violence. For a moment I thought about meeting him head-on and fighting him. What would it be, I thought—a few punches before we're separated? But then I felt fear, because of the guy's size, his

anger, his half-dozen underlings in Peehyuk, muscular and faith-
ful stooges trained to defend their bosses. The others between us
tried calming the fat man as they held him back. He took off his
sweaty baseball cap and threw it at my head. They managed to
walk him to the other side of the factory. I went meekly back to
my table and sat down. The fat man's American comments left a
bad taste in my mouth and I felt exposed, vulnerable. His words
were still hanging in the air.

The furor died away while I explained to Tracey what had happened. Like Billy, Tracey had a lot of respect for Koreans, but he
also had no illusions about how we had to defend ourselves among
them. He told me that what had happened wasn't right, that the
gangster had been out of line. In my cell that night, I was sickened by the memory of the exchange as it played over in my head
and kept me awake. I hated being spoken to that way, disre-
spected in front of everyone—the only consolation was that it had
come from a gangster whom all the inmates feared and had to de-
fer to, so it wasn't as though I'd lost real face. Still, I felt abused.
So what if I didn't squat immediately when the fat man ordered
me to? I'm not a member of his gang. I'm not one of his subordinates that he can simply order around when and how he feels like
it. I felt shaken and in danger. I was determined to get this off my
chest and speak to Panjang Nim about it the following day.

On the way out of our cells the next morning I told Tracey that
I was going to speak to the captain. He agreed it needed to be
done. We were both concerned with how we would be treated in
the factory after yesterday's display.

As soon as our first head count was over, I approached Panjang
Nim at his desk. "Panjang Nim, I'm sorry to bother you, but I
want to speak to you about what happened yesterday after exercise." I made sure that I was speaking to him calmly, with the
highest respect.

"What do you want to say?"

"You know that I try to make no trouble. I respect the gangsters in the factory. I listen to them. But there is a difference between that and being one of their younger gang brothers." I lifted my head up to see where the fat man was. I was hoping that he wasn't nearby listening. "That person," I said, referring to the fat man respectfully, "that person treated me inappropriately. I couldn't sleep last night because of the things he said to me."

"All right. I get it. I'll speak to him."

Later that day the fat man, decidedly more subdued than the day before, asked me to come outside with him so he could talk to me. We stood in the sun in front of Peehyuk's double doors. The grounds were full as another factory exercised. The fat man was wearing the same baseball cap. He said he wanted to apologize and that we should forget what happened. I thought about saying I was sorry but instead, not wanting to give away too much from my side, told him, "I agree." I thought it might have sounded less than ideal and worried about his reaction. But he was under Panjang Nim's orders now to make nice with me. He had no choice but to swallow it. Still, he had arranged it so that he didn't have to apologize to me, to lower himself as it were, in front of the rest of the factory.

PANJANG NIM WAS more powerful than all these guys, and he wouldn't allow the gangsters to abuse us: first, because he was fair and decent; second, because we were assets to Peehyuk; and third, because he would look bad if we went over his head and lodged complaints with the kaejang or other prison officers, or, if we were really pressed, with our embassy. All the gangsters obeyed Panjang Nim. They all bowed deeply to him before every meal ("Hyung Nim, have a delicious meal") and whenever they had to step out of the factory ("Hyung Nim, I will go to the visiting room and return"; "Hyung Nim, I will go to the infirmary and come back"; "Hyung Nim, I will return quickly"). When Panjang

Nim called to them, they came immediately. While we knew Panjang Nim was a line of last defense between the other gangsters and us, we had to tread very lightly around them and give them the respect they demanded. They were not only something to fear and avoid, though. They were a positive force, too. They were the glue that held Taejon together. They held down the factories and all the regular inmates. Anytime an inmate acted up, fought, argued too much, made too many problems—over space on the racks for laundry, seats at the worktables, space for things in the boxes below each table, dishwashing duty—the gangsters would squash it. Putting aside the obvious incentive they had in taking bribe money from the gangs, the authorities were smart, I think, to allow the gangs to operate as they did, to allow them to continue to collude, because overall they were more of a constructive force than a destructive one. They didn't bring in drugs; they weren't murdering other inmates; they weren't plotting escapes or rebellions. Instead, they supplied the backbone of obedience and respect that the guards couldn't completely achieve—due to the lack of manpower, funds, and will. The gangsters were down in the trenches, living as prisoners, but functioning in many ways as an organizing authority in Taejon, just as they did in many of South Korea's other prisons.

≡≡

IN THE SUMMER of 1996, after a basketball game one day—I had steered clear of the game and practiced by myself instead—Bong Tae showed his true colors. Bong Tae was the paragon of a certain type of Korean gangster: good-looking, with perfect unblemished skin, hands that looked like they had never done a day of physical work, and an attitude of gross superiority and barely disguised contempt for nearly everyone outside of his own gang elders. They were like dandy princes. Bong Tae thought he was something special, and no one ever told him otherwise. Arnel, the

Filipino who sat at my section, had kept score during the game that day. Bong Tae, hoping for some athletic achievement, had made a rare entry into the game and had managed only a series of pathetic misses, blown layups and other wide-open chances. Predictably, his fragile ego was stung and he was going to make everyone feel it. Back in the factory, he huffed and puffed. He said Arnel must have made a mistake or cheated on the score. He cursed him. Arnel cursed back. Several minutes later, when it seemed that both had cooled off, Bong Tae called Arnel into the locker room. He said he just wanted to talk. When Arnel went in there, he found Bong Tae accompanied by two of his underlings, and Bong Tae wasted no time in jumping on Arnel. We were all getting ready to shower, but when we heard the scuffle, we ran into the locker room, grabbed Arnel, and took him out.

It seemed to me that the Filipinos had been too accommodating with Bong Tae. They had let a relationship develop in which Bong Tae often cursed and mocked them. Even though this was usually done jokingly, the dynamic was clearly headed for no good. I had learned that it was better to avoid those types of relationships in Taejon. I was angry that Bong Tae had gone after Arnel, and I still had Billy's advice from the Seoul Detention Center in my head: to do nothing in response would probably mean more trouble. If we sat back and did nothing, it would affect all of us foreigners in Peehyuk. Bong Tae might feel more emboldened in the way he dealt with me, with any of us. It could, in the Korean style, be to all our shame. I sat at our table with Arnel as he held a cold juice over his eye. It looked bad, bloody and bruised.

I had seen Bong Tae in action for more than two years. He thought he could curse anyone he pleased, disrespect whom he pleased. He tried to intimidate us. The plan I came up with in those moments after the incident was to put a scare into him, to show him that he wasn't untouchable and couldn't treat any of the foreigners this way without repercussions. I told Arnel that he should ask to go out to the *kwangosheel,* the kaejang's central out-post overlooking the grounds and the factories, and see if they might not give Bong Tae some time in solitary. If it really looked like this might happen, that Bong Tae might actually be punished, I thought, then we will have accomplished something. The threat of such action might put a little fear into his head. So I resolved to push for this up to a certain point, when I knew things had gone far enough, and then relent. As far as the other inmates in the factory not liking us, the gangsters hating us—well, that was a risk we had to take, I thought. Most important was for them all to see that we couldn't be run over.

In the outside world there are almost always escapes, ways to avoid problems and conflicts, safety valves for sublimated release. In prison there really is no such luxury. An inmate is continually thrust back into the same arena, surrounded by the same people. We would be back with Bong Tae and the other gangsters in the factory the very next day, and the one after that, for years. That meant that confrontation was necessary at times: Why are you staring at us while we eat? Don't come and disturb us while we're working. If you help someone out, make sure they honor that. Talk inmates down, back them up, show them a harder exterior. These were tough lessons, and I was wary of the way they might change me. I felt better after finding an old American Indian saying in a book: Do what you will with human beings, but never shut them out of your heart. This was a revelation. It helped free my conscience when I was faced with the job of rejecting the many parasitic characters in Peehyuk who, unable to endure or occupy themselves, strolled around the factory looking to suck the energy from anyone showing signs of life. I could reject the life-sucking, vapid thieves and common crooks. I could tell them to get the hell away from me and leave me be. I could ignore their stupid, provocative questions, ignore them as if they were not really there in front of me, their faces close to mine. I could try to make sure that Bong Tae left us alone. And I could do that externally even as I kept them in my heart, so to speak, wishing them good passage and luck in their lives. These were empowering blessings for me, necessary, satisfying rejections sealed with sincere parting shots of grace: *Get the fuck away from me and all the best to you.*

I STEPPED INTO the exposed factory office to tell Panjang Nim that Arnel wanted to go out to the kwangosheel and that I wanted to help translate for him. Panjang Nim immediately began to defend Bong Tae, of whom he was very fond. It was just tempers flaring, Panjang Nim said, trying to dissuade me. After losing, everyone gets mad; forgive and forget, he said. I had anticipated that Panjang Nim was going to argue against punishing Bong Tae. Arnel was in pain and didn't want to take it any further, either. Panjang Nim told me honestly that if we went out to report the incident to the kaejang, Bong Tae would definitely get time in solitary, so he told us to consider well whether that was what we really wanted. It was a subtle threat, but I knew we were playing a kind of chess now. I pressed the point, and Panjang Nim said, "All right, fine. Bong Tae, *ya*, get ready to go, that's it." I heard Bong Tae say, "Fucking foreigners! After I treated them so well." Panjang Nim continued barking at me, trying to get me to reconsider. Even our guard told me to stop what I was doing. The entire factory was watching. I felt my toes at the edge of a cliff.

"If you insist on punishing him," Panjang Nim shouted at me, "then from now on I'm going to make you guys responsible for everything. Do you hear me? If you make even one small error, you will also be given no mercy!" This was the first time I had ever seriously challenged Panjang Nim, and it was terrifying. I worried that I might be in too deep now, but I held firm. It hadn't gone far enough yet. While we were arguing, the final horns had sounded, and Panjang Nim had to call the final head count of the day. A few of our factory mates came up to me and told me to let the episode go, that I was going to make enemies. An older gangster approached Arnel and told him to let it go. Arnel said that was what he wanted. He had a fifteen-year sentence; he just wanted peace. But I still held out for this chance to use the situation to our future benefit, proving to Bong Tae that he would have to be more careful in his dealings with us. After our final head count and group salute, Panjang Nim dismissed everyone except Arnel, Bong Tae, and me. We remained in the now empty factory with Panjang Nim and our guard. Panjang Nim promised Arnel and me that nothing like this would ever happen again.

"What more do you want?" he asked me. This was closer, in fact, to what I wanted, and I began to relent. I couldn't help feeling a deep satisfaction seeing Bong Tae standing next to us, cowed, with his mouth shut for once, his hands behind his back as we argued about his fate. I told Panjang Nim that Bong Tae was often disrespectful toward us, and I pointed out that Panjang Nim had said barely a word to Bong Tae about the incident. He assured us he would get to that. Arnel finally said, "Please, I want peace. It's forgiven." Everyone agreed. I told Panjang Nim respectfully that I was leaving to go to my cell, and Arnel and I bowed to him and the guard. As Arnel and I left Peehyuk, joining the last stragglers making their way toward the long halls, we could hear Panjang Nim beginning to rain down his verbal assault on Bong Tae.

I felt a thrill racing through me as we made our way from the space of the grounds back into the stone of Taejon. I had walked a dangerous edge and come out of it. I had stood behind our extreme minority's little trembling wall of defense in those prisons against the great tidal wave of all things Korean that we had to placate and try to learn to surf as it pushed us along and threatened to crash over our heads. I had applied everything I'd learned and managed what I was sure I had to do. I thought of how much I'd struggled in Seoul and Uijongbu, how little I understood then.

The incident blew over. Arnel's eye was all right. I was forgiven for the stand I'd taken. Bong Tae never bothered us again.

# 35

AT THE HOT bath in Taejon during my first winter there, I was startled by the naked body of a young ethnic Korean from Harbin, China, who was doing five years for trafficking methamphetamine. I knew him from our cell block. He was friendly and good looking and was in tremendous shape. But I was shocked, seeing him naked now before me, dangling the oddest, most misshapen penis I'd ever seen. The poor guy, I thought, with everything else going for him, too. I wondered if he was the victim of some genetic flaw, an unspeakable accident, or maybe a circumcision gone horribly wrong. Later, in our factory's shower, I began seeing that many of the Korean prisoners, especially the gangsters, had the same strangely shaped chajees: lumps on the shaft and disks and bulbous knots of skin around the head. It looked like an epidemic, as though some hideous malady that disfigures the cock had spread through the prison. I was floored to learn that these freak pieces were actually the result of self-inflicted wounds, homemade enhancements that involved pulling the skin and making little cuts that were then filled with Vaseline or little pieces of plastic (I was told that the bristles of a toothbrush worked well). The incisions would heal over in lumps. Done with skill and care—guys sometimes performed these operations for each other in our factory locker room, out of the guard's sight—these lumps could be made to encircle the head entirely like flared petals around a flower's core. The Korean inmates proudly called their remodeled members *haybaragees*: sunflowers. Most of the gang men did it, but so did many other inmates, to conform, to feel manlier. One jolly sixty-five-year-old Korean inmate with a funny little body, spiky white hair, and a comically huge disk of distended skin weighing down his penis told me, "The women like it. It makes them scream. My wife really enjoys it. She's had many kids and is old; she needs it to be big." The Koreans were very intrigued about our foreign members. In Uijongbu my anatomy had been a constant topic of conversation among the guards. Is the American big size? was the name of their game. However crass and annoying the scrutiny was, I couldn't do anything to stop it. I had to play along, let my johnson assume its diplomatic role as genital emissary. In Taejon I once watched Joseph the Nigerian, smiling big as usual, flash his member in the sunlit corridor at a guard who'd asked him to do so as we were walking single file to the factories. The guard, impressed, exclaimed and rocked back. This vision of manhood seemed to make his day.

We foreigners were often asked how loudly we could make women scream, how many times we could have sex in a night. The thinking seemed so primitive and crude as to be a parody of itself. We were asked if we wanted sunflowers. Some of the foreigners actually gave it a thought, but I don't think any of us ever went through with it. It was amazing to see that not only was the old joke of an Asian inferiority complex regarding penis size actually very much true, but also that it was at the root of these wild self-mutilations. (I read somewhere that in the early 1990s North Korea claimed that they had found the tomb of Tangun, the mythological founder of the nation, near Pyongyang, and that Tangun's pubic bone was inordinately large.) I felt sorry for the Korean women who were with these guys, and wondered how they reacted to these things. I imagined cons back on the outside, finding romance, and eventually pulling out their jailhouse creations to the horror of unsuspecting girls.

≡≡

THREE AND A HALF years of enforced celibacy sent all the thrills of sex into my imagination. Masturbation was too common a routine. I often thought of Rocket, her little body on top of me. I pulled up every sexual image I could think of and went to town on myself. It wasn't self-love, it was all pleasure and escape, and the desire to come often overwhelmed days—it was eating, self-copulation, and sleep; eating, self-copulation, and sleep, that's all. Those little orgasm ceremonies filled time. Three minutes or thirty, what you had in your hands was an event, a little party in your cell when the lights were still on but all was quiet on the block. I'd sometimes look out into the hall and wonder how many guys were busy doing the same. I'm sure I picked up a sex addiction there, all of it of my own making, because I wasn't able to make myself ascetic, though I often thought of challenging myself to try. I'll relinquish masturbating for at least a week, I'd tell myself, but the experiment was rarely successful. I lost track of time remembering what women were, how they once felt, badly missing their thighs and hair, the bones of their hips, the smell of the skin behind their ears, the back of their necks, their apple asses. I drifted high and away in a blaze of want, my angry johnson a door whose handle I could turn to enter a room where visions burned the walls.

I felt I had a special understanding of the line in T. E. Lawrence's *Seven Pillars of Wisdom* in which he says that the only female part of his adventures in Arabia was the camels. For us it was the colorful little pictures of movie stars in *Sports Chosun* and other Korean newspapers—"talent," Koreans called them. The photos often showed the girls in bathing suits: slim girls with symmetric beauty, lush crow-dark hair; sometimes with flat butts and little breasts but enough to make you give up your god and country. I could hear their saccharine girlie voices, the sweet deference in every syllable. They'd do what I wanted in my head. I took beautiful Korean women ferociously at night in my cell, punishing them with pleasure, thinking of it sometimes as revenge for what I'd suffered in their country, at their men's hands. I stood over the cement and the trough in the back of my cell and looked out the window into the dark sky and made my body move somewhere time and again, bringing about a physical crisis outside of sleep and hunger and defecation. And for those moments the prison would fall away; there was only the hand and the mind and the tingled nerves attached to the delicious little freedom. My body was alive and I could make it do things; I could still be its master.

I raped my blankets. That's what Green called it when I told him my routine, a day after he'd come out of his cell for exercise time with a deeply worried look on his face, telling me he'd masturbated seven times the day before. That was obviously too much. I would roll my blankets into a ball, then shape out a section of one of them as a little tunnel for me to slip myself into. I could easily imagine it was a woman's body, and by not touching myself I was less self-involved somehow, less self-reflective; it was less masturbatory. Green thought it was funny as hell and that I was a sick fuck, and after hearing about it he would never let me get away with judging him regarding anything sexual, including his precious and frighteningly massive collection of Korean girlie pictures he'd cut from the sports pages. Every once in a while he would prepare a little sampling of the collection for me and have the so-jee pass it over during long lockdown weekends. He was a great friend in that way.

KEE BAEK, AN earnest Christian nut who worked in our factory, claimed he never touched himself. He looked like the aliens drawn by anyone who's ever claimed to have seen one: a diminutive body; the head wide and swollen at the top, cheekbones prominent, and the jawline tapering down to a near point. Kee Baek's madness took the form of a blissful positivity, and he was pretty unique in that. I admired him for it. It was easy to get him laughing like an imbecile and too loud; he smiled constantly as though inwardly entertained, made absolutely no trouble at all. He went to the auditorium once a week without fail for the Protestant mass. I went over to Kee Baek's factory table a few times a week to read with him and study words in English; he'd ask me questions about some of the wild semantics in the Bible. When I began teaching English on a blackboard in our factory locker room, Kee Baek insisted on helping out. He was granted a kind of assistant-teacher status, and that meant something because not even a role carved out of nothing and as small as that was given away lightly. Before each class he would pull out two short tables and write the full date very neatly in English on the board. It was another way I counted my days.

I believed Kee Baek when he said that he never masturbated. There was something asexual about him, though at the same time he had a crazed randy look in his eyes. I always had the unfounded feeling that his murder involved a gay lover. The fact that he had killed at all could only be explained by romantic passion, I thought, though I never asked him. I admired him for his apparent self-control, but what he said made me think of Billy, who'd told me the same thing about himself. Part of Billy's discipline program in the Seoul Detention Center was to refrain from getting himself off. But without fail, he said, after just a few days, he'd be released in his dreams. The body would not and could not be denied. I found that fascinating. Sexual dreams aren't exclusive to prisoners, but the subconscious was laid particularly bare and sharpened in prison, what with the lack of things to stimulate the senses. What dreams may come when we have shuffled off and not touched ourselves? I gave the experiment a whirl and found the results to be true, and the dream sex—not unlike the blanket raping, but even more so—seemed truly to involve the presence of another, not just intangible fantasies but something closer to the thrill of live flesh, someone else next to you, the illusory, fleeting feeling of another body.

A friend of mine did much of foreign Taejon a great service when he mailed me a pornographic novel called *The Pleasures of Women*. Set in the Victorian era and written in ridiculously purple prose, it told of a shameless rake—whom all of us convicts became during the reading—who plays piano and croquet with beautiful young girls before expertly seducing and thoroughly "rogering" them. That was the word the writer used each time the deed was done, "roger." It was no wonder the inspectors in the education office didn't understand enough of it to withhold it. After I'd lent the book out once or twice and the other foreigners had heard it recommended, *The Pleasures of Women* circulated for years among us. Even Ali, one of the most devout of the Pakistani Muslims, approached me to ask very politely if he could borrow it. Five or six guys at a time would be asking me for it, forcing me to keep a careful mental list of whose turn it was so as to avoid arguments and animosity.

THE ONLY REAL sex I heard of in Taejon was of a consensual nature. Some older gang men, even several factory captains, were apparently having money put into the accounts of young inmates they wanted and who were willing to strike the bargain. Some of the arrangements were said to involve groups of inmates. I thought of the Koreans packed side by side on the floors of their cells. These scandals were exposed and met with enormous shame, the kind of shame that Panjang Nim was always talking about in his speeches to us, warning us about, threatening us with, the same shame that ordered and civilized life in Taejon and made incidents like this so rare.

There was one crazy day when Taejon officials, maybe bribed by the gangs, allowed a hot young Korean stripper to come into the prison and entertain a huge group of us in the auditorium. She stripped down to little red panties and a bra and wildly screwed the air and the floor of the huge stage around her. We were stunned into silence and awe. I'm sure many of the others were, like me, capturing and freezing these images in their heads so as to enjoy them later. I thought the girl captured some essence of Korea itself when at the end of her all-too-short routine, she scurried on her red high heels to the back of the stage and, rather than bend over—which she'd already done a dozen times in a dozen different ways—to pick up the dress she'd shed, instead primly bent at the knees to get it and quickly dashed out of sight.

## 36

ONE DAY IN the fall of 1996, a particularly zealous high-ranking officer came to Peehyuk, had Panjang Nim gather us all below him as he stood in the guard's perch, and gave us a speech. He said that the foreign prisoners in Taejon were an "opportunity," and that the Korean inmates should take advantage of that opportunity to better themselves and strengthen the country. Now that the country had become a rich nation, he said, it was essential that everyone learn English. And so our little English class in Peehyuk was born, with me as the teacher.

I had mixed feelings about beginning a class in the factory. The interested inmates, about six to ten of them at the start, were like rabid madmen in their pursuit of the language. They came at me at all hours; there was no escape, and they didn't seem to have any qualms about interrupting me regardless of what I was doing. They swept in like birds of prey, pecking, squealing. I handled questions throughout the day, about stray words and phrases, helping inmates to write bits of English in their letters to impress their friends and families on the outside. But our hour-long class in Peehyuk's locker room gave the inmates who attended it a daily purpose, a feeling of accomplishment and productive behavior. I felt that from my side, too, and because of it began to give of myself more freely. I believe that I actually became more understanding of my students in prison than I had ever been on the outside. My frustration and lack of enthusiasm disappeared. I was returning to the origins of my time in the country, the reason I came in the first place. When I taught in Seoul as a free man, however, I did it mostly for the money. In Taejon there was no money to be had, and the students seated in front of me weren't

cute little kids or businessmen or university students but convicted murderers and rapists. Now I was teaching because it was
satisfying to share knowledge with the guys, to help give us all an
identity beyond that of just prisoner and convict. I deeply appreciated the chance, and it became some of the purest and most
humble teaching I've ever done. My assistant and older brother
Kee Baek was the unsung force behind the class. He often pressed
the other inmates who had an interest in studying. He went around
Peehyuk telling them what time our class would be each day. He
encouraged them to keep it up when their interest or confidence
waned. It was from Kee Baek's own English books that we drew
many of our lessons. We wrote simple dialogues on the standing
blackboard the authorities supplied us with—English on the
right, a Korean translation on the left. I read, the students repeated. I stressed commonly used expressions, tried to explain in
Korean the situations in which particular words and phrases were
appropriate. We did pronunciation drills focusing on *th* and *r* and
*f,* all the things I'd spent so much time on with students in Seoul.
We ran through verb conjugations, present, past, past participle,
as our flawed pasts still held us tight and kept us in our present.
Subject, action, consequence, the raw and natural syntax of our
sentences.

Min Chul would lead the other students in bowing to me at
the end of class. I thought of telling them not to do this, as I saw
it as unnecessary. They started calling me *sonsaeng nim,* teacher,
with that incredible respectful *nim* at the end. I felt more like a
sonsaeng now, and so I humbly took what they gave me and accepted my new status.

THE NEW SECURITY chief of Taejon, who'd arrived sometime in
1996, was a short man with glasses and an austere bearing. He
pulled everything tighter. Part of his strict campaign was to de-
clare that all drug cases were prohibited from receiving packages,

clothes, books, or newspapers. The Americans protested these new restrictions—among the six of us there at the time were four Korean Americans who were also down on drug violations. Our embassy put a word in for us with Taejon officials, and the new security chief eventually relented. Soon after, he called me personally to his office. Peehyuk had just finished our exercise when our guard informed me that the prison's number one man wanted to see me. It came as quite a shock. I had no time to shower and could only struggle into my uniform and try to make myself look presentable. Another officer entered our factory to escort me through gates and manned posts, across grounds, through halls, to the central security office, the brains of the place. In a corner of the large room was the top man's office, Taejon's final frontier. I wasn't nervous. I knew why I'd been summoned.

A guard led me in to where the security chief was sitting in a black leather chair. He had a book open in front of him and a radio on his left with voices reading dialogues in English. He told me to have a seat and had coffee brought in. He seemed kind and not nearly as arrogant as I might have guessed. He asked for my full name and my release date, then asked about the teaching I'd done in Seoul before prison and the lessons we'd been having in Peehyuk. He wanted to know how long it had been going on, what topics we were studying. I blissfully sipped my coffee. He said he wanted to study with me and wanted me to help him with his English. No fool, I said I would like that. He would call for me when he had time, he said, and send a guard to Peehyuk to bring me here to his office, just like today. Then he turned the radio off and showed me a dialogue revolving around an insipid exchange in a restaurant. "What would you like?" "Well, I haven't decided just yet. Can you give me a few more minutes?" I took one part and he the other and we ran through the conversation once. He smiled, closed the book, and said he was sorry that he didn't have more time. It was late in the day, and the final horns were soon to go off over the prison he ran and in which I was just one among thousands. The security chief stood up, shook my hand, and saw me out the door. I left floating on a Taejon cloud of being wanted and favored and fortunate as hell. When I got back to Peehyuk, Panjang Nim wanted to know what had happened. He and the others couldn't believe that the boan kwajang had called me personally to his office, that I'd shaken his hand. There was no better ally to have in the prison, they said.

Two weeks later I was called out to the kwangosheel by a chooeem, who informed me that the security chief regretted that he couldn't call me to study with him as he'd hoped. The chief had recently committed himself to a new prisonwide campaign of making all the inmates equal. All special sneakers, for example, obtained through bribes by the gangsters, had been taken away and outlawed. There was also the matter of the thick, specially made winter uniform jackets. Before, these were available only to those with good connections to the garment factory. The security chief said the jackets could be kept, but that new ones would have to be made for all the inmates who didn't have one. So, the officer in the kwangosheel relayed to me, although the chief wanted to study with me, doing so would risk the appearance of favoritism. He wanted me to know that he was sorry for the change in plans. When the security chief came into Peehyuk on an inspection not too long after, he came right over to my table. He leaned forward, his subordinates at his sides wondering what the head man was up to, glowering at me to make sure I was going to behave. As the rest of the factory watched, the security chief held out a little bottle of medicine that he was taking for a cold he had and asked me, "What does it mean, 'Suggested use, one tablet with meal, as desired'?" I explained as best I could, telling him that "as desired" meant it was up to him whether to take one or not; it was his decision. He gave me a smile, then turned and, as we all saluted, exited Peehyuk with his minions behind him.

SOON EVERYONE SEEMED to want a piece of English. An engineer who oversaw work in the carpentry factory, where inmates could learn basic architecture, came by one rainy day with liquor on his breath to ask for my help with a speech he had to give in English. Following him out of the blue was the prison chaplain, who called me to his office in the education department one day, plied me with a little paper cup of coffee, and asked if I would help him prepare for an English test he had to take in several months. Knowing a good thing when I saw it, I said yes right away, just as I had with the security chief. The chaplain was a short, serious Korean man in his late thirties. He always wore a suit and tie. The next day, we began the regimen he had arranged. At one p.m. every day a tamdang would come across the grounds to Peehyuk to escort me to the chaplain's office. The chaplain and I would greet each other respectfully. He would carry over the bare room's electric heater and place it near us at his desk. He'd bring us cups of coffee, and we'd go through reading-comprehension exercises from a book he had: essays and articles on things like photosynthesis and the Suez Canal that were followed by a series of questions about the material. He'd ask me the definitions of words he didn't know. A little warmth and a cup of coffee, that was all I needed in the world to be happy. That was living large in Taejon, or as the Koreans said it—and it was on their minds a lot, just as it is, perhaps, for any people who have suffered much through history—"living well." They talked about their country as a whole being able to "live well" now. That meant everything. A sarcastic yet playful Korean expression that was used often in regard to something good someone else had—a new uniform, frequent visits, a delicious kimchi stew (our winter staple, cooked in the kettles on our coal stoves)—translates as something close to "Well, look at you living well, huh!" It was said with a blend of mock jealousy and admiration. That's what many of the guys in Peehyuk said to me after they saw me meeting a man in a suit, saw me keeping my daily appointment with the chaplain. I was living well and gaining status.

After I'd been meeting with the chaplain for about a week, I asked if he could help me retrieve the personal effects that were never returned to me after the investigation: my passport, wallet, and trusty Bartholomew mini world atlas. I hoped Prosecutor Shin's office still had them. For more than two years I'd been trying to recover these items and have them sent to Taejon, where at least I knew they would be kept safely in storage and would be there for me when my time was up. It felt as though parts of me, and some of my favorite parts, were still being held at Shin's whim. I was still waiting on his orders, just as I had in those squalid holding cells all those mornings in Seoul. I loved that atlas, and I needed to see it; I wanted to have maps—maps in my cell would have been amazing. They would have been among those rarest of things that had power over the walls, like magical cloth that when pressed to the walls would allow me to walk through them.

For more than two years I'd been writing letters to the courts, to the U.S. embassy, to Shin himself once—although as soon as that little aerogram to Shin was out of my hands and on our factory guard's desk, I regretted it; I kept thinking, Better to let sleeping dogs lie. Despite my efforts, nothing had budged. I never heard a word in response. Having listened to my sad little story, the chaplain told me to hold on for a moment, leaned over his desk, made a phone call, talked for a couple of minutes, hung up, and turned back to me to tell me that the Seoul Prosecutors' Office would be sending my things to Taejon in the next few days. I was dumbfounded: that power, the access, the speed with which he'd sent the information flying down all those open avenues! All the world seemed to be at the chaplain's fingertips, even from that cold, bare office. He was a wizard of the massive free world from which I was held apart.

Seeing it peek open for a moment like that in front of me almost carried a sound, that of an electric charge, as though I could hear the lines of freedom and movement throbbing with life just beyond me, outside the office, through the phone on the chaplain's desk, past the closed doors, a limitless universe pulsing just out of sight. It was a breathtaking glimpse of how far away I was buried, and before I could assess the moment, the little breach closed up, the pulse of the world outside faded, and I was left once again in our closed camp on the edge of the moon.

# 37

ON THE WALLS in Taejon were lists of the kinds of books that were banned under the National Security Law.

*Stories that praise or support communism or socialism*
*Stories of class struggle, revolution, or peasant movements*
*Stories that can create chaos*
*Stories that are critical of society and can prompt disobedience*

Looking through the books in my cell, I saw how broadly and arbitrarily those prohibitions could be applied. According to them, much of what I had was suspect. Whitman seems far outside convention, beyond all but the most natural laws. I had Thoreau's "On the Duty of Civil Disobedience"; the chaotic writings of Nietzsche; Solzhenitsyn, that tireless critic and enemy of the state. Just like the old woman in Thoreau's formulation, the Korean state still seemed to be holding too tightly to its silver spoons, and there was the undeniable reflex to want to knock her over and spill the precious silverware all over the floor—or at the very least to read what the hell you wanted, to make up your mind for yourself.

Every year on the anniversary of Korea's independence from Japanese colonial rule, the justice ministry granted an amnesty and let a number of prisoners go early. In cell 6 on our floor in Taejon was a sixty-year-old man who'd done ten years for being a socialist and an advocate of the North; he had five more to go. On August 15, 1996, guards unlocked two or three doors on our floor, including the old man's. I was told he'd signed an official statement renouncing his communist ideology—through his apostasy, clemency. It seemed like the oddest equation in the world, that so much could ride on just what you said you believed. (This was the same day that Kim Sun Myung, who'd been convicted of spying for North Korea during the Korean War and was considered the longest-serving political prisoner in the world, was released from Taejon after forty-four years in prison.)

I watched the old man go slowly from cell to cell, saying his good-byes, before the horn released the workers to the factories. When he crossed over to the row of cells on my side of the block, he disappeared from view, but then suddenly, I heard the wooden cover of my food hole being flipped open. I crouched down and saw the old man's face beaming at me from the other side. We shook hands through the hole, across the divide, and smiled. I wished him good luck. After ten years of standing on principle, what had changed his mind? I wondered. And if he was going to break, why hadn't he done it five years earlier?

IRONICALLY, LIFE IN South Korea's prisons in some ways fit my image of what a communist work camp might be like. Cell blocks were assigned to work groups, with the inmates from each factory placed together on the same floor. And there was a pretty successful attempt to make everyone equal. Whatever benefits the gang men or we as foreigners received were small in comparison to the vast sameness of our lives. Signs in the halls, the guards, our factory Panjang—all exhorted us the same way: help each other; work with each other; believe each other. They told us to do things *tan chae chuk-u-ro,* as one body. There was this constant collective urging. All the workers in a factory had to pull together. If a work section failed to make quota, then the whole section was penalized. If something went wrong in a particular factory or cell block, the whole factory or cell block would pay. Shame, success, blame, and punishment were shared by all. But while these dynamics may have resembled those of a communist work camp, their true roots were Confucian. Even in North Korea, it seems, Confucianism may be at work as much as any Stalinist ideology. In his chilling and important memoir, *Aquariums of Pyongyang,* Kang Chol Hwan, recounting the ten years he and his family spent in a North Korean concentration camp, writes that the "camp's policy of maintaining the cohesion of the family unit merely testifies to the resilience—even in a supposedly Communist country—of the Confucian tradition." That Confucian tradition is far deeper in the soul of the Korean people than any modern political or economic principle. Along with race, it is what still unites all Koreans, be they Northern or Southern. It was fascinating to see how often South Koreans would become sensitive or get offended when foreigners criticized North Korea. In most cases, they agreed in principle with what you were saying, but they didn't like hearing it from non-Koreans. They took it personally, as one would when one's family was being judged, and would sidestep the conversation or would even begin defending the North. North Koreans were still closer to them in spirit and blood than any foreigner could be.

When referring to their country, South Koreans most often use the phrase *oori nara,* which means "our country," instead of the actual name, Tae Han Min Gook, or the Republic of Korea. We often saw "oori nara" in print, heard it on the news and in many conversations—our country this, our country that. It embodied a deep nationalism and always struck me as dreadfully and wonderfully extreme. North Koreans call their half of the peninsula the same thing, oori nara.

I remembered talking with one of my classes at ELS about North Korea. When I asked the students about their feelings on Korea's split, most of them had no comment. A few believed the tension was just a political game. A kid named Yong asked me if I felt like I was in Bosnia—he was being ironic. H. J. Byun, another student, told me that his mother had advised him to fly to America with his wife to avoid the terrible violence that would

befall Seoul if war broke out. To the relief of many of her class-
mates, Hae Sun asked me if I could change the topic.

≡≡

AIR-RAID HORNS sometimes blared across the prison. Panjang
Nim would order us to put on our uniform jackets in case of an
inspection. It was the Civil Defense Exercise, a war drill. While
teaching in Seoul, I'd once gotten caught in a post office during
this national exercise. I'd licked my stamps and turned to go only
to hear the horns blaring and see dutiful employees pulling several layers of grating across the post office exit. I waited with
about a dozen others in silence for ten minutes before the radio
stopped its broadcast and the grates were thrown open again. In
our shoe factory, with the horns going and the radio voice sternly
advising us, the Korean inmates barely paused. They continued
strolling around, sat on stools and teased one another, prepared
food for their sections, scrubbed clothes in the shower room,
played Chinese chess, taking their time. I heard no one talk about
the North or the prospect of war, nothing on the divorced nature
of oori nara.

# 38

FROM THE FLOOR of my cell I could hear the birds outside and the first tentative grindings of the food and water carts as the so-jees maneuvered them into our hall. It was mid-October 1996, daybreak on Taejon's finest day of the year, the final day of our annual fall sports competition. I was to be dressed in a traditional Korean hanbok and juggle in front of the entire prison. It was Panjang Nim's idea; he'd seen me juggling one day in the factory and turned to me and said, "Tomasuh, do that during the sports tournament." That was all it took to seal my fate.

After breakfast in Peehyuk, carts were wheeled from table to table, depositing an autumn harvest of gifts donated by guys in our factory: milk, juice, candies, biscuits, ramyun, yogurt, bags of peanuts, and apples. Each of us was also given an illegal packet of instant coffee, which erased any doubt about the spirit of the day, the only one of emphatic celebration in the entire year.

A few days before, I'd been run upstairs into the garment factory—immersed suddenly in the strange confines of that world—to have my inseam and other measurements taken for my costume, which I now slipped on: baggy white cloth pants that tied at the ankles with a matching jacket-vest that tied at the sternum. Three crisp new tennis balls, highlighted with lines drawn in red marker, had been prepared for me. I got my hands warm and practiced, pacing in the factory. Everything was electric.

More than three thousand inmates were gathered in a sea of blue in a huge circle around the perimeter of the dusty grounds, each factory in an assigned section, seated on chairs or pieces of cardboard. A stage and viewing stand had been set up. It was a beautiful day with a high blue sky and plenty of sun. Hundreds of guards, soldiers, and men in suits stood at the edges. Our factory had built a lion with a great gaping mouth and dilated eyes, a colored mane, and a hairy flowing body—like the dragons and other fierce monsters at Chinese New Year celebrations. The life of the beast was the two Peehyuk men with hairy leggings who crouched beneath the lion's form, giving it shape and movement, making it leap and shake. Kee Jung, our doorman, was dressed in a white hanbok like me. Two others, lion tamers, walked beside our monster in colorful shirts and headbands. I tied a headband across my forehead—"Peehyuk" emblazoned on it, and in its center, the Korean national symbol, the red and blue yin-yang, that harmony of extremes and opposites.

There were speeches by the security chief and other officials, some mass saluting. Guests arrived, including an odd group of elderly women, and were hailed as they took their honorary places on the center stage. Then it was time for the national anthem:

*Rose of Sharon, thousand miles of range and river land*
*Guarded by her people, ever may Korea stand!*

Tracey and I had memorized some of the verses and we tried to sing along. When the anthem was done, a band of inmates swung into the open space with drums and let loose a primal beat. They were dressed in white topped with blue vests, red and yellow sashes tied like bandoliers around their torsos, colored tassels and balls of cotton hanging from their hats. The criminals' masquerade had begun. Our troubadours set off, out from our factory's section and into the open arena. I juggled out in front. Kee Jung, now sporting a grotesque mask, held a red rope, our lion's leash, and led the beast forward. The two tamers danced and jumped around at the lion's sides. Cheers and laughter went up. We circled slowly until we were in front of the stage, where we mingled with the pounding musicians, who had formed a circle. Two large puppets from the printing factory, white with huge dangling tongues, joined us, shaking, competing for attention. Inmates dressed like imperial guards held long poles with colorful banners inscribed with Chinese and Korean characters. *Take action to improve your life!* one of them read.

Improvising, I jogged in circles around the outside of the drummers, juggling as I went. Then, with the musicians and monsters behind me, I stopped, faced the warden and other officials and guests on the stage, and attempted the trick I'd been practicing. I flipped one ball high in the air and behind me, while keeping the other two balls up in front, then in one motion caught the two balls in front with my left hand and bowed at the waist to the warden while catching the third behind my back with the right. It was a gratuitous bit of showbiz deference, but I nailed the trick dead-on.

A great hush fell over us when a group of young female dancers in tight black uniforms dashed out in front of the stage, lined up in rows, and began to lunge and twist. We were in awe. There was almost a solemnity to it. The girls seemed comfortable in front of us, until the end, when they ran quickly back out of sight as if they were being chased: a general mistrust of convicts made combustible by the concentrated heat of all our deprived eyes.

A singer performed. Races were run, the athletes in the special and, for us, fancy uniforms of their respective factories. Peehyuk's uniform was white nylon shorts and jerseys with red trim. There were sprints, relays around the circle with batons and weighted sacks. My friend Sun Jae, a lifer and a promising professional track star before he committed murder, swept his events. A young, friendly guy, he was untouchable in the short and middle distances and a legend in the jail. When our factories had exercise at the same time, I sometimes ran laps with him and his pack of fellow runners. They trained all year for this day. Kwon Ahn, Taejon's best athlete, was so far ahead in the sack race that he got cocky and turned around to admire his lead, dropped his sack, and was passed. An inmate fell to the ground in another relay, throwing up a cloud of sand as the crowd let out a collective moan. He bounced up and chased the pack. I wanted to see him come all the way back to win it, but it wasn't meant to be.

In another contest ten inmates stood in front of the stage and held over their heads sandbags weighing more than sixty pounds. Activities went on around them while they remained planted, firm and mute amid the tumult. They seemed unaffected by their burdens until, after about five or ten minutes, they all began to falter. One after another, the arms swayed and slowly buckled, the contestants finally surrendering, dropping their sacks to the ground. It was the shortest man who prevailed. He was like an iron post under his bag and didn't show any sign of wearying.

Women in red dresses performed the traditional fan dance for us. The volleyball final was played. In the circle for *shirum*, Korea's traditional wrestling, stocky inmates were clutching, hoisting, and toppling each other into the sand. A smooth-faced, smooth-legged Korean inmate pranced around the arena all day wearing a wig, a short black skirt, and a huge pair of false breasts under his shirt. At first I thought it was really a girl and caught myself staring. I hoped that I wasn't the only one.

From the stage trophies were distributed to the winners of the competitions that had been held over the previous month. Man Yong called on me to run out across the grounds to collect our spoils. I was to accept something for our second-place finish in the basketball tournament. I felt proud heading out there. A smiling woman at the front of the stage handed me a neatly wrapped box of soap and toothpaste. She leaned her head forward slightly as she shook my hand. Confused, I thought she might be delivering a kiss, so I leaned my head forward, too, with my cheek ready; but she just whispered in my ear something I couldn't hear. In a single-elimination tournament of twenty teams, we'd won four straight games to reach the final. The body got beat up. My morning yoga had really helped me. I'd mentally prepared myself before every game: They're going to hack and provoke you, I told myself; you're not going to let that disrupt your flow. That mental work had done the trick for me, and our ragged squad nearly won the championship game against the powerful garment factory. We didn't give up despite the big lead they had on us early. We struggled back to within two points only to lose the game by that slim margin. I was proud of Peehyuk, and so it was with a true feeling of achievement that I held that box of cheap toiletries and jogged back across the space, past all the other prisoners, with our humble prize cradled in my right arm like the honorable trophy it wasn't. I felt even prouder toward the end of the afternoon when our troupe of performers, our lion and accompanying masquerade—which made runs into the arena throughout the day—was named the best out of all the factories. Our first-place trophy, a golden woman with wings, was placed on a special shelf at the front of Peehyuk.

When the festivities ended that afternoon and we'd gone back inside for our final head count, Panjang Nim announced that the warden had given Peehyuk an extra prize—a box of ramyun— "because of the guy who tossed all the balls," he told us, as he playfully pantomimed my routine, making everyone laugh.

==

FOR A THOUSAND days I marched on, paying my debt to Korea. The truck came less often with the bags of soles and heels. We went several weeks with little work. One day around noon Panjang Nim took a call in the factory. It seemed serious. After he'd hung up, he called for us to line up at attention. Our mother company outside had gone bankrupt. It was as if, there and then, we had been given notice, fired. Even our meager prison jobs were pulled out from under us. It was terrible news because it meant we would now have to stay in our cells as nonworkers. We were going to lose a lot. Bankrupt? Not good old Peehyuk. We had been a Taejon stalwart for so long, a humble, hardworking factory, led by the best captain in the place. And shoemakers, cobblers—show me a society without them. We should have been indispensable. What had gone wrong? Why wasn't our supplier or the Korean army or police buying our shoe parts anymore? After all, Korea was booming outside.

Panjang Nim announced that all the Korean workers in Peehyuk would be moving to a new cell block and that all of us were going to assist with the move right then. Off we marched on this completely novel activity, led en masse by our factory guard and Panjang Nim to block 7, where we began to clean out their cells, loading all their stuff onto carts or carrying things away by hand. These were places I had never been. It was a rare good look into the larger cells in which my fellow workers lived. I thought about how the Koreans not only had to be with one another all day in the factory, but then also had to pass the entire night with some of the same guys, side by side on the wood floors of these workers' cells, twelve, fifteen guys to one or two porcelain troughs. I'm sure the Koreans tried to give one another space and knew when to let one another be, but there were always bodies all around them, breathing, sniffling, farting, moving, disturbing, distracting. I realized that prison life for Koreans was very much about being forced to cooperate in extremely close community with their fellow man. We foreigners were allowed to remain somewhat separate because of single-cell life—the luxury of our quiet solitary nights. But Koreans were great at group living, it seemed to me, much better at it than we foreigners would have been. They almost never ate alone; that was just bad form. I recall times when I made ramyun for myself and sat there at our table, only to have inmates approach me to ask incredulously why I was eating alone. Was there something wrong with me? they wondered. Probably. Korean inmates sang together, wrote letters together.

They held hands and walked arm in arm. They gave hugs and grabbed their buddies. They shaved each other or sometimes used tweezers to pull out each other's facial hair. I remembered how guys scrubbed each other in the saunas in Seoul, and how even university-age men would sit on each other's laps when there weren't enough seats available on the subways. That wasn't weird or uncomfortable in any way for them. It was a level of camaraderie and brotherhood that seemed beyond me, and part of me envied them that. I thought that this was where the confidence of the average Korean came from, his ease and self-assurance, group assurance really: each man was very aware of belonging to a whole, aware that he was, through all the things shared, part of a large family; and because he knew the ways and words of the family so well, he was deeply, inextricably included, forever. It is a kind of assurance and strength that Americans don't really have. Unlike America, Korea is not just a nation; it's also a race. From that comes pride, nationalism, and prickliness—and identity, strength, and sacrifice.

So there were Jang Soo, Slim, Chang Ho, Panjang Nim, and I, along with all the others, in the late afternoon, going cell to cell, helping amid the confusion, caught up in a kind of welcome panic. Someone handed me a large wall clock to carry. It had been hanging in Peehyuk for years. I felt honored to be the time bearer, and held the clock firmly against my chest as we moved like a band of refugees through the halls toward block 13.

In the days that followed we found ourselves unemployed and back in the cells on lockdown. I got up to watch with some envy as the other guys were released in the mornings to go off to the factories. I wondered if I'd have to try to get into another one or whether I wanted to go through such a transition again, to deal with a whole new set of challenges. I was established and comfortable in Peehyuk. On a Wednesday morning, as I was readying myself for another submerged day in the cell, I was surprised by the sight of Panjang Nim striding into our hall. "Peehyuk workers, get ready!" he called out. "We're going back!" It was a miracle, and it rippled down the corridor. We were going back! We had cast off our employer and now were about to occupy his work space like squatters, like revolting proletariat. A victory for the workers! Panjang Nim had persuaded the security chief to allow us to continue to go to the factory during the day and conduct ourselves as usual even though there was no work there to be done.

But Taejon authorities soon found us a new employer and got us back to actual labor. We'd now be arranging the electrical wiring for Daewoo and Kia cars. On big boards we ran intricate patterns of beautifully colored wires, crisscrossing them over, under, and around metal brackets arranged to create various paths, plugging them into complex boxes full of slots with matching colors. The automobile industry is one of Korea's largest and most essential. It was and is a big reason for the country's economic strength. And I can say that as a prison laborer I was part of it. When I see Daewoo and Kia cars now I laugh to myself, wondering if my hands arranged the wiring in them, if these vehicles, modern, imported, good-looking, might not contain good ol' Peehyuk products. The U.S. embassy in Seoul was interested when I told them that we were working for some of Korea's biggest car companies. The consular officials wondered if their use of prison labor was legal. It was an interesting topic, and I wanted to know more, but it meant nothing compared with getting out of the cell.

These car companies had a lot of work for us, and we were asked early on to work overtime one weekend. Of course, we had no choice in the matter, but again, because it represented time out of the cell and brought with it that singular excitement created by any change in our eternal routine, I went willingly. So it seemed with everyone. And Daewoo compensated us, the easily pleased, by bringing us on Saturday, along with truckloads of wires, boxes full of bananas, enough for three bananas for each man. In the afternoon on Sunday, we had a celebration, in order to bless the new venture. A Daewoo representative set up a little altar by the front doors. There were little towers and pagodas of apples and melons on plates and, in the center of the low table, a pig's head with colorful Korean money in its mouth. This was supposed to bring good luck. It did: just a few hours later we were eating a special meal of *gook soo,* long thin noodles with onions and a hot red-pepper sauce. We ate like bandits, many of us three or four bowls' worth, competing to see who could eat the most, flaunting how full we were. One of the most common phrases I heard in Korea was, "Did you eat a lot?" I always thought it must have its roots in the era after the Korean War, when the country was poor and eating a lot was important. It meant survival and continuance, at least until the next time you were hungry. Volume was more important than questions of taste. And when you answered, as we all did that day with Daewoo's noodles, "Yes, I ate a lot!" it meant the most essential thing: that you'd be around for at least a few more hours.

WE SOON GOT warning that there was going to be an inspection of Taejon by the director of South Korea's prisons and other men from the justice ministry. A massive prisonwide mobilization, carried out cell block by cell block, factory by factory, began. Everything had to be put in order, made to look good. It was dizzying to see the lengths that would be gone to in order to create the desired appearance. Pockets in pants—a privilege many of the gangsters had—were to be sewn shut. The numbers and factory badges that we wore on our chests had to be immaculately sewn on. All winter clothes had to be stored out of sight. We were only allowed to have three T-shirts, three pairs of socks, etc. Shorts, which most of us had for exercise, had to be hidden away in storage boxes under our factory tables, as they were technically illegal. No medicine could be kept in the cells; whatever pills or other remedies a prisoner had were to be brought to the factory, where a shelf was cleared for them and given a spiffy-looking label. All books had to have inspection slips inside them. We were ordered to clean our little wood lockers, the boxes under our tables, our cells. Anything irregular, prison-made, makeshift, jerry-built—get rid of it. If you had more than two blankets in your cell, you had to bring them to the factory for storage. The so-jees and kitchen workers who piloted the carts of food around the halls were given white aprons to wear. So-jees in white frocks! This was radical and cracked us up. Amazingly, potted plants were put down the side of one of the main halls. That much green life up close made a palpable difference, and Taejon never looked better. (The plants were removed right after the inspection was over.) Panjang Nim explained to us how, on the days when the justice ministry inspectors would be making their rounds, we should be ready at a moment's notice to spring to our stations, even though we had no work then, and pretend to be hard at work. On each board we set up a network of wires and completed it halfway so that when we jumped to it we would appear to be right in the middle of our task. Even though we had forgone our English class for several weeks—due to the change in our work and the lack of interest among the current crop of Peehyuk in-mates—Panjang Nim asked me to set up the blackboard in the locker room, where we normally studied, and to fill it with writing so that it appeared that a lesson was in progress.

These were essentially deceptions, I thought. It was all a sham. But then I considered that these weren't stupid men. The officials from the justice ministry must have known that much of what they encountered during inspections was artificial, an act. But they didn't see that as a problem. An act was preferable to a lack of respect, for sure. Indeed, an act was a clear sign of respect, and the lengths to which the act is taken, the extent of the sham, is a measure of the respect being given and a reflection on the standing of the men for whose sake it is being done. We make a conscientious show of fear and appeasement; they shake their heads that all is well.

The day arrived when the ministry men came into Peehyuk. Of course, thanks to our state of readiness, Kee Jung watching the door and the grounds like a hawk for signs of the approach, we had advance warning. We were at our boards, pretending to be buried in our work, as though we'd been at it for hours. Our uniforms were tip-top. We were the model of model prisoners. We were diligent, well-behaved, penitent cons, Confucians through and through. An honor guard was with the officials, four young tall and impressive soldiers in full regalia. The ministers had suits and medals and puffed-up power oozing from them. The pack of them entered and stopped, looked around, scrutinizing everything. Panjang Nim gave the order, and we turned where we stood at our boards, saluted in unison, and shouted, *"Keng seng!"* That was what they wanted to hear. That was the ultimate surrender and the great goal of Taejon's punishment. No matter that it was as artificial for many of us as the new shelf for medicine or the plants in the hall. One perfectly pressed official strolled over to the board where my work partner, an older Peruvian who was in for stealing, and I were keeping our hands moving, and asked me, in Korean, "Do you work well?" I was glad I understood him. It meant that we were going to put on a great show, because even the foreigners in Taejon were with the program, speaking Korean, immersed in the native way. "Yes, I work well," I told him, using the most respectful form. The official turned to the other potentates and said something about how good it was that foreigners were functioning well in their country's prisons. They all nodded their agreement to one another and soon were gone.

For a week life had been tight due to the inspections. Everything had been taken to the rigorous letter of the law, all slack taken up. If we had been forced to live like that customarily, the way the laws actually stipulated, we would have had it much worse. That was the one blessing of the inspection: that when it was over, and our normal prison life returned, it seemed wide and almost pleasant in comparison.

# 39

DURING MY LAST year in Taejon I found out that my parents had divorced—that had been expected. They'd grown far apart before I ever left for Korea. Stuff went wrong; I knew that. You had to let things die, make changes, adapt. They'd been through a lot, their own Uijongbus and Taejons and worse: deaths, bankruptcies, infidelities, separations. Four kids to deal with, and some of them were downright criminals! I respected their battles. I'd been living in a world where one of the most glaring and obvious truths, one that was pounded home daily if you had eyes to see it, was that everyone had his story and that everyone, at one time or another, ate bitter. No one was without his battles, and when you saw each man in that light, you could feel empathy and respect for him. He was in the same fight as you.

Pops had sold 90 Webster, the house we'd grown up in. I'd thought that this would make me sad, but I felt strangely unmoved when I found out. So much had happened since I'd left that house, right off Main Street, as quiet as a suburban dream in that settled Long Island town. It was too far in the past to have an emotional pull for me. I was beyond it, and not just the house. So much had fallen away like dead skin.

Mom, who already had a master's degree in philosophy, had gone back to school and become a registered nurse. My brother had done well for himself in the world of desktop publishing and graphic design. I wasn't so confident that I knew how to turn a computer on. He said he'd teach me. Since I'd been gone, the twins had graduated from high school and were just months from finishing college. I'd been away doing my postgraduate work, they joked. They wondered how I'd be when I came out.

IF I HAD to be imprisoned, it was my good fortune it was in Con-fucian Korea. I was told of the possibility of being transferred to the States to complete the remainder of my time. A provision on the Korean books spoke of such a chance for an American inmate after he had served one-third of his sentence in Korea. But even if the authorities on both sides had agreed to such a move I would have refused to go. The decision in my mind couldn't have been clearer. As a prisoner in the States I might have been able to wear regular clothes, watch television, eat familiar food, sleep on a bed. It would have been easier for friends and family to visit me. I would have had a Western-style toilet, hot water, and heat in the winter, access to libraries and special facilities for exercise and recreation. No doubt my life there would have been more com-fortable in many ways, more modern, physically less restrictive—but also seedier, I'm pretty sure, more decadent, and more dangerous.

As incongruous as it may seem, my preference was to stay in South Korea, seven thousand miles from home in a country whose modern history had been scarred by militarism, authoritarianism, and a not-so-distant third-world poverty. In Korea I didn't have to constantly think about my survival, about being raped or as-saulted. While the authorities may not have reached men in their hearts or heads, and while we lived relatively bare and rough lives, we weren't surrounded by brutality and violence. I've often thought about prison reform and what could be done to try to help society through the system's opportunity with criminals. I've often wondered if there might be some way to take from Korea those Confucian qualities that made her prisons more humane, more civilized perhaps, than ours in the United States—as if you could take a cultural syringe, suck out of South Korea the good, carry it over the ocean, and inject it into America's veins.

Maybe the United States could use a little shot of Confucian shame, a better sense of collective living. But you can't inject

Confucian ethics into America's bloodstream. There's no catalyst for it. It's too late. Korea's one race has been marinating in a code of behavior and propriety and well-defined roles for centuries. She lives and dies by it. There are so many races in the United States, so much room to invent ways of relating, so much free-lancing with behavior and language. We have no uniform code. It's a cauldron of competing codes. America lives and dies by it. Some brilliant life gets born out of her complexity and chaos. But so do some scary prisons, and a two-million-man American world in need of attention.

AS SOUL-DRAINING and difficult as Taejon could be, I kept trying to take it like an adventure, to see that my situation, however un-desirable, was rich with challenges. I was in deep and far away in a place that few foreigners have ever seen or will ever see. Often that sensation came to me all on its own. Out of the monotony would emerge something wild and exhilarating. I'd be staring out at the rain drenching the empty exercise yard or at the cell blocks in the morning mist, and be visited by the same sense of wonder that came to me in Siberia and Mongolia, the feeling that I was completely removed from my world, from what I had known and seen before, and that there was not a thing, not even a Coca-Cola sign, to break the spell. Everything before me was authentic and unspoiled, and so the journey was pure. It was the real thing to mark and scar you. Even the statue of the Virgin Mary tucked into a little grove near the factories seemed new. It wasn't the same old Mother of God; this was an exotic Korean-prison Mary, there under the Korean wall, shrouded by distinct Korean pines. I was at the end of the earth. No one could reach me; no one I knew before would ever see these places. There was excitement in that, and it wasn't hard for me to imagine then that like my hero Burton I'd entered a forbidden city, lived among a bizarre and wondrous people, gained knowledge of a province previously unknown to my race. I told myself to keep my eyes and ears open.

I fasted every year on May 27, the day I was arrested, putting my kimchi, barley rice, and ramyuns aside. The lesson of the day was always "Don't ever again be so stupid." Where holidays and birthdays used to send me tumbling into depression, thinking about what I was missing with family and friends, now they passed like any other day, and I liked that feeling. I liked that they no longer had any power over me, that I could see through the construct and treat it as just another day, waking with the horns, eating my meals at the same time, scrubbing my clothes by hand on the stone floor, looking for the moon in the Taejon sky at night.

Everything became remarkably, discernibly dual in nature. Cell as coffin, cell as sanctuary. Korean keeps as peaceful and innocent, then wicked and warped. Other inmates evoked my pity, the next day my scorn. History was similar: I thought of stories of Magellan's death. In heroic versions he was killed as he bravely covered the retreat of his men to their ships—in others, cut down in shallow waters in a moment of hubris and greed. The Peruvians often described our circumstances as making us *más preso* or *menos preso,* more or less prisoner. One was not fixed, one could still fluctuate between extremes. You either dealt with the cold and the heat or you didn't. There was no middle ground. You either accepted your lot or caused yourself misery straining against it.

It was just like the Magic Eye books Mom had sent me. Look at the pictures one way and you see nothing at all; but with patience, a shift in your perspective, a mental release of resistance and struggle—suddenly, out of the confusion and the jumble on the page, the secrets and hidden things would appear. My perspective was crucial and I could always flip it. The prison, I came to realize, was simply showing me life in a bottle, life concentrate. This was proved out in the most fantastic way by the fact that

Taejon, as implacable and unchangeable as she was, was not the same place to all of us. In fact, she was something different to each of us, according to how we viewed her, and that was the only thing we had control over. That was it, how we viewed her, how we took it—her reality flowed from there.

I can't tell you how I may be different from someone who has never been to prison, but I know that little gets me down. I don't sweat small things, but so many small things bring me joy. So much of what we let burden us is small, tiny as hell. Maybe everything is like Taejon to me now, and I choose my positions positively. It's simply the easier way to go, the cleaner, less taxing way to move through time.

When I thought of my family or Rocket, I no longer felt any pain or sadness. It was a mighty sensation. I felt armored with new steel. There were reasons for the change that I could point to—life in the factory and teaching and basketball, all helping to restore my sense of who I was, to build myself over—but it was still a feat of magic, because I felt I loved all the people in my life more, not less. I loved life more. But the outside, the United States, and my prior life had faded so far away that I no longer missed them much. I no longer felt as if I'd lost them. I looked more at the small but great options still open to me, such as how I was going to take the day. I could see a thousand freedoms remaining in Taejon. If I compared life there with the outside, then I was a tightly held prisoner. But as long as I kept my head focused on what was at hand, on Taejon and nothing outside her, like a horse with blinders on so that it doesn't look off to the sides but only straight ahead, then I was no longer acutely aware of not being free. And that was a form of freedom.

Prison was the most implacable force I've ever faced, relentless, indifferent, monstrously solid and unalterable. I'd been pounding against her walls, searching for a solution in her empty halls, in the ideas that bound us by law. But she refused to budge or listen. In a cruel and brilliant way, Taejon kept forcing me back to myself. Every time I tried to run or look somewhere else, attacking the system and its stupidity, daydreaming painfully of being free, I was slapped back. An animal either goes mad or finds the only route left. If Taejon wasn't going to move, then I would have to move myself in relation to her. She was the control group, my straight man, the Magic Eye puzzle on the page, and I finally learned to play off her.

I wrote on my wall, *You cannot change them. You can keep your peace.* I had to see this idea in a physical form for it to really sink in. So there it was on a ragged sheet of blank paper written with a weak pen in capitals and stuck to my cell wall at about eye level with a bit of toothpaste. I couldn't miss it; I read it every day. My own calm and peace of mind were more important to me than any argument. I wanted no more part in the debates and wrangling over policy and procedures. I watched another American, an older man with a heart problem who had been cashing phony traveler's checks, come in and rage about Korea's "barbaric prisons." He was going to report it to the United Nations. I saw a reflection of my earlier self in him and knew I'd broken from that. And all the fighting over laundry space and hot water, food and blankets, hot-water bottles in the winters, uniforms and seats at the factory tables, all the greed and need, the tide of misery and suffering, the power games, the humiliations doled out mercilessly—I wanted no part in any of it. I stepped away from that shit then and there and have remained at a distance ever since.

I went back to Nietzsche's line that Billy had added to a letter he wrote Mom: "What is the seal of attained freedom? No longer being ashamed in front of oneself." I felt I understood what that meant now. The essence of the freedom Nietzsche was talking about was forgiveness, I thought. It was all right that I was a convict, a kid paying for a stupid stunt, and not being ashamed of that or torturing myself over it anymore was a true liberation. It was all right that I'd failed so spectacularly. I was fallible and still decent, capable of real idiocy and yet still smart enough. I was mortal, even, and that was acceptable.

AT THE BEGINNING of 1997, I moved up to cell number 1 on the top floor of block 6. It was the cleanest cell I had ever seen, with walls pasted over bright white with paper from the printing factory. And it looked over the high outer wall onto the little farming village and its plots of rice. I sometimes shouted through the bars out my window, projecting my sound over the wall into the air above the houses, not to scare or disturb anyone but to release my energy, to shout my existence out into the world. I wondered how those Koreans felt living next to the prison, whether they spoke of us when they ate dinner together. Did the parents point to our windows as a lesson to their kids? I watched the families plant rice in the spring and harvest it together in the fall. I remember the woman guarding the green rice beds in the early mornings, driving away the herons and storks that would glide down into the fields. "Woooaaa! Hwooaaa!" she cried, waving a red towel above her head as the beautiful, long-legged birds scattered into the air, lifting themselves away with their broad wings.

I gave myself a new name, Brother One Cell, and started signing my letters home with it. I was the monk of cell 1, an army of one, made new by Taejon's fire. That fire had burned away the last of my resistance. I'd let everything go. I hope that when I have to deal with the death of loved ones, with the tectonic shifts that life can spring around us, with the task of reinventing myself as relationships die and circumstances realign and my body and who I think I am change, through all the struggles with impermanence, that I'll think of Korea and Taejon and remember how to let go, how to be far away and alone and empty and at peace.

I got up every morning at five to write and follow my breath, when our camp was sacredly still and quiet—all the pain and troubled memories, the sad journeys of uncomfortable, disastrous lives, paused mercifully in sleep. The distance from the world in that silence seemed complete. As the sun rose and threw light into the cell, I would face my window and the outer wall, the village beyond it. "Thanks for today," I would say while bowing low. It became my daily ritual. I thought of the "patient endurance" my great-great-grandfather Costello had written of from his cell in Ireland more than a hundred years before: "Even in the midst of our difficulties we have much to be thankful for." His words were mine now. The brothers and priests who taught me in high school often said that singing hymns was like praying double. Well, by the same sort of calculus perhaps, saying thanks in Taejon was being doubly grateful. It was power-packed, concentrated gratitude, and I felt it for what I had and for the day at hand. I understood that nothing is guaranteed, that life doesn't owe us anything. The feeling has never left me.

# 40

Oftentimes I have heard you speak of the one who commits a wrong as though he were not one of you, but a stranger unto you and an intruder upon your world . . . And still more often the condemned is the burden bearer for the guiltless and unblamed. You cannot separate the just from the unjust and the good from the wicked; for they stand together before the face of the sun even as the black thread and the white are woven together. And when the black thread breaks, the weaver shall look into the whole cloth, and he shall examine the loom also.

—Kahlil Gibran, *The Prophet*

DOWN IN CHINJU, Green found himself the lone foreigner among mentally ill Korean inmates. On several occasions he said he could hear the muffled sounds of guards beating them. He had it good, though. Better medicine than in Taejon, better food, all the fresh vegetables he wanted, a big cell. They let Green watch videos of recent movies. He said he brought one Chinju guard to tears by telling him his life story.

As Billy had when he was transferred, Green sent letters to me through my mom. He hoped Rocket and I would make it. He encouraged me in my writing. He had his aunt send me a hundred dollars as I had finally spent the thousand I came in with. (Three years on a thousand dollars—that was the simple life!) In one of the last letters Green sent to my mom, he wrote:

When Cullen and I first met, mentally I was a basketcase, I had a lot of anger and blaming people for what happened. We would talk for hours and if I said something that should be corrected (way of thinking) he would tell me. He would say no your wrong, look at it this way. Slowly I started seeing my mistakes (problems) but it was because of him. He spent the time and listened to me. For that I'll be forever grateful. It's taken me a long time to get where I am. I still have my brains dragging the ground, but for the past three days I've been doing real good, thinking positive. I've forgiven everyone but me, I still can't let go. Some say it's because of Satan, but I say it's because I was too stupid to see the right Green.

They let him go after just five and a half years—early release, rarer in Korea than white tigers. He went to live in Koreatown in Los Angeles. I liked that he was living there, and that he'd invited a Korean friend of his to live in his apartment almost rent-free. Freaky white man from Milwaukee that he was, he still liked to be surrounded by the Korean milieu. I visited him once out there, in 2001. We still had an easy rapport, as if we were back on the block in Taejon. He was fatter and slower than ever. His hips were stiff; the metal in his left leg made it all but useless. I could still see a bit of the capable air force man in him, but he also looked like a brother from another planet. He clearly had been somewhere else, far away, and come back. His limp and everything about him seemed more extreme out there on the street, in the free world. The manager of a hotel in Koreatown liked Green enough to give him a shot as a security guard. He was good with the guests, especially the Asians. He'd stand in the lobby and chat them up. I took a bus into Koreatown and met up with him near his apartment, in front of a fast-food joint, which I thought was crudely appropriate. Green still loved beer, and we ducked out of the sunny afternoon into a seedy bar to have a couple. We tapped glasses and smiled at the good fortune we had to be able to sit there together outside in the free world and share a drink, something we'd dreamed of doing so many times in Korea.

He was doing some one-on-one English tutoring with several private students. He'd met a Guatemalan woman who liked him. He took her to the movies. I teased him about having a date. I tried to imagine what a woman who fell for Green could be like. Not that Green didn't deserve it, but I thought that he might not be fit for it. He was certainly an unlikely candidate, and his record with women hadn't been good. He had often talked about his future with women, whether he could ever get a girl, whether he'd ever have sex again in his life. I wondered if it was safe for anyone to get close to Green, and thoughts of him killing someone out there in L.A.—a girl, a child—sometimes flashed through my head. I considered my own responsibility to him and to those around him, because I was one of the few caretakers of his story, the knowledge of what he'd done. But I didn't seriously think he would ever get violent again. I just didn't see him being capable of it now. Just as I didn't ever see him being able to construct, much less maintain, an intimate relationship with a woman. He didn't like violence; he wasn't looking for fights. He minded his own business. All he wanted were his cheap cases of beer from the local Korean supermarket and movies on his laptop. He was asking life for very little. Green never did get violent again. The Guatemalan woman faded away quickly.

After our beers, Green led the way to a Korean restaurant, where we ate well. We kept talking about the cute Korean waitresses, the sounds of their voices. He told me that when he first came back and wasn't doing so well—living in a men's shelter in a bad part of L.A., scraping by with little or no money (I sent him the little I could)—he tried crack a couple of times. He laughed at himself. We talked about his depression and his medication and how he was getting by. Money was always tight, but he didn't need much to support his simple lifestyle. I knew Green wasn't going to go much further than he had, but I thought he'd done all right, all things considered. I even felt proud of him. He supported himself and was a decent member of his community. He still showed moments of real ambition. He would take a class here and there, and tried to keep up with current events in the newspapers. He still read about Korea, and often asked about how my book on our prison lives was going. He still wanted to study Chinese characters. It was a small and sad life, but it was placid and clean compared with his recent and distant past, and it was more than either of us had had back in Korea. We both knew that implicitly, and that unspoken understanding was part of the heart of our bond, why I still felt connected to Green, why I knew that I'd always be friends with him, no matter how different and separate our lives were now.

He used to call me in New York several times a week, then I wouldn't hear from him for months. He liked to call early, around three or four in the morning out there, six or seven my time. He knew I'd be getting up for work. Giggling, he'd ask if my woman was in my bed. He would tell me about his latest conversation with Mr. and Mrs. Lee, the preachers who used to visit us in Taejon. They had set up a school and an orphanage for North Korean children in the northeast of China. They said that they could use us as English teachers. Green and I were planning to go visit. We were both interested in meeting North Koreans and in the possibility of entering the South's strange other half. Green clung to the plan; it gave him a purpose.

Soon after, he found a small lump in his thigh and hoped that it was skin cancer. He said he wasn't going to the doctor. Cancer would be his ride out. He told me that he and I could go nuts and run up his credit-card bills before he died. When his energy began to ebb and the thing in his thigh had grown larger and changed color, he went to a VA hospital and had it diagnosed. Skin cancer, sure enough. There was the eerie impression that he'd called it to himself. He was happy with the results, and he coddled the disease at first. He told me that he was content to let it go where it wanted, and if it spread, so be it. I knew he meant it. I always told him to be strong and to do what he felt was right.

Part of me wanted him to live, and it was sad to hear a man so beaten that he had resigned himself to letting cancer eat away at his body. This was the sweet black death he'd been talking about since I'd met him, that seemed to follow him like a friend. The tumor grew bigger than a golf ball. He used to try to describe it for me. Part of him was fascinated by it, and he took digital photos of it, noting its changing colors and the way it felt. It was slowly draining more and more of his energy, until he couldn't move much and had to check into the VA hospital. I had no doubt that this was the beginning of the end, and when Green did, too, it spooked him, alone there in a bed in the VA, the wreckage of his life behind him. He wanted to get treatment now, put his death plan into remission. He still wanted to live, a little. He wanted to make that trip to China, to visit me in New York. He was in a lot of pain, taking morphine. Green's uncle and father, whom he hadn't seen in more than twenty years, visited him. His father told Green that he loved him, and this meant the world to Green. It seemed to give him his final peace. He had given me his father's phone number just in case, and I thought about calling him to tell him that I knew his son as a good man, a kind and good friend. But what had been his dad's contribution to the typical tragedy that Green had lived as a child, the abuse and neglect? Could I tell him that however much he and his wife had fucked up, however much those early years had fucked Green up, his son had battled to the end for a little love and help? How would he take what I wanted to say? I never made the call.

After his father's visit, Green and I went several weeks without speaking. I could usually get him on his cell phone, but when he didn't pick up over the course of several days, I called the VA hospital. When I was told that the hospital couldn't help me un-less I was a family member, I knew what that meant and asked the man on the line if he could please tell me if my friend had died. He gave me the date, just an ordinary day in May. Green was forty-five years old. I put the phone down as memories of Korea began flashing through my head. I didn't think I would cry, but I did, there at my desk where I was paid to write biographies of famous and accomplished individuals—politicians, athletes, businessmen, Hollywood stars. Green's life was still more interesting to me than any of theirs.

# 41

FRED, A FORMER U.S. soldier, goes home tomorrow. His ten
months are over—customs violation; he was illegally importing
televisions. Today at the factory he was in that ecstatic state that
comes upon the departing man and fills him as the freedom dream
at last becomes real. Fred was free of the anxiety and tension that
he'd had over the last two months, the effects of what the Koreans call "release day disease": it's easier to pass the days when you
have years remaining than when your sentence grows short. Calm
and patience are harder to come by then. It seems that the discipline the inmate has forged in keeping his head down in the day
at hand, his thoughts on what he has and not on what's outside,
breaks loose and leaves him. He begins to stumble. The shields
of tolerance, patience, acceptance, dull metals one has held up
for so long, begin to slip. Want and wish come creeping back.
The mind, so close to its goal, starts to think of ways to leap what
remains and fly to the open door at last. Time, which had steadily
worked for him before, with such unerring consistency, suddenly
becomes a plodding, torturous force, weighing on the expectant
man heavily in the final weeks, upsetting the tides of his moods
like an approaching moon.

Fred looked up at September hanging from Peehyuk's wall and
put his finger on the twelfth. I'd watched him spend a lot of time
looking at August, and as we reached the start of September, he
was there even more, sighing, stroking his dark face, pointing to
the twelfth. Today he didn't say what he'd been saying for weeks:
"Just a little more and I'm out of this place! I can't wait to get out
of here!" He'd been using these statements as weapons, to silence
anyone who wasn't going out, to sting us. His response to all the

arguments and uncomfortable situations in which he'd found himself recently had been just that: We could keep our shitty little lives. He didn't care. He was leaving.

But he didn't say that today. Instead, he was shouting something in Korean that some of the guys in the factory thought would be hilarious coming out of his mouth: *"Chowt bangee chora! Naega jib ae kan da!"*—You guys keep slapping your cocks, I'm going home! His pronunciation was mangled, and I don't think he knew what he was saying, but when all the Koreans cracked up, hearing this black American utter such a thing in their language, Fred sang the phrase to everyone he saw, even to the guards, who burst out laughing, pushed him down the hall, or kicked him in the ass while cursing back at him—"Ya, you stupid fool . . . Son of dog, don't talk like that!"

Fred had often danced in the factory, to the delight of the Koreans. They loved him for that. (Safe to say that many of them had never seen, much less spent time with, a black man before.) And with a look of innocent joy on his face he danced now in the hall as we walked single file back to our block. He broke free from our tight line and, while we all laughed and marveled at his untouchable status, shook his hips and sang for us to bang away while he skipped free.

≡≡

MOHAMMED AND JAMIL had their death sentences commuted to life. I took that as good news. Before Tracey was released, he was visited by an acquaintance, another Pakistani who recognized Tracey's brains and charisma and wanted to recruit him to his gang, which ran the same sort of manpower business, immigrant smuggling, that Tracey had done before. He was released, deported, made a new fake passport, and within a month was standing on the other side of Taejon's walls, the free side, in that same little village we looked down on from our cells. He stood there on a late summer day in the lane next to the rice fields and called out to his compatriots still inside, Hussein and Ali. They rushed to their back windows, shouted down to Tracey, and cried.

FOR A LONG time I had carried in my head an ideal image of my-self as being so wrapped up in life in Taejon that I had forgotten when my sentence was up, and that when the day arrived I would be out in the grounds deep in a game or in the factory hammering away, oblivious of the moment, and that they'd have to come get me, to tell me, "Hey, don't you know, it's over, it's done, your time is up." And in that moment Taejon, which had commanded all of me for so long, would drop away, slipping away into the other world of memory, and freedom and home would leap out of mem-ory and come rushing back to life.

When I hit the two-month wall, I received my little yellow cloth triangle with my number and release date on it. I was now an official *mangee ja,* a "man set to expire." Many guys stitched the triangle above their numbers. You'd see these lucky men in the halls smiling, with a wedge of yellowish gold on a mass of blue. I didn't want to stitch mine on, but in my cell at night I lay on the floor and turned the golden triangle over and over in my hands, threw it up into the air, and let it fall on me, like Rocket's leaves. There's an end to everything, I thought, sweet release from the worst and the best and everything in between.

MR. WANG, THE fat Korean-Taiwanese businessman, invited me to have lunch with him and the others at his section on my final day in Peehyuk, my last full day in prison. He served a stew with dark meat full of small bones. After we'd eaten, Mr. Wang told me with a loud laugh that it was pigeon. As he sometimes did with departing men, Panjang Nim made me lead the factory in a song after the last call to attention, my final "new life" salute. I knew the lyrics to a few Korean songs by heart. I chose the easiest, a children's tune with the simple title "Beautiful Song." I stood in front of the rows of inmates, Panjang Nim off to the side, our guard looking down from his perch. We clapped in time as I led us, off-key, through the verses:

*Beautiful song, what a happy song, its echo comes to our village*
*The darkness in my heart flies far away*
*Let's sing this song!*
*In every mountain valley, its sound arrives, whenever it is heard*
*Happy, joyful song, hey!*

I thought we sounded horrible. I shook hands with Slim and Man Yong. I told them to stay healthy. I gave Chang Ho a hug. Gang Guy, Kee Baek, and other members of the factory came over to say their good-byes. "Go well," they said. "Make a success of yourself out there." I said good-bye to Panjang Nim, and he offered me his hand.

"You're a good worker," he told me, not a word more, but I knew what that meant to him, how important it was. I felt proud to have suffered for a time along with him, to have done battle as part of this Korean family, paying our respective prices with as much grace as we could manage, to have lived with them for a time through the *ko saeng,* the hard living that men like Panjang Nim knew so well.

# 42

THE NEXT MORNING the tamdang opened my cell door as the workers were stepping out of their cells and heading off to the factories. Joseph, Reza, Manny, Ali—they all came over to say good-bye and wish me luck, to take the things I was giving away. My blankets, mirror, buckets, books, clothes, windows, the cell itself—all were spoken for, had been requested, reserved, gobbled up like the time. And then everyone was gone, leaving me alone on the top floor of block 6. Even the tamdang disappeared. It was amazing to me, even absurd in some sense, that because this officially sanctioned day, this arbitrary day, had arrived, I was trusted to be alone and unwatched, as if I were a chicken cooked with a timer, so that they didn't have to look in the oven at it, to question the process, but that when the timer popped, they trusted that I was done. Suddenly, though they still didn't know me much at all, I was no longer of any interest to any of them.

I opened the door of my cell wide and stared in at it. Such a tiny, empty box. I couldn't believe it had been three and a half years. I had spent the heart of my twenties there, but I had no regrets. I knew it hadn't been wasted. Maybe Prosecutor Shin knew what he was doing after all. I pictured him telling me, "This is all as it was supposed to be, to teach you a good lesson." Other than some stray writing on the walls, there was no trace of me left in the cell, no sign that I had been there at all.

THEY GAVE ME the same clothes I had on when I was arrested: green khakis, button-down shirt, black shoes. I was thinner than before—I had parasites but didn't know it yet, and they would prove excruciatingly painful; it couldn't have been Mr. Wang's pigeon, as I'd been exhibiting symptoms long before that—but everything still fit, almost as if I'd worn it yesterday. This was a moment I had kept in my head through the years. I knew that when I had these clothes back, it would mean that the experience was over, I'd be on the other side. And the moment was here. Bliss was slowly leaking from my head into the rest of my body. I felt as if I were floating above everything that was happening, even as my body acted through it. Two officials in slacks and jackets came to take me to the immigration office in Taejon City. They led me through the final doors and past several gates. As we drove down the road leading from the prison's main gate in a silver sedan, I turned to look back. It was just a glimpse. Taejon stood high, faded white, and silent, and then she was gone forever.

When we reached immigration, it was lunchtime, so the officials asked me to join them before we drove on to Seoul. They had food delivered from a restaurant: *sal bop,* the real high-quality white rice, kimchi, and beef. It was so delicious that it shocked me. I had grown to think that our payshik in Taejon, even the thick barley rice, was not that bad. I ate with gusto. When we finished, my two escorts told me there were no office cars available. We'd have to take the bus, they said. To show me that the trip was serious, they had me watch them slide pistols into shoulder holsters under their blazers.

"Don't worry. We will still make your flight," the older man told me. They put stiff, clear plastic handcuffs on me. "We're sorry, but there is no way around this."

I immediately thought that I didn't want people in public to see me like that, but everything was still fine with me. I was riding a crest of joy I'd never felt before, or since. I could have walked to Seoul or pulled a loaded cart alongside an ox. I might have been able to swim one of those Amazon rivers just as José Luis had. I managed to pull my long sleeves over most of the cuffs and kept my hands clasped together like a gentle young man. We went down to the street. The two men walked close at my sides.

"How old are you guys?" I asked.

The younger man laughed. "Guess."

I thought about it for a moment. Somehow I felt as though I couldn't miss.

"Thirty-five and forty."

"Whoa! Exactly right," the younger official said. They seemed to like me better for it.

"We have to take a picture with you," the older one said. I thought he was joking, but they walked me to a little photo shop on a busy street. They spoke to the proprietor, told me to have a seat in a chair, and then took spots on either side of me. I was smiling. I could feel how close freedom was.

"Don't smile," the older officer said as the proprietor snapped several shots. I wondered why exactly they needed to do this and what it proved. As the flash hit my eyes I thought of the custom I'd heard about: that when a man is released from prison in Korea his friends buy him a big slab of tofu, which he's supposed to throw on the ground and stomp on.

They took me to a bus station then, and we quickly boarded a nearly empty express bus for Seoul. They put me in a seat with no one around me, gave me two juices and a package of dried squid, then went and sat across from each other three rows in front of me. I said I couldn't eat the squid as it was, and the younger guy came back and kindly ripped it into strips for me. Every few minutes they turned to check on me. I leaned against the window and watched blissfully as Taejon City ran by us. About halfway to Seoul, the older man told me that we were early. We got off and they led me to a fancy coffee shop. When I told them that I couldn't go in in cuffs, they told me not to worry and helped pull my sleeves down lower. The officers seemed to know one of the waitresses, and so I wondered if this was a common stop for them.

The coffee was superb. I drank it with my wrists glued together, raising both arms up toward my head as though I were warding off a blow. I was looking around to see whether anyone noticed, smiling at how absurd I must have looked.

When we reached Kimpo airport, we had little time to spare, and the two officers held my arms and walked me quickly to my boarding area. None of the Koreans or other travelers seemed to pay us much mind. When we reached my gate, the officers became very serious. I remember thinking that I wanted to give them a polite good-bye, but they weren't interested. I had a lot of love and appreciation left in me for Korea. She had taken me to the edge and let me look over, but she never let me go and didn't leave me there too long. She didn't feel the same about me. I don't know if I can ever go back. Shin had said never. The U.S. embassy didn't know. Other foreigners told me we'd be barred from returning for a period equal to the sentences we'd served. Others said it was double that. Koreans here in New York, who know only that I was once an English teacher in Seoul, often ask me if I intend to go back. I have no plan to return right now, I tell them, but I'd like to, someday.

THE OLDER MAN put my ticket in my left hand and the younger put my black bag full of letters in my right.

"We're going to cut off your handcuffs, you're going to turn around and walk straight on the plane," the older man said sternly. "Don't look back."

I DIDN'T LOOK back then, but I have ever since. I think of Korea whenever something tests me and I feel my anger bubble up and my side ache, or when I'm in uncomfortable, claustrophobic situations, like on the subway at rush hour with sweaty bodies pressed against me. I like to think that I'm a guy who can wait out anything. I should have special powers of patience, I figure. I like to go eat Korean food on Thirty-second Street here in Manhattan, squid stew and barbecue beef and especially *bibimbop*, something of a peasant's meal—rice, vegetables, and beef thrown together in a big bowl. I'm a simple Korean. When I see people buying and consuming voraciously and wonder why I don't feel that need and still live simply, buying little, wanting little, Taejon and her bare bones cross my mind. I still pace, from one side of a room to another, almost unconsciously. It soothes me. I'll be an inveterate pacer for the rest of my life. Sometimes I squat in my tub under cold-water showers to get the feeling back, but my body isn't used to it anymore and I remember how I was tough when I had to be. I eat ramyuns at home and sometimes look up at Il Hwan's painting on my wall, the solitary fisherman under beautiful, craggy mountains. I think often of Billy, Green, Tracey, Panjang Nim. I can still see their faces. Sometimes I think I see them in the crowds in New York.

OUR LANDING AT JFK airport was rough. It felt as if we'd come down tipped over on one wheel. I got held up in customs. The agent seemed puzzled by something in my passport. Maybe it was the fact that, despite having only a three-month tourist visa for South Korea, there was a strange three-and-a-half-year gap between my last entry and departure stamps. And I had just the one little black bag. He called over another agent, and together they looked over my passport and me. The first agent asked me to empty my pockets. Then he walked around to my side of the counter and had me pull up my pant legs for him. I didn't mind at all. Search all you like, I was thinking. I had nothing to hide, and for the first time in what felt like ages no one had anything on me anymore! I had paid my debt in full. It was the cleanest feeling in the world.

My family was waiting for me among the crowds. The next day was Thanksgiving. After they'd shouted and grabbed me as if to make sure I was really there, and we'd all hugged and talked wildly and they'd remarked on how thin I was and how short my hair and how weird my accent—I truly sounded like an Asian street kid, my English words clipped, foreign, grunted—Mom hugged me again, then held me in front of her and slapped me.

"Don't ever do that again!" she yelled.

I saw Rocket that night, her great spirit, her little bubble butt. She looked just as she had that day at the post office in Seoul. It was a sweet reunion. We stayed with each other for several weeks, but we both knew that Korea hadn't just kept us apart; it had sent our paths in different directions. There was no going back. Rocket was moving to Seattle to work as a physical therapist. I needed to find my own way. She's married now, with a beautiful baby boy. Our bond was formed in that adventurous idiocy of youth, under palm trees and on ferryboats, in tropical waters and on the chaotic streets of Seoul—two kids out in the beautiful jaws of the world. It's a bond that's sure to last.

I DON'T LIKE to complain, about anything. I hope I take what I have and carry it forward humbly, vigorously, as every person has to. I feel immensely privileged in my modest circumstances—to be free and whole and writing—in large part because I know very well that things could be worse. I don't let things get to me, or at least I shake them off quickly, and I've got no time for self-pity or hatred or bitterness or regret. I refuse to carry those bags, as I know, in my own humble way, just how they weigh down the soul. I'm going to keep taking my days one at a time, each one of them counting, each one worth the same. In prison we stitched our numbers onto our uniforms above the chest, but it's as if the needle and thread had been thrust deeper, so that Korea and the people I met there are forever sewn inside my heart.

≡≡

# ACKNOWLEDGMENTS

I WOULD LIKE to thank my family for their dynamic love and strength. Without them, I might not have come out of South Korea sane enough to write this book. In particular, I am grateful to my brother, Chris, for giving me a job and a place to stay when I returned, and for his expert help with all things digital; and to Mom and Edie, for their open invitation to the wonders of the coast of Maine, a great place to write (and make fires, eat steak, drink whiskey, and run through the woods). Here's to my excellent and insightful agent, William Clark, and to the entire Viking crew, in particular Molly Stern, for seeing the worth in the story, and my editor, Alessandra Lusardi, who gracefully and intelligently saw the book through.

Also, my heartfelt thanks to Alejandra Lora, for her love and support. To Jeff Baker, a writer and a stand-up friend, for his valuable feedback on the manuscript and for being so thoughtful and so damn well read. Thanks to Charlie Gaines for the always-good conversation and the dreams of other countries. To Rocket, for still going strong and rooting for me. To Roy Isbister, Sean O'Connor, Ed Moran, and Ruth Duffy for their wisdom, advice, and support. To the sons of Mil Hirsh, I say your mom was the best pen pal a prisoner could have, which is saying quite a lot, in fact.

And my sincere gratitude goes to those fellow inmates who shared with me their struggle, pain, friendship, generosity, and grace and who helped me through my time. It was for them, really, that I wanted to tell our story.